"*Skymind* is a journey into the essential teachings of Machig Labdrön, the eleventh-century Tibetan woman who founded the Zhijé Chöd, one of the Eight Great Chariots practice lineages. Based on primary sources, the authors brilliantly metabolize these teachings in a way that can deepen our understanding of the very nature of reality. *Skymind* also offers essential pragmatic insights into daily life and meditation practices that transform our dulled awareness into luminous clarity."

—Lama Tsultrim Allione, founder of Tara Mandala and author of *Feeding Your Demons*

"*Skymind* is a radiant invitation to rest in the tender vastness at the heart of who you are. Charlotte and Pieter offer wisdom born of deep, consistent practice and attentive lived experience. Guiding us toward the spacious presence that holds everything, this book is both a quieting refuge and a clear call to awareness."

—Elena Brower, best-selling author of *Practice You* and *Hold Nothing*

"Drawing on the secret teachings of Machig Labdrön, Tibet's great wisdom Mother and founder of the Chöd (Severance) lineage, this book offers an uncompromising path to freedom from self-fixation. The profound path of open awareness is an exploration of the luminous, nondual nature of mind—a fundamental, wakeful wholeness that is always already present. This is the radical invitation of Skymind, the vast, luminous, and unconditional awareness that is our true self.

Machig Labdrön's revolutionary approach teaches that true liberation is found not by avoiding our fears but by turning toward and even nurturing what we consider most repulsive or frightening. This is a courageous journey of the awakened heart, calling us to meet our darkest shadows and recognize that wholeness includes everything—joy, suffering, and the totality of being."

—Jetsunma Tenzin Palmo, author of *The Heroic Heart* and subject of the best-selling biography *Cave in the Snow*

"*Skymind* is a spacious invitation into direct experience of the brilliance and joy of our true nature. Accepting this invitation liberates and transforms, opens and releases us from the fear, struggle, and confinement of our conceptual prisons. We live and embody this primordial freedom through compassionate activity in our everyday lives. Highly recommended!"

—Gaylon Ferguson, author of *Welcoming Beginner's Mind*

"What a precious treasure! *Skymind* elegantly guides us through the hidden depths of the severance journey, placing the dakini Machig's living wisdom in the palms of our hands. Whether we are longtime pilgrims or brand new to the path, we are empowered to turn toward the demons of our lives with tenderness and skill, opening the luminous vastness underlying everything."

—Judith Simmer-Brown, Professor Emerita of Naropa University and author of *Dakini's Warm Breath: The Feminine Principle in Tibetan Buddhism*

"*Skymind* is a treasury of sublime wisdom, transforming power and spacious vision. The writing has the virtue of precision enlivened by clarifying explanations, vivid metaphors, and personal experiences. The authors serve as intimate companions and expert guides through the mental and emotional terrain of ever-subtler layers of ego-clinging, offering at every turn ways to shift toward the realm of pure awareness, radiant compassion, and ever-unfolding beauty and bliss of the universal ocean of being. The narrative arc carries the reader forward with the immediacy and momentum of the storytellers' art. An illuminating book on every level."

—Miranda Shaw, author of *Passionate Enlightenment*

"Charlotte and Pieter have crafted a wonderful book for beginners and seasoned practitioners alike. That's not easy. A lifetime of practice and study is distilled in these pages. Heartwarming stories, illuminating teachings, and most importantly, guided meditations and exercises that bring everything to life make this a welcome addition in the transmission of dharma to the West."

—Andrew Holecek, author of *Reverse Meditation*

"*Skymind* illuminates the wisdom of ancient Tibetan masters with skillful expression that gives readers a clear understanding of their teachings. It is full of insights and offers methods to let go of our mental patterns and open our hearts."

—Anam Thubten, author of *No Self, No Problem*

"I translate old Tibetan texts just so that talented new teachers will have authentic sources to reference. It is gratifying that Charlotte and Pieter have faithfully taken the words attributed to Machig Labdrön and not only made sense of them but created an entire coherent journey for our times. Reading *Skymind*, this heartfelt guide to practices based on Machig's teachings, it's hard to imagine anyone who would not be inspired to engage the practice right away."

—Sarah Harding, author of *Chöd* and *Machik's Complete Explanation*

"The practice of leaning into the things we usually turn away from characterizes Machig Labdrön's practice of Chöd. The spirit and practice of this essential instruction is indispensable for liberating the mind from confusion and opening the free flow of compassion. The authors of *Skymind* present the view and methods of this practice in an accessible, insightful, and tender way."

—Elizabeth Mattis Namgyel, author of *The Logic of Faith*

"*Skymind* is a gentle and genuine introduction to the wonders of recognizing your natural mind. Chapter by chapter, readers are introduced to practice sequences that make possible this recognition of this mind beyond mind, offering access to the timeless wisdom and unique contemplative style of the One Mother, known as the Lamp from the Tibetan land called Lab (*Machig Labdrön*). Pieter and Charlotte's eloquence in conveying their deep experiential knowledge provides guidance that is clear and welcoming, especially to those newly entering these pathways."

—Professor Anne C. Klein, Lama Rigzin Drolma, Rice University and Dawn Mountain, author of *Heart Essence of the Vast Expanse*, *Meeting the Great Bliss Queen*, and *Being Human and a Buddha Too*

SKYMIND

The Radical Path of Open Awareness

Charlotte Rotterdam
Pieter Oosthuizen

SHAMBHALA

Shambhala Publications, Inc.
2129 13th Street
Boulder, Colorado 80302
www.shambhala.com

Cover and interior design: Meredith Jarrett

9 8 7 6 5 4 3 2 1

First Edition
Printed in the United States of America

Shambhala Publications makes every effort to print on acid-free, recycled paper.
Shambhala Publications is distributed worldwide by Penguin Random House, Inc., and its subsidiaries.

Library of Congress Cataloging-in-Publication Data
Names: Rotterdam, Charlotte Z author | Oosthuizen, Pieter author
Title: Skymind: the radical path of open awareness / Charlotte Z Rotterdam and Pieter Oosthuizen.
Description: First edition. | Boulder: Shambhala Publications, 2026. | Includes bibliographical references and index. |
Identifiers: LCCN 2025023305 | ISBN 9781645471394 trade paperback
Subjects: LCSH: Rnying-ma-pa (Sect)—Doctrines | Meditation—Buddhism | Compassion—Religious aspects—Buddhism | Spiritual life—Rnying-ma-pa (Sect)
Classification: LCC BQ7662.4 .R68 2026 | DDC 294.3/444—dc23/eng/20250923
LC record available at https://lccn.loc.gov/2025023305

The authorized representative in the EU for product safety and compliance is eucomply OÜ, Pärnu mnt 139b-14, 11317 Tallinn, Estonia, hello@eucompliancepartner.com.

For our parents, H & P and B & B,
and our sons, M & M

Contents

Acknowledgments

A deep bow of gratitude:

To all our teachers, beginning with our parents who gave us life, the spark of awakened mind, and the courage to trust our hearts. To Lama Tsultrim Allione whose teachings, friendship, and guidance inspire our lives, practice, and work, and without whom we would never have written this book; Lama Tharchin Rinpoche and Namkhai Norbu Rinpoche who ignited our love of the Dharma; and the numerous wisdom teachers we have had the good fortune to meet and learn from along the path.

To Sarah Harding for opening a direct door to Machig's words through her illuminating translations, and for her friendship and generous willingness to answer our many questions. To our Tara Mandala community and fellow teachers Lopön Chandra, Tulku Ösel, Lopön Ellen, Lopön Karla, and so many others; and to our Skymind sangha of fellow practitioners with whom we shared, developed, and honed our Skymind teachings over the years. To Monica, our heart sister, who has been an ongoing sounding board and a wellspring of encouragement. To Liz Shaw, our editor at Shambhala, for planting the seed for this book and her immeasurable patience and kind direction. To Lama Gyurme for his beautiful original drawings that bring Machig and Padampa to life before our eyes. To Sherri and Miranda for their generous help with permissions and early editing.

To dear friends and colleagues at Naropa University, especially Judith Simmer-Brown for her unwavering support over these many years; Regina Smith, Carla Burns, and Jordan Quaglia for their friendship and providing time to write; and our students from whom we never cease to learn.

To the Hemera Foundation whose generous grants allowed for a writing sabbatical and solitary retreats during which much of this book was written.

To our families who taught us the meaning of unconditional love. And to Mateo and Milan, our sons, who gifted us with joyful and steadfast support through long evenings and weekends of writing and whose exuberant life force continuously reminds us of the blessing of life itself.

SKYMIND

Machig Labdrön

Introduction

Gazing out our window, we look into the beautiful Colorado sky—a deep, endless blue without a cloud in sight. It's a magnetizing azure that invites the eye to relax into open, spacious infinitude. The sky, without any effort whatsoever, seems to hold everything; it doesn't discriminate between the lovely and the horrific. It doesn't decide to encompass sunshine but not the hailstorm, the soft breeze but not the winter gale. Whether you see the sky or not, it's there, embracing the entirety of living and dying. Contemplating the sky, we might access a sense of ease and comfort in being held unconditionally, just as we are. Without judgment, the sky embraces our pains and our joys, our brilliance and our confusion. But the sky's vast embrace is also quite radical. You can't hide from the sky. You can't get away, you can't escape. When we awaken to the sky-like nature of our being, we recognize our vast, wakeful nature and our inescapable connectedness to all. This is the potent invitation and promise of Skymind, the vast, luminous radiance of being.

If life were a video game, we'd have many books and systems to advise us on how to better play the game. Those books would tell us to set goals, and how to attain those goals—how to level up in the game of life. As attractive as that may sound, this book is not about that. This book is more about the source code and the electricity that powers the game. In other words, the teachings here, drawing from and inspired by the treasure of Tibetan Buddhism, address the existential essence and the underlying energy that powers the game of life itself—and thus also our basic nature. Although learning to recognize and rest in this basic nature profoundly influences and changes the events of our life, our primary preoccupation is not to become even better at avoiding the bad and chasing the good. No, our focus is more on *how* we view, understand, and experience life. It's about how to profoundly and stably shift our view so the events of our life—the continual ups and downs—cause us less suffering, introduce joy, and lessen the suffering of others.

If one were to search the planet for the most sophisticated systems of knowledge ever revealed or devised, the Buddhist teachings as expressed through the Vajrayana tradition of Tibet would surely be at or close to the top. There are certainly other profound sources of nondual teachings to be found, but the Vajrayana—in particular, the Dzogchen and Mahamudra[1] teachings contained within it—remains remarkable for its penetrating clarity and overwhelming richness. These teachings have been practiced, protected, expounded upon, and transmitted through many generations to reach this day and age where they are not only still relevant but perhaps more needed and applicable than ever before.

In Buddhism, which is essentially nontheistic, the view is quite simple. The *nature of mind* is at the core of this view. Simply put, it references the essential nature of reality, the ground of being. It underlies how we and the world around us came into being—actually, it arises in every moment. More will be said about this, but one important distinction is that our own nature is understood to be fundamentally the same as the nature of all things. This nature is ungraspable, beyond concept, open and vast, yet profoundly potent and radiant. By recognizing this ground, by attuning to it and learning to rest in it, we can experience naturally arising authentic wisdom.

This wisdom is not relative; it does not differ from one religion to the next or change based on individual preference or belief. It is inherently authentic as it directly relates to how things really are rather than how anyone wants them to be. Some form of meditation is generally prescribed as the best way to attune to this nature—and there are many forms—but the important message here is that this nature of mind is imminently accessible to all of us. Why is it accessible? Because it is, after all, our very own primordial nature.

The journey of this book is to come to know and live into Skymind not as a rare mystical experience but as an everyday opportunity to engage fully with every aspect of life. So when we awaken to the sky-like nature of our being, we can recognize that we can include everything in the totality of our being; we can meet every moment of life with a heart of unending compassion and a mind as vast as space. Because this journey also includes meeting our darkest shadows—personally, socially, and globally—it is a courageous journey. Courageous means to "have heart," so it is a journey of the awakened heart.

Our guide on the Skymind journey is arguably one of the most interesting figures of the eleventh century, and possibly since. Welcome to the ever-fresh, resplendent, and uncompromising nondual view of that wise woman of Tibet, Machig Labdrön. Machig was extraordinary in so many ways, but her forays into the nonordinary spaces of deep practice and the resulting wisdom made her positively peerless. Within the context of the Buddhism of her day, she came up with a profound and detailed system for transcending everyday challenges to live a liberated life of authenticity and wisdom.

We were introduced to Machig, her practices, and her teachings by Lama Tsultrim Allione, who herself was recognized in 2007 as an emanation of Machig. We are profoundly grateful for this connection, which provides a fresh and direct link to this lineage of deep wisdom.

In this book we present short verses from texts attributed directly to Machig that serve as luminous pearls of inspiration, profound guides for everyday life, and pith instructions for meditation.[2] Machig's precise, arrow-like instructions take us into the heart of the Buddhist teachings regarding our true nature and the nature of reality itself. We can imbibe them like drops of sweet nectar or use them like koans[3] to tie up our ordinary mind so that we may liberate into the mystery beyond everyday preoccupations.

Who Was Machig Labdrön?

Machig's colorful life in Tibet, spanning almost a century from approximately 1055 to 1153, infuses an earthiness into her luminous insights. Her story is marked by contrasts and extremes. Recognized for her unique realization and committed spiritual practice at an early age, Machig grew up with relative privilege but encountered poverty and homelessness at various stages of her life. She had a fiery connection with Topa Bhadra, a consort and the father of her children; a memorable story recounts their first union generating brilliant, blazing light. Yet she did not remain with him for long. For a period of time, she left her children to pursue a solitary life of meditation. Eventually she reunited with them, shared her teachings, and finally passed on streams of her lineage to each one.

As a teacher, Machig was honored and revered even by her own teachers, including Dampa Sangye (affectionately referred to as "Padampa" or "Father Dampa"), the famed Indian master who played a seminal role in Machig's life and lineage.[4] Yet she had to fiercely defend herself and the validity of her teachings, most notably in a famous debate with three Indian scholars in front of an audience of thousands. She prevailed in this exchange, opening the way for her unique lineage to take its place in the Tibetan Buddhist canon. She holds a key position in the history of Buddhism as the first Tibetan—and the first woman—to be the founder of a new stream of teachings and practices that did not directly originate in India, the motherland of Buddhism. Her extraordinary lineage of Chöd (pronounced *chuh*), meaning "to cut through" or "severance," has subsequently been woven into all schools of Tibetan Buddhism.[5] In her writings, and specifically those presented in this book, Machig's primary focus is on illuminating the ineffable nature of mind. When she writes about Chöd, she is offering us a path for severing our fears, insecurity, and anxiety, and coming to rest in fundamental wholeness, our true nature. The wisdom of Chöd is to suggest that only by meeting and even nurturing whatever we consider most "other" can true liberation be attained. As long as there is someone or something "out there," we are held in the prison walls of our own dualistic fixation.

We were first drawn to Chöd for its unnerving insistence to turn toward that which we find most repulsive or frightening, most other, most opposed to who we think we are or want to be. This view seemed so counterintuitive, so clearly different from the oh-so-human default response of avoiding the difficult aspects of life that we were instantly compelled. The traditional Chöd practice involves visualizing feeding all beings—in particular, harm-doers, disease-bringers, and other negativities—with your own body, transformed into a nectar that feeds all to complete satisfaction. Sung in ancient melodies and accompanied by drum, bell, and a thigh-bone trumpet, Chöd is penetrating and potent.

It is an invitation to go to the places that scare us with an open heart and a spacious mind in order to recognize that fundamentally there is no enemy out there. Machig challenges us:

> *Don't you consider the enemy in your dream*
> *as coming from yourself?*[6]

In Machig's view, true freedom lies in the lived realization of nonseparation. Through compassionate engagement with our perceived enemies, we begin to taste this liberation. Her teachings on severance are about cutting through the fundamentally mistaken duality of self and other—and the resultant isolation and claustrophobia of self-fixation.

Machig Labdrön was inspired by *Prajñāpāramitā*, the teachings on transcendent wisdom from the turn of the first millennium. The Prajñāpāramitā teachings suggest that the basic nature of reality, the ground of our being, is infinitely open, innately awake, and so profoundly interconnected with all things that it is actually "empty" of solidity and separateness. It is the radiant source of all.

A beautiful story recounts a potent event in Machig's life. She had just withdrawn from her role as an acclaimed spiritual teacher, left her partner and children, and entered into solitary retreat in a cave. In deep meditation, she has a vision of Tara, a female deity of compassion, who illuminates for Machig who she really is and what her purpose is. Machig expresses uncertainty regarding her own capacities, being a "weak, stupid woman."[7] But Tara is fierce in her encouragement. Tara speaks of Prajñāpāramitā,[8] the Great Mother, the source of all wisdom, the ultimate ground of being from which all things arise. And this Great Mother, this primordial ground, says Tara, "is no other than yourself!"[9] This is a pivotal moment in Machig's life as Tara calls her to step into the empowered fullness of her being without doubt or hesitation, not for her own sake but for the sake of others.

Tara's affirmation points to the inherent wakefulness and radiant wholeness that lies within us already, the most precious jewel we've forgotten even as we go searching outside for abundance and fulfillment. Years later, Machig offers a similar message to her students, gathered by the thousands:

Once one's mind is recognized for sure,
there's no need to establish buddha from elsewhere.[10]

Buddha is "the awakened one," referring to the radiant, aware, and self-perfected nature of our being. And although we may spend our entire life searching for who we truly are, Machig invites us to contemplate that it is not actually "elsewhere."

There's a traditional Buddhist parable of the poor man who goes out begging every day. When he dies, his neighbors find a large bag of gold under his pillow. He had been immeasurably wealthy all along. The gold is our true nature, which is radiantly aware, supremely vast, inextricably connected to all, innately compassionate and loving. The journey of life is to discover, uncover, recognize, and embody this very ground of our being. There are grand terms to describe this journey—*awakening*, *enlightenment*, *realization*. Put simply, it is to be as we truly are.

This book is an invitation to recognize, like Machig, that you are already awake, that there is nothing elsewhere or in the future that is more complete, more whole. There really is nothing to fix. There is nothing you're going to get that you don't already have. The nature of mind, the basic reality of all things, is fundamentally unborn and undying; it is complete and whole as it is, right now. As you are. Skymind.

This message is a wonderful relief. On the one hand, it's an invitation to acknowledge and savor the already-always wholeness of life. *I have what I need? The world has what it needs? Not somewhere else, not "elsewhere," but here, now?* Yes.

On the other hand, it's a supreme wake-up call to the absolute reality of no escape. Wholeness includes everything. The sky holds everything. We have to be with all things—and all things include great suffering and pain, hardship, loss, injustice. All things also include joy, intimacy, humor, lightness of being. It's all there. Nothing is left out. As Machig suggests,

The realization of the nature of mind
Includes all phenomena without exception.[11]

This book is for you, whoever and wherever you may be. If the ground of being is my true nature, is your true nature, then we will recognize it in any number of languages. In this case, we will use the language of Buddhism, as it is the tradition we are most practiced and versed in and the one we have been drawn to for its clear precision, deep wisdom, brilliant beauty, and practical helpfulness. If you are new to Buddhism, we hope to offer a view that is accessible. If you are a seasoned Buddhist practitioner, we hope these teachings will support, deepen, and expand your ongoing path. Above all, we hope the insights and practices of this book may be applied to your everyday life so that the gold beneath your pillow may be recognized, enjoyed, and shared with others.

Tracing the Skymind Arc

In this book we provide a framework on which to hang Machig's exquisite insights: a cohesive system whereby we can hopefully integrate this timeless wisdom in a way that brings about profound change for ourselves, and through us, the world around us. We employ the time-honored arc of *ground*, *path*, and *fruition*, a progression traditionally used as one of a variety of ways to describe the Buddhist path to liberation.

Ground refers to the ground of being, the nature of mind, always already present. All phenomena arise out of this basic, luminous, potent space, including us. When we realize and live in Skymind, we actualize the recognition of our inseparability from the ground. Because it is not other than our true nature, it is best recognized through Machig's instruction to "rest." In chapters 1–3 we offer insights into this ultimately nonconceptual and ineffable reality.

Because most of us, most of the time, don't recognize the ground as our primordial nature, we enter the *path* where we encounter our confusion, ignorance, and insecurity—but also the possibility of developing insight, awareness, kindness, and altruism. According to Machig, the *path* is initially defined by "self-inflation," which is our pervasive sense of a separate self, which is perpetually attempting to establish and prove its own identity and is the fundamental cause of our suffering. We explore this in chapter 4. Chapter 5 introduces Machig's practice of "severance," in which we cut through our mistaken notions of duality, separateness, and insufficiency, thus opening us to Skymind.

Traditionally the path is further divided into *view*, *meditation*, and *action*. Chapter 6 is about view, which is essentially the application of our understanding of the ground to everyday life—it becomes the lens through which we view our reality. Vast in scope, the view embraces the totality of all that is, excluding nothing. Nothing exists independently of anything else but only always in a web of unending interconnectivity and interdependence.

In chapter 7 we look at *meditation*, through which we practice to embody and stabilize the view. Meditation is the skillful means to recognize Skymind. While there are countless forms of meditation, here we emphasize the cultivation of attention, the awakening of awareness, and the embodiment of loving radiance, combined in a single accessible practice in chapter 8: the Skymind meditation. Chapter 9 offers further refinements and subtler reflections on open awareness–type meditation.

Finally, *action* manifests the view through compassionate conduct. Action is where Skymind meets the grit of everyday life. Certain truths become evident: Because we cannot hide from ourselves, we recognize the need for radical honesty (chapter 10). Because we are inescapably connected to all beings, we embrace profound responsibility (chapter 11). Because avoidance is actually suffering, we awaken to the wisdom of radical acceptance (chapter 12). Because we wish to liberate from the prison of hope and fear, we practice going to the places that scare us (chapter 13). As it opens our hearts and minds, the path of action reveals our capacity for supreme compassion (chapter 14) and awakens us to our inherent fullness (chapter 15) and innate dignity (chapter 16). We end the "Path" section with reflections and teachings on ways we can meet death and dying within the view of Skymind (chapter 17).

Fruition is essentially a return to the ground that we had never left in the first place. We don't necessarily "figure out" the existential questions; we don't successfully reverse engineer our system or situation. Indeed, as we discuss in chapter 18, we are liberated from the very notion of having to accomplish something in the first place. But somehow the questions transform, become lighter, more translucent, and finally self-liberate in the vast luminous space of wisdom-essence. From this vantage point, the ultimate view is that of no view (chapter 19); the supreme meditation is non-meditation (chapter 20); and the absolute action is non-action (chapter 21). As we discuss in chapter 22, outwardly fruition may manifest as unhurried deep ease, supremely aligned spontaneity, unforced originality, an effortless upwelling of boundless contentment, subtle bliss, and radiant compassion.

How to Engage with the Practices of This Book

We invite you to engage directly with Machig's verses, the Skymind meditation, and a variety of exercises described throughout the book. These are designed to offer a direct, personal experience of some of the concepts discussed, to integrate the teachings into your everyday life, and to support you in developing a regular meditation practice. The exercises are designed so you can lead yourself through them or be guided by someone else.

Contemplating Machig's Verses

In presenting Machig Labdrön's verses, we were inspired by the methodology of the *lojong* (mind training) slogans based on the teachings of the eleventh-century Bengali teacher Atisha,[12] which were designed as direct and applicable instructions to integrate compassion and wakefulness into everyday life. Similarly, Machig's verses can be used as reminders throughout the day to integrate her teachings into your life. A full list of the verses discussed in this book are included in the appendix.

Some ideas for how to work with Machig's verses:

- ✧ Write or print out some of your favorite verses. Choose a new verse each day or week. Start your day reciting the verse; contemplate it before any kind of formal meditation practice you might do (see chapter 8 for the recommended Skymind meditation); recall it as you are walking, driving, eating; remember it as you go to bed. How does its meaning evolve for you? What impact does it have on you—your thoughts, your emotions, your body, your actions?

- ✧ Memorize verses so that they can pop into your mind at random moments. Notice their significance as you recall them. What are they pointing out?
- ✧ Post verses in places where you'll encounter them as you move through your day: your bedside table, bathroom mirror, refrigerator, computer screen. Leave verses in random places: inside a book, in the pocket of a coat, in your clothes drawer, among your spices—anywhere you may chance upon them. When you find them, take a moment to contemplate their significance right in that instant.

Skymind Meditation

This book is intended for those new to meditation as well as those with an existing practice. Meditation is key for moving from a purely conceptual understanding to a direct personal experience of the teachings presented in these pages. Thus we encourage you to develop or deepen your relationship to meditation so that it can serve as an ongoing teacher and practice for cultivating awareness, insight, and heart.

The Skymind meditation described in chapter 8 is an essentialized practice that integrates focused attention, loving radiance, and resting in open awareness. As with any practice, the more we engage with it, the greater benefit and insights we derive from it. The Skymind meditation can serve as an introduction to meditation, as a supplement to any practices you may already be doing, and as a regular practice that you can integrate ongoingly into your contemplative life.

As with all meditation practices, while written guidelines are helpful, it is always recommended that at some point you work directly with a meditation instructor or teacher with whom you can discuss your meditation experiences.

A Note to Our Readers

The teachings of the Tibetan Buddhist tradition are exceptional, profound, and vast in scope. We have no pretense of being authoritative Buddhist scholars, and there are many others more deeply learned than us. We have the good fortune to have studied with exceptional teachers and to have had some time to practice what we received from them. And we certainly would not have been in the position to write this if it wasn't for the inspiring teachings of Lama Tsultrim Allione and her encouragement and support over many years. This book is about making available what we learned and practiced in the hope that it might benefit others. Although the entire Vajrayana is sometimes viewed as secret, we took care not to reveal any restricted practices for which transmission is required.[13] As always, we encourage our readers to seek out a qualified teacher if they decide to deepen their study and practice.

Part One

GROUND

1

The Basic Ground

Our Skymind journey begins with ground, the ground of being. This ground refers to the fundamental nature of things, our basic nature. In Buddhism, this fundamental basis of all is described variously as the nature of mind, Buddha Nature, awakened mind, basic goodness,[1] suchness, luminous cognizance, pure awareness, great bliss. To recognize the ground of being and our inseparability from it is the point of all of Machig's teachings; Skymind is the lived experience of this realization.

Why might it be helpful to recognize the ground of existence of our lives, of reality? Because—so suggest the Buddhist teachings—the root of our suffering lies in the ignorance of our true nature and the nature of all. Thus, to awaken to our true nature is to meet the fundamental wholeness and radiant brilliance that underlies the vibrancy of this precious life.

It is through this recognition that our deepest human search for meaning and fulfillment is accomplished. To recognize the ground of being is like a weary traveler finally coming home and resting in loving, enveloping peace, a peace blazing with crystal clarity and all-encompassing wisdom. So the ground of being is the starting point, the refuge, and the end point; to awaken to the ground of being *is* the point.

What Is Ground?

The ground of being is always already present. The great primordial purity, it is the empty, luminous basis of reality. Also known as pure awareness, this basic ground is alpha-original—the fundamental state, the natural state. Whatever is, whatever was, whatever will be arises from this uncompounded, infinite, and inconceivable ground and is never separate from it. Although nondual and indivisible, it can be said that the essence of the ground is empty, free of conceptual constructs or extremes; the nature is radiant clarity and spontaneous presence; and the manifestation is all-pervasive compassionate energy. Since all apparent phenomena, including ourselves, are the unobstructed display of this ground, it is also our basic nature, our Buddha Nature—brilliant, clear, and radiant. We cannot create or destroy this true nature; we can only recognize or not recognize it.

The ground of being is ultimately beyond words, inexpressible, ineffable. It cannot be grasped by thought or concept. It is no-thing. Yet it is the source of all. Machig points to it in this way:

it abides inherently
it occurs naturally
it is unborn
it is unceasing
it is all-pervasive
it is oneself
it is without contrivance
it is without meeting or parting
it is like space[2]

Thus this self-occurring vast expanse of being is not constructed or manufactured, is neither created nor destroyed. The primordial essence of all things, it cannot be lost or found. Like space, though empty in and of itself, it pervades everything.

Āryadeva the Brahmin, the ninth-century Indian master whose teachings are influential in Machig's lineage, writes,

The meaning of [ultimate reality[3]] is not to be looked for elsewhere.
It exists within yourself.
Neither real nor endowed with characteristics
The nature of mind is the great clear light.[4]

Thus our own awareness, our own clear light of wakefulness, is the doorway to a direct experience of the nature of all things. The point is not to go searching elsewhere but to recognize the innate brilliance, the wholeness that is already within us and that is also the very fabric of reality itself.

The moment of recognition is captured metaphorically in Tibetan Buddhism through the union of the wisdom deities Samantabhadra and Samantabhadri. Iconographically they are represented as two elegantly entwined figures of exceptional beauty: the white, feminine Samantabhadri and the blue, masculine Samantabhadra. Samantabhadri represents the empty essence of the ground—vast, pure potential. Samantabhadra represents luminosity or spontaneous presence—the unceasing radiance of the ground that appears as all phenomena.

Is that which arises out of ground other than the ground? There is a crossroads here: to recognize or not to recognize. Samantabhadra can either experience himself as separate or recognize his inseparability from Samantabhadri. But Samantabhadra is considered the Primordial Buddha because of his instantaneous recognition of inherent unity with the basic space of all. He is original wakefulness and represents the awakened nature innate to each and every one of us.

We, too, are continuously arising as an endless parade of manifestations, activities, thoughts, emotions, and perceptions. And outer appearances are always arising in an infinite number of creative permutations of color, vibrancy, and outrageousness. Even though there is no fundamental otherness, it does not mean there is no differentiation. Endless diversity and multiplicity manifests all the time, but no one and nothing ever actually separates from the ground.

The Basic Split

We could, however, have the *experience* of being separate from the ground, which is what most of us experience most of the time! The self arises out of the ground, but unlike Samantabhadra, we don't recognize our inseparability from the ground. This is the birth of duality, and there's a split, known as *the basic split.* What arises is a sense of self as a separate entity and the ensuing birth of the ego (discussed in greater depth in chapter 4). From the relative, dualistic point of view of the contracted self, the vastness of the ground feels overwhelming—even threatening—leading to further contraction. The feeling of separateness and threat creates a profound sense of insecurity and anxiety at the core of the ego; it is our most basic experience of fear and the birthplace of suffering. The result is a perpetual striving to regain a sense of safe and stable ground.

Thus from the nonrecognition of our true nature and the resulting basic split, the journey of constructing and maintaining a relative or "false" ground of self begins. Our ego comes into play, with its mission to maintain itself against a world "out there" that is either for or against us. The experience of self and other, me and you, us and them seems completely solid, true, and real. Preoccupied with "me," we get caught in the constriction of self-involvement. *Everything* is perceived and experienced from the platform of the ego-self, even our highest ideals and pursuits of salvation, liberation, or enlightenment. No matter what we do, we seem to remain trapped in dualism. We call this trap of dualism the *claustrophobia of self-referentiality*, and this is exactly why Machig's primary remedy is to "cut through ego-clinging" (see chapter 5). Nonrecognition initiates the path on which we journey in order to find our way back to what we have always already been.

In contrast, recognition results in a profound transformation of all aspects of our life. Everything we experience is the radiance of the ground—not in the past and enduring into the future but actually in every single moment. Through our senses and relative awareness we perceive the luminosity of the ground as manifest reality and as thought and emotions.

Yet, as everything arises out of the same basic space, there is no separate, solid existence of anything. Since nothing exists in isolation of anything else, this includes our "self." The Buddha famously described this reality of nonsolidity as "no-self" (Skt. *anātman*) and "emptiness" (Skt. *śūnyatā*), which should be understood not in a nihilistic sense (as though nothing exists) but rather as a description of the essence of all things. Everything arises in relation to everything else. Everything is completely interconnected. There is no separateness anywhere in this vast sky, this vast ocean of awareness in which we are floating. So not only is there no substantial self but there is no absolute separation between self and other, self and ground, just as there is no separation between wave and ocean or cloud and sky. The perceived separation between the wave and the ocean is only at a relative level of relationship. But in the absolute sense, from the point of view of the absolute ground, we are all profoundly connected; we are made of the same stuff. Experientially, this realization is the place of natural deep ease and alignment, self-evidence and spontaneity. All experience is blissfully integrated and spontaneously complete.

We will continue to explore these ideas in this book and provide practices aimed at consciously experiencing this ground and hopefully stabilizing that experience.

Wave and Ocean

Let's use a metaphor for how the nature of mind and the basic split may apply to our human condition. We may say our experience in daily life is like a wave on the ocean. We think of ourselves as a wave, and our entire identity is caught up in our waveness. We see the other waves around us, and relating to them reaffirms our own waveness—and so we roll along on our journey. Some days are stormy and dark; others, the sun is shining in a blue sky, gulls are swooping, and we are enjoying our life as a wave together with our wave friends. But one day we hear a crashing noise, and as we look over the tops of the waves in front of us we see an alarming spectacle: A steep rock face rises out of the water, and wave after wave ahead of us crashes into it and disappears into a billion droplets of foam and spray. Now, from our point of view as a wave, this is a calamity of existential scope. We are literally witnessing our own imminent demise—inexorably rolling toward it. Try as we might, there is no escape from the fact that we will soon completely cease to exist as a wave. However, we will probably all agree that a wave is also absolutely and undeniably part of the ocean. From the point of view of the ocean, the waves crashing on its shores is not at all a problem. In fact, from the ocean's perspective, it is beautiful play, a completely natural consequence of its dynamic oceanness.

When we are limited to expressing only as a wave, when we forget that we are the ocean, we fall into all the suffering that arises from the fundamental misapprehension of separateness and the resultant cascade of dualistic perceptions and reactivities. This specifically is the suffering the Buddha taught about: the basic ignorance of our true nature and the resultant contraction around a self. It is the basis for the "three poisons" in Buddhism: ignorance, avoidance, or denial; grasping or fixation; and repulsion or aggression.

Through practices of mindfulness, meditation, and awareness on the path, we begin to identify more with our oceanness, with the vaster ground of our being; we take refuge in our oceanness while also expressing as a wave. We start to realize that the boundaries of self are permeable rather than solid; that the self cannot be separate from the ground or anyone or anything else, just as much as the wave cannot be separate from the ocean or from any other wave. How does the wave come to know that it is the ocean? By resting, by relaxing into its water nature. If the wave keeps looking outside for the ocean, it will only see other waves. When the wave looks inside, all it sees is ocean. Nothing but vast ocean. (See the Wave and Ocean exercise at the end of chapter 17, "Encountering Death.")

Another way of thinking about the self is that we are like focalizing lenses of self-awareness floating in an ocean of awareness. The innate splendor of the ground expresses through us and is experienced by us in all its magnificence, intricacy, and diversity. The invitation here is not to reject our waveness or to try to flatten the ocean. We don't demonize the ego. No, the wave keeps expressing itself in all its uniqueness, as a *naturally perfect* expression of the ocean. However, once we relax the contracted boundaries of self, we open to our actual situation of interconnectedness with all things; we see that we are made of the same stuff ultimately. Relaxing into oceanness, we start developing the bandwidth to pay attention to what else is going on around us. Not consumed with self-preoccupation, we tap into self-arising compassion and let it effortlessly express through us. Without manipulating or grasping, we engage from a place of ease and spontaneity. We don't have to change the waves; the storms are still happening. We're not trying to make everything quiet and peaceful. All of life is still happening. But our view is vast. We recognize that at the relative level, the waves are just the play of the ocean; they will keep crashing on the shore, but it's not the end of the world. It's just what the ocean does. We can rest in that and enjoy the play of the waves of life. Eventually we experience ourselves as the ocean experiences itself in all its glorious totality, which would be considered fruition.

2

Rest in Your Nature

If we are not other than the ground of being, then how do we recognize this primordial unity? How do we consciously embody the profoundly vast and luminous wholeness that is our true nature? Would a fish recognize water if all it ever knew was to be completely surrounded by it? Machig's response, reiterated in numerous versions throughout her writings, is deceivingly simple.

> *Since there is no path to traverse,*
> *rest in the basic ground, noble child.*[1]

To be on a path means that we are busy getting somewhere; we are progressing from where we were to where we hope to be. Life consists of all kinds of paths; paths give us direction and a sense of purpose. Yet there is no path to traverse, says Machig. What you are ultimately trying to get to—fulfillment, completion, wholeness, and the happiness that ensues from these—is not down the road. It is not something you can achieve by walking a path, by taking a journey. It is not something that you can work your way toward, that you can build up to or attain like any number of other accomplishments. Why? Because wholeness and completeness *are* our true nature. And our true nature—vast, awake, brilliant—has never been separate from us; it is not arrived at by a pathway because there is no distance to traverse. It was never and will never be other than what we are, what is already, always.

You might wonder why we would include an entire section on path in this book, given Machig's teaching here. Fundamentally there is no path to our true nature. Yet within the experience of nonrecognition, the path is the way by which we come to *recognize* what we have always already been. The irony is that in journeying on the path, we also come to understand that there was never ultimately a path to traverse. We'll continue to return to this paradox.

Let's return to Machig's verse: the view is that meeting the ground of being, recognizing our Buddha Nature, living in Skymind, is not a project. It's not work, like assembling pieces and putting together a puzzle. To find it is like being asked to look for your own face, a traditional Buddhist metaphor. Every day you get up and look—under the bed, around the corner, then outside; you start asking other people, you read books about how to find your own face. You travel the entire world. You will never find your own face by searching outside. You will not find it until you look back, until you see yourself just as you are—your original face.

How do we come to know what we already are? We rest. We rest in what already is.

Rest in the basic ground, noble child.

We are all familiar with conditional rest, based on completion, arrival, or fulfillment—the end of a long day of work, getting our kids to bed, finalizing a project. Yes, part of our practice of rest is to simply recognize these mundane gaps when we can relax our efforting and exhale. But the rest that Machig is speaking of is unconditional. It is not about fulfilling or completing anything whatsoever. In any and every moment we can stop and recognize the ground of being that has never been foreign to us.

When Machig urges us to "rest in the basic ground, noble child," she is inviting us to relax back into the natural state we have actually never left. In the practice of meditation, we turn our awareness to become aware of itself so that it rests effortlessly in its own ground. (See chapter 9 on meditation.) In our everyday life, this becomes a profound exercise in surrender, of relinquishing our attitude of incessant striving. If we read this verse in the imperative, it is as though Machig says, "Rest! Let go! Drop it!"

When we stop trying to get somewhere else, we arrive where we are. When we release our search for something else, we find what we already have. Thus Machig reminds us,

Leaving oneself behind and searching,
even after many millions of aeons
of practicing, [one] will not attain it.[2]

Ironically, our perpetual drive to search elsewhere, outside of ourselves, or somewhere in the future ends up separating us from the very wholeness or awakening we set out to find in the first place. Skymind is fundamentally about resting back into the always already-present sky-like wholeness of our nature.

Diogenes and Alexander the Great

Alexander the Great lived about 300 B.C.E. and is recognized as one of the youngest and most successful conquerors of all times. His battles took him from Greece to northwestern India. There's a retelling of the story of Alexander meeting Diogenes, the great philosopher and father of cynicism who had devoted himself to living in utter simplicity. Diogenes is lounging on a riverbank, taking in the warm rays of the afternoon sun. Compelled by the man's radiant presence, Alexander engages in conversation, telling Diogenes of his great journey to India where he will go into battle, expand his empire, and eventually conquer the world. "And what will you do then?" queries Diogenes. "Then," reflects Alexander, "I will rest." With a smile, Diogenes notes that Alexander need not conquer the world in order to rest. Indeed, like himself, he could rest right now.

What is it we feel we need to accomplish in order to find peace? What state or place do we need to reach in order to feel fulfilled? For most of us, the goal is less grandiose than Alexander's, but somewhere within us lurks the suspicion that our rest must be earned.

"No path to traverse" means the ultimate arrival is not somewhere else. It's right here. Literally right now in this moment, with all our messiness, undone dishes, and unanswered emails; all the parts of ourselves and the world that seem untidy, confused, problematic, unresolved.

Machig's teachings may have been helpful to Alexander as he made his way across Eurasia in search of the fulfillment that Diogenes found reclining on the riverbank. Alexander died before he made it back home. In the end, despite his immense efforts, his final dream of resting was never attained.

There's something quite lovely in Machig's tender encouragement to us as a "noble child," beckoning us to come home. Traditional teachings suggest that recognizing the ground of being is like a child running into the warm lap of their mother. The child luminosity returns to the mother luminosity; the spark of wakefulness that manifests as you and me comes to rest in the primordial wakefulness of the Great Mother. The recognition of the ground of being is a homecoming like no other because it is unconditional and unwavering. We remember the nobility and dignity of our true nature, our innate worthiness.

Don't Search

Machig's unflinching directive is further clarified in this verse:

Don't search, don't practice; rest in your nature.[3]

"Don't search"—what balm to our restless souls Machig offers here! How much of our day is consumed with one search or another—the quest for the better life, the better partner, the better work, the better idea, or maybe only the better cup of coffee. We define ourselves, in great part, by what we search for; our searches drive us, inspire us, and too often taunt us, torture us. Of course, our modern economy and the global marketing complex are built on and reflect this propensity for continual searching. We search because we have a sense of something, an inkling of something that will provide fulfillment, ease, wholeness, however small or large. But it's always "out there," isn't it? We're never quite there. Maybe soon, just around the corner. That's the hook of the search: the promise that we're almost there.

You might notice at this moment whether you are searching for something—an insight, a realization, a guide for wellness, awakening, inspiration, relief . . . Whatever it may be, Machig says quit it. Stop the search. Perhaps there's a sweet glimpse of freedom, like a tight belt that's finally been unbuckled. Or a smile of ease that crosses your lips. Or perhaps the restless mind balks: *Now what? What am I now? Who am I without my search?*

"Don't practice." Fundamentally, our true nature, the lived experience of Skymind, is not a product of practice. Once we recognize this, the ultimate practice becomes one of releasing even the idea of practice. On a more relative level, this instruction uproots the subtler but often more enticing search embedded in spiritual practice. Whispers of striving and achievement can lurk within any spiritual endeavor. We hope for an awakening, a grand attainment of insight, an ultimate arrival. There is beauty in this ancient longing that is shared across religious traditions. Yet it, too, can become a golden chain, laden with goals and targets. The Zen teacher Charlotte Joko Beck aptly calls this spiritual "athleticism."[4] Chögyam Trungpa calls it "spiritual materialism."[5]

Alternately, Machig notes,

Once one's mind is recognized for sure,
there's no need to establish buddha from elsewhere.[6]

Once we recognize our own embodied, heartful awareness (what Machig calls "mind") for what it is—the radiance of the ground of being—our attempts at finding truth and wholeness elsewhere dissolve like ice in the warm rays of the sun. Perhaps then, like Diogenes, we might simply rest, just as we are.

"Rest in your nature." What remains when we stop searching, when we stop practicing? What remains when we release the tight grip on a path, whether external—with its sweet promise of accomplishment in the human world—or internal, providing a refuge for heart and mind? At first there is perhaps the subtle tightening of fear. We're being asked to drop the complex identity we've spent our whole life assembling. Maybe there's even a feeling of voidness, loss, meaninglessness. But here again Machig says "rest"—rest in what remains when we let the reins drop; rest in the open space after all the juggling balls have fallen to the ground. We release, surrender, relax back into the warmth and radiance of the compassionate ground. Not to be searched for because it is not ever somewhere else. Not to be practiced because it is always already present.

Sometimes we may feel that we need to be safe before we can rest. But from this perspective, the way to feel safe *is* to rest. Resting in our nature comes first, is more fundamental. It's not resting because we have something to grasp on to. We're resting beyond any grasping. We can let go because we are held deeply, profoundly, unconditionally. Machig is saying rest, and rest more because you are in the lap of the Great Mother, the ultimate ground. This is the supreme safety.

This may sound like some grand mystical experience, and to some extent it is. But we can rest in our nature at any moment. I like remembering this slogan when I'm doing the dishes. "Don't search." I notice the miniature purple orchids blooming at my window. "Don't practice." I feel the hot water running over my fingers. "Rest in your nature." The cast-iron pan drips glistening in my hand.

But what of our life's path? Do we stop our searching? Do we stop practicing? No, probably not and maybe never. As humans we strive and search, just like children play hide-and-seek. But when we rest, we can let go a bit. Our searching becomes more like play—divine play. Perhaps we can enjoy both the finding and the not finding. We are playing hide-and-seek with our Buddha Nature, and we can be sure that we will find it again and again, sometimes in the most unlikely places.

To rest in our nature means to trust our basic nature, to trust our inherent wakefulness, wholeness. We don't need to prove ourselves worthy of our lives. It is the desire for approval, from others and from ourselves, that drives so much of our searching, after all. If we can rest, over and over again, we can begin with worthiness as our starting point in whatever we endeavor. You are the ground of being. What will you do? What will you manifest? What will you dream?

3

Groundless Ground

Charlotte's dream: *I am falling, plunging down into space, frightened and terrified. I desperately grab onto magically appearing ropes one by one, but each, it turns out, is short and not attached to anything at all. I try all my well-practiced techniques—I breathe, I try to remember it's just a dream. But I keep falling, and the panic remains. And then, as though from nowhere at all, the voice of my first teacher Lama Tharchin Rinpoche comes to me: "Just rest, just rest." I let go. I stop trying to hold on to bits of rope in vast infinitude. I release. I surrender. In an instant, space becomes luminous, warm, radiant. I am held in unconditional embrace.*

We have been talking about the "ground"—the all-encompassing basis of experience and phenomena—but in some ways it's a misnomer. There really is no ground in the literal sense of that word. The ground is groundless. Even as we take respite in its all-pervasiveness, Machig reminds us that this ground is not solid. It is not a thing. Like space, like the sky, it is without handles or footholds.

Given the pervasive melancholy of the basic split, we are primed to strive for a firm foundation. Much of our lives is spent trying to build a sense of security, to find stability, to establish things we can depend on, whether material, psychological, or spiritual. This is the literal basis of fundamentalism. But here, the radical notion is that our ultimate refuge is actually the *groundlessness* of the ground. We are invited to tenderly relinquish our grasping for finality, fixity, certainty—even the notion of some absolute reality. We can surrender, release, and expand into this vast view, into Skymind. The good news is, even though it is a radical leap, we can do it bit by bit—with gentleness and self-compassion.

Let's return for a moment to some of Machig's verses describing the ground, which we introduced in chapter 1:

Since it is unceasing, don't construct a support.
Since it is transparent, don't be biased.
Since it is all-pervasive, don't take sides. . . .
Be utterly certain that it is like space.[1]

The ground's unceasing, all-pervasive transparency points to its substanceless nature. It's not *there* in the way that everything else in our experience seems to be. It's not a thing that we can hold on to or stand on for the firm footing our insecure "small" self craves. In case we think we are looking for some*thing*, Machig notes,

In fact there is nothing to see . . .[2]

Machig warns us not to "construct a support" because in the groundlessness of the ground, any attempt at creating solidity is futile and ultimately becomes the very source of our suffering. If we're looking for definiteness or a concrete foundation, we're looking for support in the wrong way.

The Refuge of Groundlessness

The notion of refuge is central to Vajrayana Buddhism. What can we truly depend on? What can we ultimately rely on? We turn to all kinds of relative refuges in our everyday lives—food, entertainment, our favorite activities. And there are deeper, more profound relative refuges—a healthy body, meaningful work, nature, friends, community, family. These bring joy, meaning, and relevance to our lives; we turn to these in times of confusion, uncertainty, need. Indeed, offering daily gratitude for the multitude of small and large blessings that grace our lives is a worthwhile practice in its own right.

However, as we know, many of these refuges don't satisfy quite as much as we might have hoped—the glass of wine only temporarily makes me feel more at ease after a stressful day. Even our most beloved friends and family members can't always ease our worries as we had hoped. Ultimately these refuges are impermanent, changing over time, and finally passing away, just like ourselves. We, too, can only serve as temporary refuges to our loved ones. While there may be some sorrow in this consideration, it is also a reminder to appreciate and savor the beauty of connection and support we experience day by day. Contemplating impermanence can actually enliven and invigorate us.

What remains when our relative refuges, our temporary supports, fall away? What remains, says Machig, is the vast expanse of beingness itself, the basic space that is unceasing. Ironically, it is the ground's very ungraspability, its groundlessness, that makes it the most profound refuge. It's the only ground that is actually unassailable because the rug cannot be pulled out from under us. There is no foundation to crumble. There's a classic quote attributed to Chögyam Trungpa: "The bad news is you're falling. The good news is there is no ground." This unchangeable refuge—the vast and luminous basic space of all—cannot be taken away because there's nothing to hold on to in the first place. And yet it holds us and everything unconditionally.

Machig's poetry beautifully transmits the essence of this idea:

There is no intention within the unborn.
There is nowhere to go within the unceasing.
Still, once naturally liberated without reference—
*Just vivid, quiet, radiant (*lhang nge lhan ne lham me*).*[3]

The Art of Letting Go

As with Machig's previous verse on "resting in the basic ground," the invitation is for us to relax back into the groundless ground. But because we are relaxing into groundlessness, this is really about letting go and surrendering—radically and completely. We call this "the art of letting go" because it entails expanding beyond the habitual boundaries of the familiar self—beyond our comfortable identity. In this process we come up against things we've been holding on to, often unconsciously, but also the things we have been conditioned to believe we should be holding. In discovering these boundaries, we get to know the subtle textures of ourselves, our ego makeup: our sensitivities, fears, belief systems, and conditioned reactivities. Here we are invited to gently let go of the holding. And yet, from the view of groundlessness, we realize that just as there is nothing to hold on to, there is also ultimately nothing to let go of. Everything is an unending expression of the ground of being.

Even though the infinite nature of basic space may feel intimidating from the ego's contracted point of view, it is this vast totality that offers absolute, incontrovertible refuge. We expand our awareness, which is the same awareness as the groundless ground, the same awareness as the Buddha, the same awareness as the greatest deity you may imagine: that awareness. We surrender into that, and there we rest.

Machig refers to it like this:

Awakening is actualized by realizing rootlessness.
So then, rest relaxed . . .
Rest just so with everything.[4]

Clinging to our habitual ego-identity makes us feel rooted in a solid sense of self. "Realizing rootlessness" is surrendering this grasping. We could rephrase the verse simply as "take refuge in groundlessness." In the vast view of things-as-they-are, we "rest just so with everything." When we surrender our own preferences, biases, and agendas (our "roots"), we have more bandwidth and energy to pay attention to what's actually going on around us. We have the capacity to be responsive rather than reactive and to engage with naturally arising compassion.

Fear and Fearlessness

Of course, we are deeply conditioned not to surrender. It's not an intuitive and smooth transition to go from experiencing the close-in self to resting back into our much vaster true nature. From the point of view of the ego, it feels like there's a lot that will be lost in this practice of surrender. As a result, any number of fears may arise—from the existential fear of losing the familiar self, sometimes called ego death, to the fear of being lost in overwhelming nothingness.

Regarding the reflexive fear we may have of this seemingly overwhelming space: Remember, you are not the small self, the identity self, the habitual ego-self, falling through space and trying to surrender to the unending vastness surrounding you. No, you are that vastness. You are that spaciousness. You are made of the same stuff you are letting go into. You are made of awareness, and you are relaxing into the space of awareness. By surrendering your clinging to your ego-identity, you are able to experience your larger nature—your fundamental nature—which also happens to be the nature of everything else. When you "rest just so with everything," you recognize it. Machig recommends it because the groundless ground is the only true refuge, and you can find profound ease resting in it. That's why it's such a wonderful refuge.

Thus Machig says,

> *The measure of freedom from inflation is fearlessness.*[5]

"Inflation" here refers to self-inflation, our clinging to a pervasive sense of a separate self. And "freedom from inflation" points to our capacity to see beyond the duality of self and other that leads to the whole range of dualities that lie at the root of fear. The more we are able to rest into the unconditional embrace of the ground of being, the more we can access our innate fearlessness. In the most absolute sense, there's no one and nothing "out there" to fear; realizing the unified ground of being integrates everything and opens us to the experience of genuine fearlessness. When we experience ourselves as all things, then we need not be afraid of anything.

What Surrender Is Not

Radical surrender, letting go, and resting should not be confused with giving up or letting others take advantage of us. It's not about becoming a rag doll and letting life run roughshod over us. It's also not about detachment, passivity, or nonengagement, a critique that is sometimes leveled against Buddhist teachings.

When we really let go into Skymind, we find that we don't stop showing up. We don't stop engaging. The radiance of the ground manifests through unceasing compassionate energy. There is nothing dull or passive about it—a common misconception. We don't shrink away from life. We just engage from a much different place—vaster, more expansive, less self-involved. We are less compelled by our ego machinations, our perpetual cycles of hope and fear, our struggles for validation. In Skymind we open to radical non-avoidance, acceptance, and profound inclusivity of everything that is happening. (See the chapters 4 and 5 for more on this.)

Rather than taking us out of the messiness and pain of lived reality, the experience of resting into groundlessness elicits a heightened state of presence and awakens us more fully to the raw beauty and subtlety of existence, the so-called zing of reality.[6] We realize that we cannot actually escape the challenges of everyday life, community, or society. Surrendering and resting are not exits from reality. They are the doorways for entering our lives and meeting others with presence, wakefulness, and an open heart.

Realizing Rootlessness: Charlotte's Reflections from Retreat

I contemplated Machig's emphasis on "realizing rootlessness" for many days during a solitary retreat in a ramshackle little hut, tucked in a dip between hillsides, with a mucky pond of croaking frogs and a wild green meadow that was home to a small herd of deer.

Machig's whole lineage of teaching is about severance (Chöd), cutting the root of suffering. She often uses the metaphor of a tree for the spiritual path. We can keep cutting the branches of all our particular forms of ignorance and confusion, but it's an endless task until we've cut the root of self-clinging, the mistaken notion that we exist as a separate self in a dualistic world. That's the rootlessness she is referring to here.

When we look at who or what we truly are—you or me—there's nothing solid there. We don't have a basic root that makes us some *thing*—solid, independent, immutable. This is the no-self that the Buddha taught. I only exist in relation to other relative things, which themselves have no permanence or independent existence. This is the truth of interdependent co-arising. It's not that I don't exist; it's that "I" don't exist in the way I normally think of myself, as fundamentally distinct and apart from others and the world around me. I'm far more permeable and ephemeral than I usually take myself to be. Just as the wave never exists apart from ocean but only ever as an arising *of* ocean, so too the self is ultimately not an entity unto itself but only always a conglomeration of various patterns, conditions, and relationships, never separate from the ground of being.

To realize rootlessness is to let go of my continuous attempts at reaffirming my separate existence, at creating a defensible "territory" of identity. Who I am, what I do, what I believe, what I like, what I don't like—these are the cornerstones of my identity and also the golden chains that bind me. To realize rootlessness is to open the tight clasp on me-ness, like a fist finally relaxing its vain attempts at grasping air.

Thus, Machig says, whatever you grasp, let it go, let it go, let it go. Realize that ultimately you are rootless, all things are ultimately rootless. And that, believe it or not, is good news! Because in letting go of grasping our tiny bit of seemingly solid yet strikingly temporary territory, we open ourselves to the far more immense and empowered groundless ground of our being that is "without meeting and parting."[7]

Listening to the spring rain drumming on my tiny roof, I realized that rootlessness awakens me more readily to the coo of the evening dove, the chirping of the crickets, the gentle gaze of the deer. I'm not trying to build a mini empire of my life. "I" am simply passing through just like all these beings. That's the resting, not outside of the movement of things but right within them, more present and awake.

To truly realize rootlessness is an ultimate view. At a relative level, we all have roots—our family, friends, animals, beloved places. Looking out at the tall ponderosas reaching high into the sky, I thought more about the very nature of roots themselves. Roots are like tentacles reaching into the very heart of the earth, drawing nurturance and sustenance from their connection to myriad forms of life. Rootlessness is to let go of the idea that our roots have an endpoint, that they are holding us firmly to a solid base. "This is mine, this is me." The invitation to rootlessness is a call to keep reaching our roots so deep until they connect us with all beings, until roots open us to rootlessness. Until we realize there is no ground because we are the ground.

When we stop grasping to rooted solidity, when we release the grip on our territory, then what? Then "rest relaxed. Rest just so with everything." Rest in this way—rootless in vast groundless ground, the source of all—at all times, with everything, everywhere. We begin to intimate that we are very much *not* alone. We are with all things; we are all things. Inextricably. Always.

~ EXERCISE ~

Rest in the Way of a Corpse

This contemplation is intended to give you an experiential taste of resting in the groundless ground we've been discussing. These are Machig's instructions:

[R]est the body in the way of a corpse.
Rest in the way of being ownerless.
Rest the mind in the way of the sky.[8]

The practice is best done while lying down on a comfortable surface, in a way that allows you to most easily relax all parts of your body. You might set a timer for yourself so that you don't need to worry about time (20–30 minutes is ideal). You may say the words silently to yourself or have someone guide you, taking appropriate pauses between instructions.

- ✧ Close your eyes and bring awareness to your breath.
- ✧ *Rest your body in the way of a corpse.*
- ✧ Let your body release any and all tension. Scan your body, allowing every part to relax, surrendering into the support of the ground beneath you. Let your feet fall open, thigh muscles relax, belly sink into the spine. Arms roll open, hands at ease, releasing the tiny muscles in each finger. Limbs become heavy. Notice the weight of your head on the ground. Let go of any strain in your body, as though you were falling asleep at night. Whenever you notice any kind of tension, release it gently into the ground.
- ✧ *Rest in the way of being ownerless.*
- ✧ Consider that nothing and no one owns you. No one is watching; no one is keeping score. Let go of whatever has its grip on you: concerns, hopes, fears. Become aware of what you're currently trying to hold together in your life—elements of a relationship, work, health, money, spirituality. Let go of anything you think you have to hold. As though you were letting go of a handful of golden leaves, gently release all the things you are grasping, letting them ride out on the outbreath; see

them drift away into the open space around you. Whenever you notice a point of stress or worry, see if you can simply drop it, just for now, like a fist opening, releasing its contents into the wind.

✧ Finally, see if you can let go of even the sense that "I" am resting, "I" am letting go. Let efforting go. Let "doing it right" go. Be like one who is owned by nothing and who owns nothing. That way you become everything.

✧ *Rest your mind in the way of the sky.*

✧ Become aware of your conscious mind. Let awareness expand as though it were vast like a bright blue summer sky. There is no edge to this sky, so your awareness can simply open without any limit. At first, you might even imagine relaxing your brain, as though it were a muscle that you could release. Then let awareness itself relax. If thoughts arise, see them as clouds moving through the open sky of your awareness. Rest deep into that sky-like awareness.

✧ Allow yourself to feel absolutely held without doing anything. If you reach an edge of fear or contraction, bring a tender attitude of kindness to yourself. Accept any boundaries you encounter, and gently explore how you might compassionately relax just a bit more.

✧ Continue this contemplation as long as you like, relaxing your body, emotions, and mind at ever subtler levels.

✧ Now gradually bring movement back into your hands, feet, and limbs. Make the aspiration that your contemplation may be of benefit to yourself and others.

Part Two

PATH

4

The Problem of Self-Clinging

One thing that has always fascinated us, much more than how much we know or how to acquire more knowledge, is how much we *don't* know. With all of human history, and eons of iterative knowledge, we still don't really have definitive answers to the most basic existential questions. How did we get here? What happens after death? What is consciousness? And where does it go when we sleep? We may have beliefs about this—religious, philosophical, or otherwise—but we don't really know firsthand, experientially. Assuming there's a larger reality, a larger truth to our existence, it seems that truth is pretty effectively veiled from us on a day-to-day basis. It's as though our experience of this world is set up in a way that cocoons us from our true condition. It's like living inside of a dream, without any idea whatsoever that we are dreaming. Thus the dream becomes all-consuming, all-important. This general ignorance pervades and conditions all of humanity, and the whole of human reality is necessarily conditioned by it.

As said before, Buddhism considers the ignorance of not recognizing our true nature as the root cause of suffering. This nonrecognition leads to a persistent preoccupation with a self whose existence to us seems self-evident and separate from everything "out there." Machig calls this preoccupation "ego-clinging" and sees it as the root of all our neuroses and unease. In addition to physical pain and emotional distress, suffering also refers to a pervasive sense of unease or "unsatisfactoriness."

We may experience this unease as a vague, underlying sense of incompleteness or anxiety, a core insecurity that something is not quite right. Deep down there's a faint awareness of our fundamental wholesome nature, but it's covered up by a very real, everyday experience of separateness. Now we want to find our way back. One could say the spiritual journey is fueled by a longing to recapture completeness, a yearning for reunion with the Mother, an ultimate homecoming. We enter a path to find our way back to what we vaguely feel we have lost.

Thus the search begins. At the most basic level, following the hierarchy of needs, it could be just about surviving. We look for more comfort, less pain. Then we start aspiring to greater fulfillment, living a more meaningful life, following spiritual paths, engaging in practices, and so on. Ken Wilber, the integral philosopher, notes, "The separate self is, at bottom, simply a sensation of seeking."[1] We are seeking some kind of refuge that offers comfort, peace, and happiness in our everyday life or, at a more exalted level, salvation, final union, or enlightenment. We take all sorts of trips and journeys looking for answers. But the ultimate refuge, the real answer, is finding our way back to our true nature—the radiant, compassionate, nondual ground of our being. To come to know again the all-good ocean of nondeluded awareness out of which we all arise in the first place.

If we could effortlessly and continuously rest in the lucidity of unconfused awareness, that would be wonderful. We could skip the path and jump from ground to fruition. Just rest in your true nature! Thank you very much. That could be the end of this book. But it's not quite that simple, right? We turn to our email and suddenly it's not so easy to rest our minds in the way of the sky anymore. There's a stark contrast between a romantic idea of some vast ground of ultimate deliverance and the actual intensity of everyday life. It's wonderful when we take a moment in our busy day to relax into spacious, compassionate awareness. But then the potatoes are burning on the stove, and we feel we have to come back from our reverie. These two extremes, the absolute and the relative, seem very far apart. The question is: Do they really meet—not just conceptually—and if so, how?

The Predicament of Dualism and the Birth of the Ego

In chapter 1 we described the luminous ground of being and how all phenomena are a compassionate manifestation of this empty ground. This includes the complex patterns that make up our physical being, our intellect, our psyche—in short, the so-called *self.* From the point of view of the self, the primordial ground out of which it is born is so vast, so other, so overwhelming that the self contracts against that ground and essentially takes refuge in itself, including its constructs and belief systems. This basic split of the self from the nondual ground it arises out of is the beginning of dualism: the *self* experiencing itself as separate from *others* and phenomena *out there.* We experience life from the point of view of the wave rather than as the ocean.

Namkhai Norbu Rinpoche describes this predicament of dualism:

> These paths all have the common aim of seeking to overcome the problem that has arisen as the individual enters into dualism, developing a subjective self, or ego, that experiences a world-out-there as other, continually trying to manipulate that world in order to gain satisfaction and security. But one can never achieve satisfaction and security in this way, because all the seemingly external phenomena are impermanent and furthermore, the real cause of the suffering and dissatisfaction is the fundamental sense of incompleteness that is the inevitable consequence of being in the state of dualism.[2]

The self, once "split off," continually tries to establish a platform or safe ground for itself, and incessantly grasps at strategies to maintain itself in the face of what it now perceives as the world-out-there. This is the birth of the ego. The ego, and by extension the psyche, can be seen as latticework, a self-reifying frame of reference constituted by countless overlapping patterns. This self-identity is partially seeded by past actions[3] and further reinforced by all our experiences, memories, traumas, belief systems, personal narratives, and so on—some conscious and many unconscious. The conscious and unconscious patterns, referred to as "shadow," drive our behavior and often show up in the form of reactivity in our life. We experience this as deeply ingrained tendencies and triggers—our personality, in short. This complex matrix—what we think of as our *self*—also includes our body. So, we don't just contract against the ground; we contract in an endless variety of very specific ways. This further fuels the sense of unique individualism at the heart of our self-absorption—what Machig calls the demon of inflation or ego-fixation.

Buddhism offers a detailed description of this development of self through the teachings on the twelve *nidānas* or links of causation that outline the mechanics of dependent origination. It goes something like this: As a result of ignorance and karma, we experience and perpetuate ourselves as separate individuals carried by consciousness, the mindstream, much like a current in an ocean. Through dualistic experiences of form, senses, feelings, perceptions, emotions, and thoughts, we construct a sense of self that is driven by previous causes and conditions and propels itself through craving and grasping into a supremely convincing form of perceived continuity. We will always be thwarted in our attempts to establish this self once and for all, however, because it is only a conglomeration of facets that themselves exist only in relation to everything else but never separately or permanently. Its true nature is pristine awareness, just like everything else's.

As with the ego, the constellations of overlapping patterns can also be seen to apply to the "external" world, providing relative continuity and a semblance of permanence to everything we see around us. One might think of it as resonant patterns that repeat throughout the nondual realm of clarity, expressing vividly as the unendingly rich display we see all around us.

When we look at the world in this way, we might see it as an infinitely complex, ever-unfolding fractal of unfathomable scale. And we are a small but inextricable part of it, our ego like a tiny iteration, a tiny reflection of the larger whole. Whether completely preoccupied or lucidly present, we are a part of the dance; we participate in the magnificence. Through practice and realization we expand our view and become more conscious participants. At that point we don't have to be radical or do radical things—the scale of our participation becomes so vast that being effortless is the most radical thing we could do.

Machig's Four Demons

Machig describes the basic split and our experiences of self and duality through the device of the "four demons."[4] (We use the term "demon" rather than "devil," found in the original translation, since it is used more widely and can be understood in a psychological context.)

[Demons] are classified as four:
tangible [demon] and intangible [demon],
the [demon] of exaltation, and the [demon] of inflation.
All are included in the [demon] of inflation.[5]

Tangible and intangible demons are also known as outer and inner demons, the demon of exaltation as the demon of elation, and the demon of inflation as the demon of ego-fixation or ego-clinging.

She defines "demons" as follows:

That which is called ["demon"] is not some actual great big black thing that scares and petrifies whomever sees it. A [demon] is anything that obstructs the achievement of freedom.[6]

Freedom means to live within the stabilized, embodied recognition of our inseparability from the ground of being. Without this realization, we are bound by the whole slew of insecurities, doubts, fears, and hopes that drive our endless search to find comfort and peace—our demons.

Another way we can understand our demons is as the protective mechanisms developed around the core wound of not recognizing our inherent wholeness. The basic split is an experience of losing home, which creates a shakiness and instability within us. For example, the demons of fear—not being loved, not being recognized, not being enough—and the innumerable behaviors we develop to counter these fears all arise from this underlying loss of connection with the ground of being. We think we're alone, moving through a world of otherness, and so all our ideas about reality, all our feelings, and all our actions are infused with this basic flavor of separateness and a deep preoccupation with finding safety and ground.

Thus it makes sense that Machig's "root demon" is the *demon of ego-clinging*. It is the core demon that arises from the fundamental mistaken notion that "I" exist separate from everything else. Machig says,

> *[T]here is no greater [demon] than this fixation to a self. So until this ego-fixation is cut off, all the demons wait with open mouths. For that reason, you need to exert yourself at a skillful method to sever the [demon] of ego-fixation.*[7]

And,

> *The root [demon] is one's own mind.*
> *The [demon] lays hold through clinging and attachment*
> *in the cognition of whatever objects appear.*[8]

But why does she say the "root demon" is our own mind? What she is *not* saying is that there is something fundamentally wrong with us—like a Buddhist version of original sin. No. It is our mind's *clinging* to a dualistic self that forms the basis for our suffering. And that condition is entirely workable.

Once we fall into and remain in dualistic fixation, it becomes the totality of our experience. We become very involved in this relative world of self and other—we take it on face value, and we take it very seriously. This is Machig's ego-clinging, or *self-inflation*. We naturally become supremely attached to ourselves as the primary platform of perception and experience: as a familiar haven during the ups and downs of daily life or as a desperate refuge in what we see as the vast emptiness of meta-existence. And we are attached to everything that supports this platform and affirms our separate identity. According to Machig, this is the root of all our hope and fear, and thus the beginning of suffering: not getting what we want, getting what we don't want, sickness, old age, and death. Such hope and fear, born out of the dualism of clinging to a self in the face of a perceived *other*, are like the marionette strings that control the puppet of the ego. Thus this attachment to self is called the "root demon," which naturally gives rise to the other three demons.

Looking out our kitchen window, it seems most self-evident that our three beautiful ash trees are really "there," separate from "me." In that moment of perception, one easily falls into what Machig refers to as subject-object cognition: the notion that I am distinct from and fundamentally other than what I perceive—the tree. This dualistic perception in relation to objects external to us gives rise to outer or tangible demons, and inner or intangible demons in relation to internal objects, like thoughts or emotions.

With regard to *outer demons*, Machig says,

> *[J]udging the appearances that arise to our senses,*
> *negating or affirming them, is the tangible [demon].*[9]

So let's say the trees are the appearances that arise to our senses. (From a dualistic perspective, we would think the tree is actually substantially there, and because we also really exist, we are able to see it over there with the help of our eyes.) She's calling them "appearances" that "arise" because she's pointing out that the trees arise from the basic space of awareness and only appear to exist substantially. Furthermore, the one who's sensing it, also arises simultaneously from the basic space of awareness. There's no absolute substantiality, no enduring permanence to either of them. We know this same dynamic intimately from our dreams: When we see a tree in our dream, it looks like it's really there. But what is that dream tree actually made of?

Seeing, hearing, and perceiving, we decide what we want to have (affirm) or not have (negate), what's for us or against us, grasping or rejecting. This is not merely dispassionate preference. We believe what we see. We judge; we become involved, attached, driven by the powerful feelings of hope and fear. It's an incredibly tiring enterprise when we're continually in an offensive or defensive posture in relation to a reality that is coming at us. From a developmental point of view, outer demons correspond to our tendency to blame people or circumstances outside of ourselves for our own discomfort and suffering. We project on the other person in a difficult relationship, for example, and refuse to take any responsibility.

About liberating from outer demons Machig says,

Decisively cutting through inflation liberates fixation to real things.
As in cessation, appearances do not stop.[10]

Here again, "inflation" means ego-clinging, Machig's root demon. "Cessation" refers to the Buddha's Third Noble Truth: complete liberation from suffering.[11] In other words, by cutting through the notion of the self as substantive and real, we also liberate the outer demon of clinging to objects as real. What happens then? Does reality go *poof!* and dissolve into an empty void? No, Machig says, "Appearances do not stop." Phenomena keep naturally arising in an unimpeded way. We don't have to reject anything. It's our relationship that changes, our contraction and grasping that release. So, what to do about the trees outside our window? Open our awareness, relax, accept, enjoy. Emerald leaves, gnarled bark, soft gray sky.

Inner or *intangible demons*—also demons that run on and on relate to our internal world. They are the belief in the truth of our own thoughts and interior narratives, the ways in which we take ourselves so very seriously. Machig describes them in this way:

[A]ll thought-provoking mental hopes and fears
are one's own [demons] rising up to oneself.[12]

The supremely convincing experience of duality and a separate self persists in our internal world. When we think, *There's the thought itself and the one experiencing the thought*, that's a self-reifying mechanism—a literal experience of "I think, therefore I am." It's the same for emotions. The anger we feel seems very real and solid; it's telling the truth about who we are.

So much of our suffering is driven by our own stories, beliefs, and judgments, both positive and negative. This is the bondage of inner demons. Developmentally, recognizing our inner demons represents taking more responsibility for our experiences; we realize the role we play in creating pain and joy in our lives. With greater self-awareness, we accept our own part in a difficult relationship, for example.

Finally, the *demon of elation* or *exaltation* refers to the arrogance, attachment, or distraction caused by worldly or spiritual success. At a subtler level, it refers to any kind of grasping to the attainment of "great" insight or the "perfect" meditation: that little voice in our head that says, *Aha! Now I've got it* or *Wow, what a great meditation this is*. However wonderful these experiences are, when we cling to them, they become forms of spiritual materialism. Machig describes the demon of elation arising from these material or spiritual accomplishments as

> *mental attachment in which one delights or exalts . . .*
> *causes great arrogance and pride and becomes*
> *an obstacle on the path to freedom.*[13]

The radical view being presented here is that anything that reifies our sense of self, our ego-clinging, however spiritual it may be, is ultimately a demon, a cause of suffering.

Ego-Clinging in Everyday Life: The Claustrophobia of Self-Referentiality

We are reminded of an inspiring exchange in Carlos Castaneda's *Teachings of Don Juan*:

> "You're plagued with problems," he said. "Why?"
>
> "I am only a man, don Juan," I said peevishly.
>
> I made that statement in the same vein my father used to make it. Whenever he said he was only a man he implicitly meant he was weak and helpless and his statement, like mine, was filled with an ultimate sense of despair.
>
> Don Juan peered at me as he had done the first day we met.
>
> "You think about yourself too much," he said and smiled. "And that gives you a strange fatigue that makes you shut off the world around you and cling to your arguments. Therefore, all you have is problems. I'm only a man too, but I don't mean that the way you do."
>
> "How do you mean it?"

> "I've vanquished my problems. Too bad my life is so short that I can't grab onto all the things I would like to. But that is not an issue; it's only a pity."
>
> I liked the tone of his statement. There was no despair or self-pity in it.[14]

Interpreting everything in our dualistic world in relation to the self leads to a high degree of self-preoccupation. This may be more for some and less for others, but the more contracted and self-preoccupied we become, the more isolated and lonelier we feel. For some this may manifest as depression, insecurity, or feelings of inadequacy. For others it shows up as arrogance, usually also born from insecurity. We call this tendency the *claustrophobia of self-referentiality*. We feel like a project that needs to be upgraded or fixed, and we don't quite know how. Or we have strong ideas about how, but it seems like a never-ending project.

As an escape, anything that takes our attention away from ourselves offers temporary relief, like scrolling on our phone. Or reality TV, which is about other people's problems. A further example of this claustrophobia is awkward social interactions or a difficult relationship. You second-guess yourself: *Should I have said that? Is it me? Is it her?* You get caught in self-reflexive entanglements—feeling awkward, having regret. Or being triggered and reacting in a way you've told yourself a thousand times you would not—but there, you just did it again!

This same claustrophobia can play itself out in terms of spiritual ideals: *How can "I" improve myself? Which books do "I" need to read, which teachings do "I" need to receive, what practices do "I" need to accomplish?* The project of enlightenment gets very tight and constrictive. And of course, there is no way for the "I" to become enlightened anyway.

The prospect of releasing our self-referentiality, or cutting the root of our clinging to a self, may initially evoke a fear of loss or even a deeper fear of voidness, emptiness. But we are not really losing anything, except perhaps a small-minded view of a self that at best provides only temporary refuge. Through releasing we gain a much vaster perspective, expanding into a direct experience of the nature of things as they are. We gain access to energy, which you might also call wisdom, insight, freedom. This resource of energy helps us to compassionately nurture the smaller parts of ourselves that want to stay attached.

Is Self-Awareness Self-Absorbed?

It may be helpful to consider the relationship between self-awareness and self-absorption. When we lack self-awareness, we are easily preoccupied with the world outside—objects, other people, events. We are dualistically fixated—perceiver and object—but we tend to be more preoccupied with the objects of perception rather than with ourselves, the perceiver. It's like watching a movie and being completely engrossed in the story without being aware of oneself as the watcher. This is also where Machig's outer demon comes most into play: the problems all seem to be outside ourselves, happening *to* us.

With self-awareness we start the journey of contemplating the subject, the so-called self, the one perceiving. The ancient maxim of "Know thyself," as Socrates advised, was regarded as the first step in self-mastery, leading eventually to the good of society. Self-awareness is the basis for exploring our shadow aspects, our trigger points, and our unconscious reactivities. Here we become aware of Machig's inner demons, which are active within us regardless of outer circumstances. This is the realm of psychotherapy, and also of contemplative practice. Meditation, as we'll discuss more in chapters that follow, cultivates the awareness that lights up the dark corners of our psyche. Through practice, we infuse space, self-acceptance, and compassion into our constrictions, liberating the energy held in our tightest knots. We develop greater spaciousness and less reactivity in our approach to life, and greater tolerance and more consideration of others, more compassion. In its full progression, this journey eventually leads to the stabilized realization of no-self and resting in the nondual nature of mind.

However, at some point our engagement with shadow and the good work of bringing awareness to the inner recesses of the self could lead to being overly self-preoccupied. We actually start reifying the self with its revealed patterns, vulnerabilities, protective mechanisms, and so forth. If we become too self-involved, too preoccupied with our own shadow and what needs to be *fixed*, we end up further solidifying the self instead of severing the unhealthy preoccupation with an essentially nonexistent self. Machig's third demon, the demon of elation, creeps in here as we start to take pride in our psychological or spiritual accomplishments. Thus, one has to find the line between healthy self-awareness and unhealthy self-absorption. Ultimate liberation is about cutting through this construct of self or ego-clinging altogether. Machig's suggestions for how to do this are discussed in the next chapter and throughout the following chapters on path, but for now we could say it has to do with letting go of grasping and radical acceptance of the way things are.

Don't Demonize the Ego

Ego-clinging is very subtle. Calling our small self our ego-mind the *root demon* may lead us to think the ego needs to be subdued or overcome. But demonizing the ego will not take us very far. We can wax lyrical about how we want to transcend the ego, but it is *us*; it is our entire identity. We can't liberate around it or in spite of it—we liberate *through* it, use it as a skillful means and integrate it into a vaster view. The ego is not the problem; it is the unconscious *clinging* to it that is. Machig says,

> *Conduct yourself without fixating on yourself.*[15]

At the relative level, I do exist. This self is a magical vehicle for experiencing all kinds of joy and deliciousness. We don't need to demonize anything. The self is the mechanism that makes all of this rich experience possible. Appreciating the beauty of the leaves outside the window, watching them turn different colors every season. Falling in love, cultivating friendships. Getting older, watching our children grow up.

The self is like the pocket of the ocean through which this particular awareness is coming to know the entire ocean. Can I come to know this body, this heart, this particular web of patterning so well that I begin to see reflections of the entire universe within it? The invitation is to feel so fully, see so completely, hear so unequivocally, taste so profoundly that we recognize the immense spectrum of life flooding through us and are suffused by the unfathomable knowing of all things. Consider the great Zen Master Dogen's beautiful teaching:

> To study the buddha way is to study the self. To study the self is to forget the self. To forget the self is to be actualized by myriad things.[16]

When we let it all in, the fixation drops. There is no self to hold on to. There never was because the self is made of the infinitude of the universe, the myriad of beings, the myriad of things.

This too is Machig's invitation. Fixation makes us want to accumulate and accomplish through our actions, our conduct. Fixation means there is a solid container that I must fill up. Make something of myself. No, Machig suggests, don't make something of yourself. Act. Conduct yourself, awake, aware, present. Then let it go.

In summary, then, we work with the self as our vehicle for the maturation of wisdom. At a relative level, our bodies, thoughts, and emotions—even our neuroses—become gateways for transformation and realization. This understanding is at the heart of the Tantric view,[17] where ego with all its seeming imperfections and foibles becomes a skillful means to awakening. Poisons are transformed into wisdom through the recognition of fundamental emptiness, nonsolidity.

From the relative point of view of wanting to gain liberation through the realization of the true nature of reality, the trap of dualism seems like a bad thing. But from the perspective of already having gained that liberation, the mechanism of dualism is pure delight. It is after all as a result of this profound mechanism that we can participate in this world of magical illusion and sense pleasures. Once liberated from the *trap* of dualism and the resultant self-clinging, this same mechanism provides texture to our fully integrated experience of blissful inseparability.

At the subtlest level, nothing remains to *be done*. Nothing to transform, nothing to overcome. This is the great perfection of things just as they are. We don't have to beat duality. In fact, we can't! How do we overcome subject-object cognition? By relaxing. Relax into the very awareness that is manifesting the world in its momentary just-as-it-is-ness.

Ego-Clinging at the Collective Level

The personal claustrophobia of self-referentiality translates at the collective level to cultural self-absorption, expressed in fundamentalist ideologies such as tribalism, nationalism, and racial supremacy. Fixed notions of "my" nation, "my" culture, "my" race, "my" religion preclude the possibility of being wrong or of including other views as potentially valid. Machig says,

> *[O]ne errs in the distraction of loving and hating friend and foe. Attachment and aversion are the [demons] of self-fixation.*[18]

Our seeming individuality is not as unique as we think. We are continuously impacted by the context within which we function—from the people around us to the larger culture. This does not only extend to what we perceive through our senses, like media and conversations. Because everything is interconnected, we may assume this permeability also impacts our internal world of thoughts and attitudes. When I have a thought, it seems to me I am the originator of that thought. It is *my* thought. But so often we will be driving in the car and one of us will say something about a friend, and the other will respond, "I was just thinking about her!" So who thought of her first? Both of us feel like the thought originated with us. (Or was that friend actually thinking of us?)

Thoughts and ideas may come to us from the "outside," but the *way* we think them is based on a complex frame of reference that we have been constructing over a lifetime and that *is* very unique. So our propensity for self-referentiality results in a tendency to be very subjective in our thinking and attitudes about the world and others in it. As a result, it is difficult for us to walk in someone else's shoes.

Through an evolutionary lens, one could say we evolve from a very "solid" self to a much more permeable self. From a dualistic, self-centric view to progressive levels of collective understanding. Cutting through ego-clinging by relaxing into the ground allows us to break out of the contracted small self and access a more universal view, Skymind. Because we are less preoccupied with ourselves we are less fearful and we have more bandwidth to be curious about the world and others. And because compassion naturally self-arises in that space—yes, you guessed it: We are more kind and compassionate.

5

Cutting Through Self-Clinging

The cold rain came driving up the valley in sheets, veiling and revealing the steep barren mountainsides and dancing on the surface of the river. We sat way out in the open of the valley in a lazy loop of the river, right on the flat alluvial plain, facing the fuss and fury of the oncoming storm. Our little group was practicing Chöd in all earnestness—drums rotating, bells ringing, texts fluttering—but we were not even halfway through and here comes the rain! I (Pieter) was in remote Zangri Khamar in Tibet, tracing the life and times of Machig Labdrön in the way of pilgrimage. But what to do now? Do we interrupt the practice and tuck our instruments and pages from the rain? Scramble for frail and thin cover on the banks? Or do we continue with upturned faces glazed by the cold rain, belting the ancient melodies with fervor, glancing at each other as we smile and surrender to the soak? Zangri is a spectacular place: a little monastery hugging the top of a high cliff, overlooking the broad and shallow headwaters of the Brahmaputra river. This is where Machig lived out the second half of her life, meditating in a cave underneath the monastery. This is also where, on that same visit, Lama Tsultrim was recognized as an emanation of this eleventh-century yogini.

Machig is most famous for this powerful practice of Chöd. It appears very shamanic in nature and involves the singing of evocative ancient melodies and the use of a drum, bell, and human thigh-bone trumpet. The practitioner visualizes ejecting their consciousness, then virtually chopping up their body, offering it in a ritual feast to their "demons," enemies, disease-makers, karmic debt-holders, and so forth. After the intensity of drumming, singing, and piercing shouts, the practice culminates in utter silence, a point of arrival when all beings are completely satisfied and the distinctions between the one who offers, the offering, and those offered to have melted into an experience of primordial inseparability. All rest in the inherent wakefulness of their true nature.

Chöd means "to cut through or to sever." Beyond the practice described above, severance is Machig's remedy for the root problem or core suffering of dualistic perception, ego-clinging, and its accompanying fixed notions.[1] What we're cutting through are all the ways we reify and solidify dualities of all kinds, the primary one being the sense of self and other. We're cutting through the self-inflation (which can show up as self-denigration as much as through self-aggrandizement) that separates us from the truth of our radical interbeing[2] and our fundamental wholeness. Thus Machig writes,

> *Other than your own decisive cutting through inflation,*
> *nothing at all will happen externally.*[3]

Like a sharp blade piercing the veil of confusion, severance lays bare the clarity and radiance of transcendent wisdom, Prajñāpāramitā, revealing the basic goodness and brilliant wakefulness that is the true nature of all beings.

The path of severance leads from self-absorption to radical inclusivity, a direct experience of interdependence, and the embodiment of awakened compassion, all of which are the full expression of Skymind embodied in everyday life. How do we sever the root of ego-clinging? How do we work with the afflictions and encumbrances that hamper our clarity and wisdom?

In the following chapters on path, we will discuss a variety of skillful methods and the applicability of severance to everyday life. In the remainder of this chapter, we lay out some frameworks and guiding structures that will create a road map for our exploration.

Three Levels of Cutting Through

Machig's extant writings focus on radical, high-level nature of mind teachings, with an uncompromising approach of resting in our nature just as it is. Yet her pointers on severance—ways of cutting through—also offer helpful insight on how we can skillfully work with our persistent preoccupation with *self*, the ultimate source of suffering.

As is common in Vajrayana teachings, Machig refers to three levels of practitioners—*superior*, *middling*, and *inferior*—that reflect three different approaches to understanding and practicing severance. If you're anything like us, you may start wondering where you fit on that scale, perhaps hoping to rate superior, but then thinking, *Eh . . . I'm probably in the inferior camp.* (That in itself could lead to some egoic entanglement!) Even though there may be a larger arc of progressing on the path, the truth is, most of us experience all three levels but at different times. Some days we have peak experiences where we effortlessly *get* the superior insight. Other times we're dragging the bottom, crawling through the muck, feeling much more like an inferior practitioner.

One of the most common questions we receive from practitioners and students is, "What do I do when I'm really struggling?" To start with, we want to suggest that it may be more helpful to reframe Machig's three levels of practice to pertain to *levels of affliction* rather than levels of accomplishment. The more contracted, stuck, or encumbered we feel, the more the healing guidance of the so-called inferior approach will benefit us; the more clear and liberated we are, the more we are able to engage the superior way. In this way, we can apply the appropriate remedy or approach on a daily basis, depending on our level of struggle or affliction. For our purposes, we will rename the approaches *instantaneous* (superior), *direct* (middling), and *gradual* (inferior).

The Instantaneous Way

> *Those of superior scope rest within nonconceptual equipoise without fear or anxiety no matter what [demons] arise.*[4]

The instantaneous way corresponds to an absolute approach in which the path is that of no-path: simply relaxing and resting in uncontrived inherent wakefulness, the radiance of intrinsic nondual awareness. There's no contraction whatsoever, no preoccupation with doing or not doing—just complete presence and acceptance of everything as it is in the great perfection of its arising.

Thus, the instantaneous approach is to directly connect with our basic nature, which is clear, spacious awareness—Skymind. We generally cultivate and stabilize this view through meditation and then integrate it in daily life. When we are able to completely rest in a direct experience of our nature, anything that arises is immediately recognized as the display of the ground itself, and any obscurations self-liberate in that space. Because there is no contraction around a separate self, there is nothing for appearances to hook on to; so there's no grasping, no stickiness, no manipulation, no contrivance. There is only complete, open, vast surrender into things just as they are. When we rest in the nature of mind, perceptions and thoughts naturally arise and fall away, like clouds in the sky. Emotions arise as the adornment of our mind; we experience their pure energy; and they fall away, liberated in their own ground.

We have to be careful here to not fall into the mistaken notion that the real solution is to escape into some kind of never-never land, some vast refuge that is outside the sphere of our personal problems and the challenges of the world. Sometimes called "spiritual bypassing," it is the concern that resting in the nature of mind could be used as some kind of big escape trick, an evasion into the romantic absolute, far from the gritty weight of everyday reality where real suffering takes place. *Don't worry, just rest; it's all good*—this can certainly be just another form of neurotic avoidance.

Actually, resting in the nature of mind is not that. You're not escaping anything because there's no *elsewhere* to escape to. You are resting in the totality of all things.[5] And things do self-liberate here because there's no stickiness. That's why *escaping into the absolute* is a nonstarter in the first place. Resting in the nature of everything is the path of radical non-avoidance. Everything is included. All phenomena, all afflictions are the manifestation of the ground itself.

Practically speaking, this view results in tremendous relief. The relief lies in the vastness of the view, not the avoidance of perceived points of pain. The ego's propensity for self-fixation leads to contracted awareness; our problems and preoccupations are front and center, dominating our immediate mind space. Then the only way to get relief is through distraction or avoidance: we pick up our phone, flick on the TV, or indulge whatever go-to addiction or coping mechanism we have going on. But when we expand our awareness, there's suddenly a lot more space. We don't have to avoid anything; it is included in that vast view.

Imagine being caught in a frightful storm on the open ocean. In the immediacy of the storm, all you can do is fight to keep your little boat afloat under the onslaught of the massive waves. But if you could zoom way out, you would see the storm from the perspective of the entire ocean. That particular storm does not stop raging, but it is just one storm on the expanse of a vast ocean. Elsewhere the sun is shining, the waves are mellow, and whales are peacefully lolling in the shallows. From this expanded view, you're not trying to run away from the storm and constantly chase sunshine. No, you are resting in the totality of the entire situation—resting in the way things are—including all the flux and dynamism of the entire ocean, of all of life.

A vast, all-inclusive view directly impacts our approach to everyday life. Because there's more space, we become less reactive and more responsive. We're not riding on a hair trigger, we're not knee-jerking. We're less self-involved and more curious about others and the world. More at ease. More compassionate.

When we encounter someone who's aggressive toward us, for example, our normal tendency might be to meet them with either defensiveness or aggression. We're triggered, hooked, and thus reactive. But meeting them from a place of zero contraction, we immediately see their suffering. Our understanding is clear, and our response is suffused with self-arising compassion. Rather than shutting down in reactivity, we actually open our heart even more.

Within the instantaneous way, life becomes more like divine play and less like a serious and heavy burden. The dark cloud just as much as the rainbow are met with curiosity, openness, and kindness, recognized as equal manifestations on the spectrum of appearing phenomena.

The Direct Way

Those of middling scope seek the one who has the feelings [of demons arising] and understand that [demons] are their own mind and rest within mind's unborn nature itself.[6]

In the direct way, afflictions arise, but we have the presence of mind and wherewithal to cut through them. We notice a thought, a distraction, a narrative, and as it arises, we recognize it as dualistic fixation and apply the remedy of severance: We decisively cut through the duality by realizing it is not *other* than the workings of our own mind.

Don't you consider the enemy in a dream
as coming from yourself?[7]

When you dream, you believe what's happening in the dream. But when you wake up, you're relieved because you realize, *I was just dreaming. That monster was a creation of my own mind.* Now if you could have that realization while you are dreaming, the monster would instantaneously become less threatening. It could even transform and become a fluffy cat or a teddy bear or disappear altogether.

At an everyday level, the direct way is an invitation to drop our story. I (Charlotte) remember running up to our young son's bedroom after we had had an irritating exchange. I was filled with frustration, anger, and some sense of motherly righteousness about setting things straight. As I neared the top step, I realized that it was I who was carrying the issue; there wasn't actually a problem. It had simply been a little whirlwind of energy, ultimately signifying nothing. I caught myself and thought, *Actually, you could just drop it.* It was an incredibly liberating moment because I realized I didn't have to play out a drama simply because I had adrenaline coursing through my body and stories flying through my mind. I could cut through.

This remedy works particularly well in meditation as a way of working with distracting thoughts and emotions—that is, you have enough awareness to recognize a thought just as it arises, and before you compulsively jump on that thought train, you cut through the distractibility and rest.

Decisively cutting through inflation liberates
fixation to real things.[8]

In the Chöd tradition, the vocalization of the sound *phet* (often with a loud, cutting quality) can be used to cut through mental and emotional fixation. It is a unique practice in its own right, whereby the sound pierces distraction like a warrior's sharp blade. There's a moment of nothing at all, in which discursive thought ceases. In the gap, the liberating view of sky-like mind appears.[9]

Our ability to recognize and cut through affliction comes as a result of our practice: basic mindfulness, the resulting presence of mind, meditation, and the cultivated habit of turning toward adversity. So, at the middling level, the direct way is to ask ourselves what we might just let go of, what we are holding and dragging around with us unnecessarily. What story, belief, or memory could we perhaps quite simply liberate, like releasing a balloon into the clear blue sky?

~ EXERCISE ~

Remain like a bunch of straw cut loose.[10]

This exercise invites us into an experience of cutting through, as is described in the direct way. We work with the image of straw that has been tightly bound together in a bale and which is then cut loose. The straw falls open onto the ground, completely released from its bond. We use this image to tighten our attention and then release it into open awareness.

- ✧ Take a few breaths to bring yourself into presence. It may help to close your eyes for this exercise.
- ✧ Become aware of thoughts, perceptions, and emotions moving through your awareness. Imagine that you begin to tie these together like pieces of straw, gathering them into a bale. Use your attention to bind them, as though your attention were twine or a sturdy string. As additional thoughts, perceptions, and so forth enter your awareness, also bind these into your bale.

✧ Continue to wind the string of your attention around this bale. Wind the string tighter and tighter so that your attention is wound around the bale as tightly as possible. Stay in this tightening of attention for some time.

✧ Then all at once, cut through the strings of the bale. Let your awareness open like straw falling onto the ground. Relax completely. Rest in naked awareness for as long as you like.

The Gradual Way

The nondual view of the nature of mind espoused in Machig's superior remedy is a radical view—let's not pretend it is not so. Even though it is our actual primordial nature, most of us are so deep in the jungle of dualistic fixation, so profoundly preoccupied and compulsively distractible, that a direct experience of our true nature often remains practically inaccessible—or at best few and far between. At other times we may be so deeply afflicted or overcome by emotion or adversity that it feels like it's the last thing we can access. Or it could be as simple as waking up on the wrong side of the bed—we feel misaligned, out of sorts, swimming in a fog of uncertainty.

In the relative approaches of the gradual way, we're working directly with our experiences of emotional or mental pain and skillfully applying awareness and insight in order to find resolution and healing. If the instantaneous way is continuously abiding in Skymind, the gradual way is more like moving through all the clouds and storms of our experience until we recognize that they, too, are not other than the sky, not fundamentally separate from our true nature. Generally this means embarking on a path that integrates basic mindfulness, attention, and compassion; we learn to work with our thoughts and emotions so that we are not overrun by incessant inner dialogue, plaguing narratives, and afflictive reactivity. We cultivate moral integrity and radical honesty,[11] all of which leads to a more wakeful, aligned life informed by wisdom. The vast majority of advice, techniques, and modalities that deal with mental and spiritual health function at this relative level, within the realm of dualism—self and other, neurosis and insight. This includes most of Western psychology and theistic religions as they're commonly practiced. Of course, this can be deeply helpful, especially when we are contracted and afflicted.

Prayer and Devotion

In spiritual traditions, the primary dualistic remedy takes the form of prayer and devotion. It can be tremendously helpful to put our faith in a divine being that is *outside* of ourselves and is also *superior* in all ways. Just by invoking it, we feel immediately held, protected, and supported by a higher power not subject to the vagaries and insecurities of everyday terrestrial life. In theistic religions, the divine is seen to be at work *in* and *through* us (i.e., the Holy Ghost of Christianity), but we remain fundamentally separate and inferior to it.[12] Thus we supplicate and pray for blessings, protection, and salvation.

In Buddhism, and particularly in the Vajrayana, there is also a devotional relationship to a wide variety of deities, wisdom beings, and accomplished teachers that are supplicated for their blessings and wisdom. But in Buddhism this is seen as a relative refuge (dualistic), with progression on the path resulting in the eventual realization that the deity or teacher is no other than one's own primordial nature, our Buddha Nature. This collapses the dualism and thus becomes the absolute refuge.

Turning into Darkness and the Practice of Chöd

A key principle of Machig's severance is radical non-avoidance and a courageous and compassionate engagement with all that we consider other, challenging, and even terrifying. Her teachings are a direct invitation to turn toward and lean into darkness rather than to avoid or fight that which we fear. We are so deeply conditioned to reflexively avoid unpleasant or negative emotions that we have made an artform out of distracting ourselves. Even when our affliction is so strong that we can hardly avoid it, our rational mind starts to tell stories about it rather than just feeling what we're feeling.

The wisdom of the gradual way, or the relative approach, is to engage with the totality of our lives, rejecting nothing and including everything; to show up with presence and mindfulness toward whatever is going on, even if it is extreme discomfort or suffering. This is like a farmer who, rather than getting rid of manure, uses it as compost to fertilize the soil. At this level, the practice is to work with our shadow and reactive patterns until we arrive at a place of full integration, where we can rest with fearless ease.

This basic gesture of turning into darkness lies at the heart of Machig's renowned Chöd practice, described at the beginning of this chapter. This is her teaching for the level where our self-fixation, contraction, and affliction are most intense:

> *Those of inferior scope give over the body to the dangerous obstructors and rest in non-action within the state of mental nonrecollection.*[13]

The traditional Chöd practice of visualizing the offering of one's own body strikes directly at our attachment to our body as the most visceral, seemingly solid manifestation of a separate self. In giving what is most precious to those whom we fear the most, Chöd upends our fixed concepts of self and other, and our ideas about safety and protection. The ultimate protection against any and all fears is radical compassion even toward that which is most terrifying, arising from a view that includes and transcends any dualities whatsoever. When we enter into a compassionate relationship with our "demons," true liberation becomes palpable.

You may remember that Machig's instructions on Chöd were inspired by the Prajñāpāramitā teachings that describe the basic nature of reality as inherently empty and open, and continuously manifesting as the display of interconnected phenomena. Chöd enacts the realization of Prajñāpāramitā in which everything and all beings are recognized as fundamentally not other than oneself—indeed, that we are all not other than the ground of being itself. Thus, having made the most generous of offerings, the practitioner realizes there is nothing more to do ("non-action") or think ("nonrecollection") but finally to rest in the embodied experience of inseparability. Here, the gradual way joins the instantaneous way in primordial, spacious awareness.

The Feeding Your Demons[14] process, developed by Lama Tsultrim Allione, is based on this same approach and is a remarkably effective way of working with our afflictions and shadow aspects. Drawing on Chöd as well as Jungian and Gestalt psychology, it comprises a five-step process to engage skillfully with our inner "demons" and transform them into wisdom. Using this process also encourages and conditions us to develop the willingness and courage to turn toward, rather than away from, our neuroses and afflictions and thus uncover the intelligence and insight that lies dormant within them. Like the traditional Chöd practice, Feeding Your Demons ends with an experience of dissolution in which the practitioner rests in naked awareness beyond any notions of demons or allies, neurosis or insight.

Absolute and Relative Approaches to Affliction

Machig's three levels of severance give us a framework for understanding different ways that we can apply her teachings, moving from a more absolute to a more relative view. Traditionally the absolute refers to the unchanging basic space of the nature of mind. The relative is the dualistic display of phenomena that we perceive as our 3D world, including our sensations, emotions, and thoughts.

A great way of understanding the relationship of absolute and relative is the metaphor of a mirror. Namkhai Norbu Rinpoche clarifies:

> In this analogy the clarity, purity and limpidity of the mirror represent the Absolute, while the reflections arising in the mirror which have no concrete substance—represent the illusoriness of Relative. Yet Relative and Absolute are shown to be inter-dependent and mutually arising because a mirror cannot exist without reflections, nor reflections without a mirror.[15]

Machig's three levels of cutting through are skillful means of engaging with the vast array of our physical, emotional, and mental experiences (the reflections) in order to awaken to innate luminous, radiant awareness (the mirror, inseparable from its reflections).

On the path, we can thus move from the absolute to the relative, or the other way around. The absolute approach is resting in the nature of mind. But since that's not always accessible depending on the severity of our affliction and degree of caught-upness, we work with relative remedies, starting right where we are. We recommend doing both.

This kind of tiered and flexible path offers a more sophisticated, customized approach based on our particular situation and state of mind. It also resolves the apparent contradiction and paradox between the instantaneous (absolute) and gradual (relative) approaches above: Machig's advice to "just rest" in the natural arising of any and all experiences, on the one hand, and the encouragement to turn toward one's greatest challenges, on the other. It's incredibly helpful to be aware of this full spectrum of ways that we can practice, as we will certainly find ourselves traversing the entire arc of confusion and wisdom over the course of our lives.

A Road Map for the Path: View, Meditation, Action

Traditionally, *view*, *meditation*, and *action* are considered the primary components of the path, and we have used this helpful structure as the organizing principle for the chapters that follow, related to path.

View

View is the most important because it entails a direct experience of the nature of mind and provides the basis for one's meditation and one's actions. Traditionally, particularly in the Mahamudra and Dzogchen traditions, such an experience is introduced by a master to their student through skillful methods commonly referred to as *pointing out*; the student is directly guided to a recognition of the nature of mind.[16]

Since the nature of mind is also the nature of *our* mind, it stands to reason that we should be able to directly experience it, whether formally "pointed out" or not. The truth is, we are always and constantly experiencing the nature of our mind, even in our most deluded moments! But suppose we haven't had even a conceptual introduction to the view, in a Buddhist or any other context. In that case, it may be difficult to not perpetually and instinctually act out our karmic-dualistic propensities—forever and a day.

Either way, we all may have had an experience where the world seems to stop in a moment, and we access a kind of self-arising clarity and quietude that eludes us in the everyday. For many, just being in nature can bring on those kinds of experiences.[17] The Scottish singer Donovan popularized an old Ch'an (Zen) teaching: "First there is a mountain, then there is no mountain, then there is."[18] First we see things in a conventional way, then we realize the true nature of things, and finally we integrate the understanding into ordinary life. So, once the view is established, it becomes the guide that informs every aspect of our lives.

In the next chapter, we lay out what is revealed by the view: the realization that in the totality of existence, everything and everyone is inextricably included and interconnected. Nothing is or can be rejected. Carrying this view into our everyday lives informs how we engage and relate, particularly with aspects of our experience that may be challenging or difficult. It opens the way for the path of awakened compassion.

Meditation

Since we know that our true nature is absolute and nondual, we develop the means to directly experience this nature and to condition ourselves to rest in this vast ground. This is the path of meditation. Here meditation refers not simply to sitting meditation practice but to any method that allows us to cultivate and sustain the view. By familiarizing ourselves with the essence of our mind, our view changes, and with it our experience in daily life. The spacious nature of our true being begins to permeate our daily experience. We become more at ease, less reactive, and more compassionate, among other benefits.

We offer the Skymind meditation and various contemplative exercises in this book as more structured meditation techniques to cultivate familiarity and nurture confidence in our direct, embodied experience of the view.

Action

Having established the view through meditation, we bring it into post-meditation, into our everyday lives. We learn to rest not just on the meditation cushion but also while we are walking, driving, doing the dishes, and perhaps most challenging, while we are talking. Traditionally action, sometimes also referred to as "conduct," relates to morality and karma, and overcoming our habitual dualistic patterns. So, in a more relative sense, we don't want to conduct ourselves in such a way as to create more intrigue, drama, and obstacles in our lives. That just leads to more self-entanglement. Less self-entanglement usually leads to the joy of altruism.

Some of these teachings may seem well and good on the meditation cushion, but what about the roller coaster of emotions and afflictions of daily life? Or running into serious adversity, like a terminal disease, divorce, or the death of a loved one? Are these teachings applicable then? And if so, how? We will explore this in the chapters below, particularly those on action.

In summary, when we talk about Skymind, we are referring to the view that recognizes our true nature, inseparable from the ground of being; to meditation as the practice and cultivation of that view; and to action as the integration of the view into all aspects of our lives. We turn now to these three aspects of the path as a way to live into the full experience of Skymind.

6

Radical Inclusivity

Every summer I (Charlotte) hike up the wild mountain behind our house and spend a few days in solitary retreat. One of my favorite spots is under a tree on the edge of a cliff. In one direction, I look down onto the sloping foothills, the city of Boulder in the distance and the plains stretching to the east. In the other direction, I look at the majestic and rugged Rocky Mountain peaks. I remember arriving one year in the late afternoon, laying out my tarp and blankets, and looking out over the darkening town and mountains. A loneliness came over me as I settled into the stillness, and I wondered why I had chosen to be away from my family and friends on what could have been a pleasurable evening with them. The loneliness stayed with me through the night and the following morning; I wished for a deer to walk through the forest, a bird to fly past, some sign of life to ease my feeling of isolation. But nothing came—only silence, only me. It was later at dusk that my senses began to awaken to subtler, quieter forms of life. I finally noticed the line of ants that had been moving back and forth all day from the rock in front of me, under my blanket, and up the tree trunk at my back. I watched the dragonflies settling for the night into the branches of my ponderosa tree, their tiny front legs hooking onto a twig, their body hanging downward, wings outstretched like a Christ figure. The coo of a dove. The world slowly came alive. Bit by bit, my eyes and ears attuned to the rich orchestra of life that surrounded me. I realized I was not alone at all. I couldn't actually be alone.

What happened was an expansion of view. I had moved from a tight, self-referential perspective, feeling alone and isolated, to a more spacious view, transmuting my experience into one of intimate relationship and interconnectedness. I had tapped into a deeper aliveness that permeates all of existence.

From a more absolute perspective, the view refers to the recognition of the ground of being, the realization of the nature of mind. To hold the view means to abide in spacious awareness, to rest in inseparable totality, to know everything as not other than a manifestation of the ground of being. The view recognizes the inherent radiance, goodness, and wakefulness—the Buddha Nature—of all beings.[1] From a relative perspective, we cultivate and stabilize the view through meditation, developing total confidence in it. It is literally our understanding of the nature of reality that then becomes the lens through which we "view" all the events of our hopefully long and beautiful lives. Thus it informs our behavior and actions; it serves as the fundamental basis of our beliefs and ideas that in turn guide our decisions and conduct.

Machig describes the view in this way:

The defining characteristic of mind
Is to be primordially empty like space;
The realization of the nature of mind
Includes all phenomena without exception.[2]

Or we could say: Include everything! (You don't actually have a choice.)

To say that mind is "primordially empty like space" suggests that mind is inherently open, unimpeded, unrestricted, and all-encompassing. This is not conceptual or thinking mind but rather mind understood as basic, fundamental awareness, the very nature of mind. Just as Machig characterized the groundless ground to be "like space," so too our basic awareness is boundless and ungraspable, yet embraces everything. Skymind.

Of course, our everyday experience of our mind is generally quite different—mind tends to be filled with all sorts of perceptions, thoughts, and ruminations. But what is the nature of mind itself, beneath all its contents? When we look at mind—when awareness looks at awareness—we do not see anything. Mind is actually no-thing. And in this no-thingness, in its "emptiness," it is actually profoundly and immeasurably spacious. This vast openness is the true nature of mind, the "defining characteristic" or essence of our awareness.

The spacious, empty ground of being is sometimes described as primordial purity, a pristineness that has existed since the beginningless beginning. Just as space is not perturbed by that which arises within it, just as a mirror is not stained by what it reflects, so too mind is not altered or affected by that which moves within it.

We might fall into the mistaken notion that this primordial emptiness of mind exists somewhere else; that we need to "get" to it somehow apart from the myriad of appearances, perceptions, sensations, and so forth that fill our ordinary experience. But the emptiness of mind is not vapid; the spaciousness of mind is not inert. It is awake, cognizant, vibrant, or as the traditional teachings suggest, luminous. What appears to mind—trees laden with snow, a tremor of anxiety, an inspiration—are the movement, the aliveness, the wakefulness of mind showing up as appearances. But just as nothing that moves in space—the cat, the wind, the traffic—is separate from space, so too all the appearances of mind are not fundamentally separate from the spacious, empty nature of mind. Appearance and emptiness are ultimately one; they never exist apart from each other.

The ultimate objective in all these teachings is to end affliction, delusion, and suffering for ourselves and others. The supreme remedy is to realize the nature of one's own mind, a realization of the union of emptiness and awareness. Emptiness points to the absence of inherent existence—the ultimate nature of all phenomena—and a sense of spaciousness, expansiveness, and totality. Awareness points to the clear, luminous nature of mind, vivid, wakeful, limpid.[3] And these two are inseparable.

So what does all of this mean for our everyday life? It means that within the problems, questions, pains, and joys of our lives, we can become aware of the imperturbable open sky of awareness that is the ultimate ground of all of them. Not only will we not be destroyed by that which moves through our awareness (that is, all our experiences of life) but our ability to hold all things in vast view—the view—is a reflection of our truest nature. This in itself is an incredible refuge, the profound refuge of Skymind.

The view is not something we have to manufacture, make up, or effort our way into. We ease into it, relax into it, just as my view expanded simply by abiding on the mountaintop. Mixing the openness of space with basic wakefulness, we begin to rest in the view, contracting less and noticing more. Our habitual mental patterns—worries, preoccupations, judgments, opinions—begin to ease, and we open to the spontaneity of fresh seeing. Reality becomes less static, fixed, and solid. The permeability, flexibility, and thus workability of things become more evident. As a famous line from the Laṅkāvatāra Sūtra[4] states, "Things are not as they appear—nor are they otherwise." When we rest in the view, this understanding becomes brilliantly clear. Life is as we experience it, yet it also so much more, so profoundly vast in its potentiality.

Meditation provides us with a tool to directly experience this aspect of mind, as awareness turns from apprehending outer phenomena and becomes aware of awareness itself. We access the "primordially empty" spaciousness of mind in open awareness meditation, for example, by resting back into the pervasive wakefulness of awareness itself. (See our chapters on meditation.)

All Phenomena without Exception

Machig continues, "The realization of the nature of mind / Includes all phenomena without exception." When we recognize the empty, luminous nature of mind, we also recognize all appearances as the display of that basic space of awareness. Within the spaciousness of awareness, nothing is left out. Just as space excludes nothing, so too resting in the vastness of awareness necessarily entails an encounter with the totality of being. This is likened to the unconditional embrace of the Great Mother, Prajñāpāramitā, the source of all, the wisdom that includes all and excludes nothing.

Everything without exception is radiating from the vast open clarity of the spacious ground. Like an ever-revolving fractal or mandala, manifestation is always unfurling in unimaginable complexity. Things we call horrible and things we call wonderful, arising and subsiding in successive waves of never-ending novelty.

Of course, in our everyday lives we come up against all kinds of things that are very difficult for us to include. We have strong feelings about what is not right or good in the world. Perhaps we can include everything, but not *that* thing. Reminding us of "all phenomena without exception," Machig invites us to a profound practice of radical inclusion, suggesting that we take everything into account, consider everyone.

When we realize the nature of mind, the all-encompassing ground of being, inclusion is not really a choice. We recognize that we can't actually get rid of anything. We can't get rid of the bad guy, the enemy, the things we don't like. We can't get rid of any part of ourselves either.

We often use the metaphor of garbage to contemplate this teaching. In our personal home, we collect our trash all week in a white plastic bag, then bring it down to the dumpster at the bottom of our driveway. Every Thursday morning a big garbage truck carts it off. The dumpster is empty, our garbage is gone. It's quite magical really! But of course, if we give the whole situation even a moment of thought, we realize that our garbage is simply being moved to another location, a landfill, possibly even being shipped off to another country. If we expand our notion of home just a little bit, we must admit that we never really get rid of any garbage. We are just moving it around. From the view of space, we can't ever get rid of our garbage. There is no cosmic dumpster.

The view of radical inclusivity is not at all about condoning but rather expanding our boundaries to include what seems other, difficult, averse. Space doesn't pick and choose what to include. You might end up slaughtering some sacred cows in the process, some dearly held personal beliefs, and ideas about what should or shouldn't belong in the world. Yet it's also not about adopting some kind of radical nihilistic agenda—that nothing matters. It's not about abandoning all our values and shrugging off everything as ultimately irrelevant or all the same. We don't have to abandon discernment. That's not the point. Everything does matter. But it matters at the same time all together.

Traditional teachings warn against falling into extremes of eternalism and nihilism, both of which can occur as we consider the notion of radical inclusivity. Eternalism views all things as solid, real, and ultimately permanent, a notion we can easily fall into when we feel stuck in our lives, burdened by our conditions and responsibilities.

From this perspective, the idea of including everything without exception may lead to a sense of utter overwhelm, being oppressed by the weight of it all. On the other extreme, we may fall into nihilism, a sense of meaninglessness or voidness, as though within this vast inclusiveness, nothing ultimately matters. *If I can't ultimately get rid of trash, then why sort out trash from treasure in the first place?* In either extreme, we shut down; our hearts and minds close off; we become numb to the richness and vibrancy of this magnificent, unimaginably diverse and complex life. The Middle Way, as the Buddhist path is often called, is an ongoing practice of remaining open and awake within the immensity of reality. We reveal our tender hearts to the fullness of life in all the beautiful and awful ways we encounter it.

Profound Relationality

Holding the view offers us great refuge on one hand, in the realization that we are held, as is everyone and everything, just as we are. We can relax into the pervasive embrace of space. On the other hand, there's incredible responsibility, because being part of totality means we are all—every one of us—in this phenomenal circus of life together. There's no way out, and everything matters. This is the reality of interconnectedness and interdependence. Nothing ultimately exists in isolation of anything else. Everything is affecting and being affected by everything else—the truth of profound relationality.

Another way of understanding radical inclusivity and interdependence is, perhaps paradoxically, through the teachings on emptiness. You'll notice Machig's insistence on the "empty" nature of mind. Emptiness suggests that all phenomena, including the self, are devoid of concrete, continuous identity. A piece of paper is never just a piece of paper. "If you are a poet, you will see clearly that there is a cloud floating in this sheet of paper,"[5] wrote the beloved Vietnamese teacher Thich Nhat Hanh. The cloud brought rain to the earth, which nourished the tree out of which the paper was made. The paper is empty of pure "paperness"; it is already always something else.

While we may perceive anything—the paper, you, me—as a particular object, upon closer examination its true nature is characterized by fluidity and relationality. Even "I" am not quite as solid as I think:

certainly not at a cellular level, which is composed of the rich banquet of nutrients I digest and which renews itself completely every number of years. My construct of self is intimately interwoven with and dependent on those around me, lending me various identities of parent, partner, friend, colleague, teacher. It's not that the paper doesn't exist or that I don't exist, but neither exists with the definitive finality we normally ascribe to their existence.

A more accurate way of understanding the nature of any phenomenon, including every living being, is that we are in dynamic relationship with each other and everything else. Or as Thich Nhat Hanh suggests, we are "interbeing." The emptiness of solid, separate identities reveals a totality in which all things are interdependent. This radical truth is most beautifully articulated by the great visionary Martin Luther King Jr. in his "Letter from Birmingham Jail": "We are caught in an inescapable network of mutuality; what affects one directly affects all indirectly."[6]

We should remember, however, that this profoundly interconnected, all-inclusive web of being is not a flat, undifferentiated sameness. "All phenomena without exception" means the particularity and granularity of manifestation persist. Radical inclusivity doesn't mean we mix everything in a blender until we're left with a colorless mush. There is tremendous diversity and uniqueness within the whole.

This realization has implications for how we engage with otherness, in whatever body, language, cultural norm, or belief system we meet those who are different from ourselves. Radical inclusivity is not about discovering sameness but about embracing the myriad forms *in their difference*, through which the ground of being self-arises.

Machig's teaching is that the groundless ground is realized *through* the rich particularity of phenomena. This is good news, because it means we don't have to go searching for some totality "out there." We don't have to go looking for space in-between phenomena. We actually are already immersed in it. And we are perceiving the grand display arising from the ground of being in everything that we perceive around us. So there's nowhere else we need to go; we have it all right here! This is how we can understand the famous line from the Heart Sutra, a traditional Buddhist text: "Form is emptiness. Emptiness is form." Phenomenal manifestation in all its complexity and intensity is a display of the vast, luminous, empty ground of being.

The recognition that everything and everyone without exception is included serves as the ground for compassion. Realizing radical relationality is the seed of uncompromising care. Just as our left hand doesn't need to be convinced to assist our right hand, so too, when we recognize our basic inseparability, we develop natural compassion for all beings. We've probably all experienced moments of grace when we are filled with that joyful heart-opening love that makes us sing, *Yes, I love the world, I love all beings.* It's wonderful. But then the next question: Do you love that person who just cut you off in traffic? Do you love the politician you didn't vote for? How do you include those whose views and behaviors are anathema to your core values and beliefs? This, then, becomes the ongoing practice of compassion, meeting our edge and gently expanding our embrace.

Any Thoughts Whatsoever

The teaching on radical inclusivity pertains to our internal landscape as well. Don't be shocked by the workings of your own mind. Or as Machig says,

> *From the realm of phenomena's great expanse of clarity*
> *any thoughts and memories whatsoever may arise.*[7]

"Realm of phenomena," a translation of (Tib.) *cho ying*, refers to the totality of being, the expanse that includes all that is. Just as everything is radiating from the vast, open clarity of the spacious ground, so too every insight, every thought, even confusion and ignorance, arise from the radiant nature of mind.

In fact, when we rest in open awareness, we must be ready for any thought or memory whatsoever to arise. It's romantic to talk about resting in the nature of mind, as though you were relaxing into some safe, profound, spiritual realm. But what you're actually doing is opening to everything just as it is. There's no guarantee that some of your old demons are not going to make an appearance. Repressed shadow aspects may arise. Old traumas, memories, unpleasant things, but also incredible experiences of bliss, clarity, or emptiness. Although generally a beautiful refuge, meditation is not a safeguard against discomfort; it's not a firewall against difficult emotion. It's creating a space of awareness in which anything may arise and developing the courage to be okay with all of it.

That is the honesty of this path. We must show up. Sometimes it's a walk in the park, but often it's not. Taking the view into meditation (the practice of looking at our own mind) and into action (our behavior and conduct) calls on the courage of vulnerability—opening to whatever may arise.

Often, of course, we don't open to whatever arises. Instead, we feel ourselves shutting down, closing off. Chögyam Trungpa described this as the territoriality of ego.[8] We may think we are very spiritually advanced and have practiced a lot, so our territory is imbued with wisdom and light. But we are still upholding an identity, a territory that we've defined as "me." On the other hand, we may have the opposite kind of territory, filled with not-enoughness, self-doubt, and low self-esteem. But either way, it's a manifestation of the same kind of claustrophobia or preoccupation with self. There is no judgment here, simply a recognition of how most of us function most of the time. We have this territory that we want to defend or maintain at all costs. Whatever that territory may look like, it creates some foundation, something to hold on to. Through practice, therapy, or simply good karma or luck, we may be able to expand our territory. But however subtly, we probably still have an idea about who's in and who's out, what's inside the boundaries and what's outside, what the right thoughts are and what the wrong thoughts are. Machig's verse is an invitation to look at what is outside—because nothing really is outside. And if you think something is outside, then you are experiencing the play of duality, the self-reification of the ego. You're in a walled garden, defending the boundaries of your territory.

This practice of radical inclusivity may seem intense—and it is. But it doesn't mean we are being asked to unflinchingly press our faces into the hurricane 24-7. Yes, there are times when we are being called to step up and show up. But really, there's a greater refuge here than what it may seem from the vantage point of our protective little garden. We don't have to avoid anything in order to find a place of rest in "phenomena's great expanse." In the ocean, we can be tossed on the waves in a storm. Or we can relax into the vast ocean. Relaxing into the ocean does not stop the storm, but it gives us the capacity to be with what is. "The realm of phenomena's great expanse of clarity" means phenomena *are* clarity, phenomena are not other than clarity. All emotions, thoughts, objects, occurrences, wildfires, pandemics, and so on are a manifestation of the ground of being. The essence of the great expanse is luminous clarity, and that is what we rest in—the totality of it all.

With the view, we cultivate the capacity to rest in vast acceptance. This acceptance is not a capitulation. But you don't have to take our word for it. Through practice you can try it for yourself. When we surrender to this extent, we find ourselves not in a space of having been defeated but in a place of profound inspiration and wisdom. This is the kind of surrender that requires courage. We have increased capacity to show up in the moment from a ground of surrendered presence. We can remain effortlessly engaged because we are not constantly contriving and judging. We are at ease. We are present. And as things arise, we are there to meet them. Naturally.

Engaging from the View of Skymind

In closing, let us reexamine the nature of engagement with our lives that unfolds from the Skymind view, which is fundamentally a view of radical inclusivity. In previous chapters, we briefly addressed the critique of spiritual bypassing, the concern that nature of mind teachings and the practices of resting, letting go, and radical acceptance are an evasion from actively working to change the ills and injustices that surround us. We'd like to suggest that it's just the opposite. Resting in the nature of mind is an invitation to release a fundamental anxiety that permeates much of our lives, an anxiety that arises out of the nonrecognition of our inseparability from the ground of being, a confusion regarding our intrinsic wholeness. This anxiety separates us from others and from our direct environment.

When we practice open awareness, we're cultivating an embodied, felt sense of inextricable interconnectedness to all things continuously. As Machig's verses in this chapter highlight, everything must be included: our joys and delights, our inspirations, our creativity. Beauty and love and intimacy. But also doubt and conflict and confusion.

Depression and sadness. Violence and war. We are not escaping the challenges of life but awakening more fully to them.

It seems inevitable that awakening our awareness to all things—within ourselves and the world around us—will crack us open. On some level, it is all too much. Our ability to rest in the fullness of all of it opens us to tenderness. I realize that I feel so very much indeed. My heart cracks a bit, or a lot. Practicing with Machig's verses, many of our students noted a quality of kindness that arose naturally in their hearts. This is the awakened heart, *bodhicitta*, the seed of compassion.[9]

The common misconception of "resting" in the nature of mind is that we are necessarily embracing passivity. But looking at the world around us, we see the ever-unfolding radiation of the ground manifesting with unlimited kinetic energy. We don't stop engaging; in fact, we realize there is no way that we *cannot* engage.

The cultivation of acceptance actually enhances the way we engage with any given problem. We hold the vast view and remain engaged. Psychologically, this means we transform reactivity into responsiveness. Reactivity arises from the narrow standpoint of personal sensitivity: I'm triggered and then I react. Responsiveness arises within a view of relationality, considering not only oneself but others, the context, and the overall environment. A response remains open to ongoing dialogue; a reaction is a one-way street. Responsiveness is engagement with a bigger view and thus can be more effective in meeting any given situation with clarity, precision, and skill.

We don't need to stop our work toward making the world a better place. Holding a bigger view, however, our point of departure is not so tightly locked in an oppositional posture. We are often conditioned to use our outrage to motivate our actions against what we perceive as injustice. Outrage, like judgment, compartmentalizes and removes us from that which we oppose; we actually cut ourselves off from the other. When we get self-righteous, we presume that the platform we are standing on is correct, right, inviolable, unassailable. From this place, we pronounce others wrong and in need of change. It's a very precarious perch. It is trying to establish a foundation of being "right" in a space where there actually is no ground. Nothing is absolutely unassailable.

Thus, we would suggest that Skymind, rather than removing us from the fray of the world, invites us to greater dedication to be of benefit to others. When we awaken to radical inclusivity, compassion naturally arises. We get out of our own way. We are willing to see not just our own perspective but also that of the other. The bigger view actually translates into us being more effective advocates. Rather than pulling us out of the world, holding the view and learning to rest in the vast ground of awareness inspire and support engagement that is profoundly committed, compassionate, and potent.

~ EXERCISE ~

Integration with Space

This practice[10] invites us into an embodied experience of totality beyond dualistic experiences of self and other, inside and outside, singularity and multiplicity.

This practice is best done outside with as wide and open a view of the sky as possible. You can sit looking out at the sky and space in front of you or lie down and look up directly into the sky. Let the sun be at your back so that your eyes can remain open with ease.

- ✧ Begin with a few breaths to settle your attention in the present moment, releasing as best you can any physical tensions and remnants of worries, concerns, preoccupations.

- ✧ Let your gaze be open and relaxed, taking in the vastness of the sky without straining your eyes in any way. Let your eyes rest back naturally in their sockets.

- ✧ Slowly let your entire experience become suffused by space. Rather than focusing on the objects within space, become aware of the space that permeates and holds all objects. Relax into the expansiveness of space.

- ✧ Let whatever perceptions arise become like space. Imagine that sounds become space, images become space, sensations become space.
- ✧ As feelings or emotions arise, let them become space.
- ✧ Let thoughts become space.
- ✧ Whatever moves in you becomes space, until there is no boundary, no separation between you and space.
- ✧ Let your awareness rest as space. Rest in this way for as long as you like, ideally for twenty minutes or more.
- ✧ When you close your practice, gently bring movement into your body.
- ✧ You can maintain this sense of spaciousness as you continue with your day.

7

Attention, Awareness, and Loving Radiance

This body of ours is impermanent like a feather on a high mountain pass,
This mind of ours is empty and clear like the depth of space.
Relax in that natural state, free of fabrication.[1]

I (Pieter) was sitting in a small church hall in a residential suburb of Johannesburg. My tai chi teacher had invited the late Chögyal Namkhai Norbu Rinpoche to South Africa from Italy. Renowned as a great Vajrayana teacher and contemporary Dzogchen master, he came to transmit the essence of the traditions he so obviously and radiantly embodied. After several days of teachings and meditation practice, on a late afternoon with the slanting African sun coloring the church windows, he suddenly shouted an ear-splitting *phet!* All my conceptual frameworks shattered in that instant, leaving a sudden gap. It was as if the gears of my rapid-fire mind had suddenly slipped into neutral. The next few moments felt vast, open, and strangely empty. Time had lurched toward the timeless end of the scale. Nothing was really happening, and yet everything appeared crystal clear and impossibly vibrant. Having been primed by days of meditation practice, complex visualizations, and teachings on the nature of reality, the effect on me was profound.

What I experienced in Johannesburg is known as *direct introduction to the nature of mind,* or *pointing-out instructions*, and is used by accomplished masters in the Dzogchen and Mahamudra traditions to do exactly that: provide students with a direct experience of the primordial nature of their mind.

Whereas this experience is certainly profound and may well change the course of one's life, such is the power of our deeply conditioned karmic patterns that we tend to soon revert to our habitual dualistic point of view. Theoretically, once pointed out, we have the opportunity to rest in this place, to rest in the already present nature of our mind and to act from that place of deep ease as we engage in the adventures of this life.

But that is often easier said than done. Thus begins the path of meditation.

Our curious, restless, and mercurial mind naturally tends to preoccupy itself with the world that appears to exist outside of ourselves. This dualistic tendency of the mind leads to sustained distractibility and preoccupation. And this is where the practice of meditation is helpful. One's understanding and embrace of the *ground*, the underlying existential nature of reality as described in the previous chapter, is often called the *view*. Meditation, apart from its many other benefits, is in essence the practice of regularly accessing this view and eventually stabilizing and integrating it into our day-to-day experience (*action*).

The Skymind meditation, introduced in the next chapter (chapter 8), is a simple and direct practice that we hope you can engage with on a daily basis to cultivate the qualities of attention, awareness, and loving radiance described below. In preparation, we offer in this chapter an overview of some key aspects and elements of meditation in general,[2] some basic techniques, the progression from one to another, and the ultimate goal of the meditation journey.

Attention and Awareness

One way of viewing meditation is as a set of techniques for working skillfully with our *attention* and our *awareness*. For our purposes here, attention is what we use to focus on a particular object, person, or thought. So, we can say we *place* or *direct* our attention toward an object. Our awareness is that which is cognizant of what our attention is focused on. But attention is also imbued with awareness, made of it. So in that sense, attention is focused awareness. In everyday life we habitually and impulsively use our attention to wield our awareness, but in meditation we use attention and awareness more consciously to gain insight into ourselves and the nature of reality. The net result is an increase in clarity and ease, and eventually an increase in compassion and a little thing we might call "wisdom."

Machig's teachings highlight the Buddhist view that the true nature of everything, including all aspects of ourselves, is inseparable from primordial awareness. In other words, what we experience as our own cognition, our own awareness, is no other than primordial awareness, the essence at the heart of reality and existence itself. This is absolutely a key point, because it means that skillfully working with our own awareness becomes the relative doorway through which we can consciously experience the vast and luminous nature of all phenomena. And, at least initially, meditation is a prime technology for accomplishing this. (If, at this point, you're still wondering why it is advisable to experience this, we would simply say try it and see for yourself!)

Meditation With and Without a Support

Most of the variety of great meditation techniques could broadly be divided into two major approaches: *with a support* and *without a support*. Meditation with support is where we place our attention on an object of choice and practice to remain focused and not get distracted. The most common, quintessential technique here, taught by the Buddha himself, is to focus on our breath.[3] Meditation without support is when we let go of the object of focus and let our awareness settle in its own ground. We are essentially relaxing into the nature of our own mind. This method is also broadly known as *open awareness* meditation.

These two approaches are not always presented together, with some techniques emphasizing one rather than both. From a developmental point of view, and even a historical one,[4] the two approaches are sometimes viewed as an arc of progressively developing one's meditation practice. This arc begins by cultivating attention through mindfulness in the moment and meditation techniques that develop our ability to place attention on an object of choice and have it remain there, unwaveringly, at length ("with a support"). And finally "dropping" the object of attention and simply abiding in the wakefulness of pure awareness ("without a support").

Let's look a little deeper at the relationship between and benefits of these two approaches from the point of view of a beginner meditator. Since meditation with support is particularly good for cultivating and stabilizing attention, and since stabilized attention is essential in all types of meditation, including open awareness, it is often the best place to start. Placing your attention on an object is also a great yardstick for your progress because you know exactly whether you are meditating or not. Either your attention is on the object or it is not. On the other hand, placing our attention on an object and keeping it there may feel overly restrictive and boring, especially early on, before we are able to experience and appreciate the simple clarity that arises from this practice. Coming to terms with boredom is not a bad thing, and there are many great resources on this topic,[5] but it may cause us to avoid meditation.

The benefit of meditation without support, if done "correctly," is that it allows for resting directly in the underlying transpersonal nature of our mind. As far as there's any objective in meditation, this could be seen as an end in itself rather than a means to an end. This way of resting our mind is the opposite of restrictive, and boredom is generally less of an issue, whether we're doing it "correctly" or not. Without the measure of a defined object for our attention, we may find our mind roaming freely or spacing out into a vaguely pleasurable neverland, detached from the sharp edges of everyday reality. Since there's an important aspect of spaciousness in this type of meditation, stabilized attention is still applicable and helpful to prevent us from getting lost in the space of our own unfocused mind. Although it's called "meditation without a support," if there is an object here, it is spacious awareness itself.

Our Skymind meditation, presented in the next chapter, incorporates both these approaches in a single practice. The idea is that one might locate oneself on this arc based on personal tendencies and level of progress. These days, we don't all get the opportunity to climb the mountain to the lonely cave where the master tells us, "My child, for the next ten years, just follow your breath. Then come back for further instruction." Most of us may need to be our own mentor and self-medicate. This arc does not only apply in terms of our current level of experience but also from day-to-day in our practice. Some days we feel more contracted and afflicted. At other times, more spacious and easeful. So depending on the particular meditation session, the Skymind meditation allows us to apply our focus in a way that is most helpful.

Attention and How to Cultivate It

Therefore you should abide without distraction in the meaning of the equipoised mind itself. Remaining undistracted in the meaning of the abiding nature in that way will bring about the power and energy of blessing.[6]

Strengthening and stabilizing our attention is a key support in all types of meditation, and also a worthwhile practice in itself. Generally, in the course of a normal day, our attention is commanded by any number of things, including our thoughts. Some thoughts may be profound, and some very mundane, but the point is we tend to just think whatever thought pops into our head. We seem to have a built-in generosity toward our own thoughts, where we assume it's worth thinking just because we find ourselves thinking it. Thus our attention jumps from thought to thought all day long, like the classic metaphor of a monkey swinging from branch to branch or a wild horse running in a meadow. The same goes for how easily our attention is attracted by the objects, people, and events around us.

This innate curiosity, this spontaneous distractibility, means our mind is basically preoccupied 24-7. In addition, this curiosity pulls our attention *out*, so we tend to be much more preoccupied with the object of perception rather than with the awareness that's perceiving it. These seemingly default mechanisms of ordinary perception work together to keep us locked in a convincing dualistic experience of reality. In fact, one might say they conspire to *create* the dualistic experience in the first place!

The very first step in taming the wild horse is to practice basic mindfulness in everyday life. This helps us to become more conscious of how we use our attention. Traditionally mindfulness includes a variety of aspects, but here the primary one is to bring one's attention into the present moment. Since this is the only place where anything actually happens, there's an instantaneous alignment that takes place.

There are many benefits to mindfulness in the moment. We become more aware of what is happening with our attention and awareness on a moment-to-moment basis. This does not mean constantly nitpicking about what we're thinking. That would not be liberating. It is gradually becoming more aware that our attention is being compelled in a particular moment rather than being compulsively distracted.

The next step is to engage in more formal meditation practices designed to cultivate and stabilize attention and focus. The first phase of our Skymind meditation (presented in the next chapter) is designed to do just that. There is also a wide variety of other meditation practices, from simpler techniques, such as those of *shamatha* (calm-abiding meditation), to more complex visualization practices, such as the deity practice of the Vajrayana tradition. Shamatha is perhaps the foundational technique for developing concentration through various stages of stabilization. It is the basis for *vipassana* (insight meditation), where one progresses by placing one's attention on increasingly subtle aspects of experience and sensation in order to realize the true nature of existence.

Benefits of Meditation

Stabilized attention and mindfulness in the moment gives rise to presence of mind—*presence*, for short. Our attention is wakeful, alert, and simultaneously at ease because it's not continuously seduced by the next flashy stimulus. It's a particular kind of settledness that also calms others. This presence of mind also allows for embodied presence—that quality of being that allows us to show up fully with whatever is happening or whomever is with us; we're not, however subtly, on our way somewhere else. Presence of mind also promotes agency; we realize we are not at the whim of every thought; we have a choice about what to lend our attention to. It allows us to wield our attention like a finely honed instrument. Imagine your focused attention was a sword—how would you wield it? Randomly? Or with the utmost intentionality? Being responsible with our attention does not mean we should take ourselves more seriously. In fact, presence of mind generally leads to a lightness of being and an improved sense of humor.

Machig says resting with an undistracted mind "will bring about the power and energy of blessing."[7] In other words, it builds energy and wisdom. In chapter 4 we spoke of how the ego and psyche consists of many overlapping patterns. Here's a great, concise explanation by the translator and teacher of Tibetan Buddhism Ken McLeod of how the practice of mindfulness and meditation interacts with those patterns:

> Attention works to dismantle patterns the way the energy of the sun melts ice. The directed energy of attention dissolves the structure of patterns, releasing the energy locked in them. We experience the freed energy as awareness and presence.[8]

Deity practice in the Vajrayana tradition also provides a sophisticated means for skillfully honing attention, in addition to working with awareness. The mind is induced into deep concentration through detailed visualization of complex deities who represent various qualities of wisdom. Machig's practice of Chöd serves as a further example. It involves generating and evolving vivid visualizations while singing the liturgy of the practice in a variety of ancient melodies—while playing a two-sided drum and a bell. It's hard to be distracted thinking about your shopping list when you're practicing Chöd.

Open Awareness

If meditation had a goal, genuinely resting as the spacious ground of awareness—the uncontrived nature of mind—could be regarded as a pinnacle. Often considered the completion phase in Vajrayana deity practice, it is also the main part of the Skymind meditation presented in the next chapter.

Here is the method of resting in suchness:
in being unimpeded and fixation free,
you rest naturally without contrivance . . .
[T]here is nothing to do on purpose . . .
Relinquish fixation and rest at ease.[9]

Once we have practiced stabilizing our attention through techniques of meditation with support, we become curious about awareness itself. Have we considered that the awareness or cognizance that is perceiving phenomena is perhaps infinitely more interesting to explore than the phenomena themselves?

When we become aware of something, we might say, *I am aware of that painting*. But what is that "I" that is aware? Open awareness meditation is the invitation to rest back into that awareness that is aware of the painting. Once we start resting in that awareness, we realize that it is actually not "me" that is aware; it is awareness itself that is aware. It is the intrinsic crystal clear wakefulness that expresses through me that is aware. Furthermore, the perceived phenomena and that which is perceiving it are in essence no different; they are both dynamic expressions of a single underlying reality. They are both reflections of awareness arising from the same ground. Theoretically, this realization collapses the subject-object duality. Practically, this means that our very own cognition is the access point to a conscious experience of the ground of all phenomena:

By looking inward, there's nothing to be seen.
Dharma[10] is ordinary, ordinary mind laid bare.
Looking outward, everything is rainbow-like.
Though forms are distinct and clear, their nature is emptiness.[11]

So how do we "rest in awareness"? As we said elsewhere, even though we really mean "rest" and "relaxation," it's not quite the same as our ordinary idea of rest as taking naps and lounging about. At least initially, we have to rest in a way that leads to the recognition of our true nature.

Machig's most famous meditation instruction suggests

Tighten tight and loosen loose[12]

In another translation, the verse continues:

> *Released by release, let go freely.*
> *Freed by freedom, rest by resting.*
> *That's the resting place of meditation.*[13]

Machig is speaking here of the balance between effort and release in meditation. We have to have some modicum of intention, presence, and concentration before we can release into the freedom and relaxed spaciousness of open awareness. We can't truly rest in the nature of mind if our attention is running all over the place or if our mind is dull and sleepy. The Tibetan word used for "tighten" in the quote above, *bsgrim*, is also translated as "concentrated," suggesting focusing the mind. Lama Tsultrim suggests that this relates to the spinning of wool into yarn, where multiple threads are twisted and tightened sufficiently so that they stay together when released. This image is a metaphor for intentionally bringing the mind into presence so that it can then relax in singular, nondual, open awareness without distraction.

Tulku Urgyen Rinpoche explains it as follows:

> "Tighten tight" means simply to look into mind essence. Unless you look there is no recognition. "Loosen loose" means to totally let go of or disown any idea of recognizing. What is recognized here is that there is no "thing" to recognize. . . . So first look and then loosen from deep within; then it is like space, wide awake. This is the samadhi of suchness, which is real and naturally stable.[14]

In its mildest form, "looking" means that we enter our meditation with the intention to recognize the uncontrived nature of our mind and rest in pure awareness. Once we're meditating, "looking" means using our attention as a tool to find awareness, before letting go and just resting. In the words of the famous seventeenth-century Tibetan author and scholar Karma Chagme,

> Right now, look! Look inside. Look into your own mind.
> By looking into your mind, you'll not see it, for it's not a thing.[15]

For the mind to remain at rest for any amount of time can be challenging. One way of working with this is to relinquish any and all thoughts and distractions as they arise in your mind, as soon as they arise. With practice, you end up resting in the space of awareness from which those distractions arise in the first place. Remaining wakeful there, you start to notice thoughts as soon as they arise. Here you may clearly experience the way awareness contracts into a dualistic experience as your attention is compelled to follow a thought. Of course, as soon as your mind jumps on the train of that thought, you are no longer meditating but rather just thinking. However, since thoughts are also made of awareness, they are not fundamentally a problem in themselves. It is their compelling nature combined with our mind's distractibility that pulls us into a dualistic experience, which then becomes the obstacle. For this reason, once your resting becomes stabilized, thoughts tend to self-liberate in that space.

Tulku Urgyen continues, "This watchfulness is necessary until you are used to it. Once that has happened you don't need to look here or there. You have caught the 'scent' of the nature of mind. At that point, you do not need to struggle; the nature of mind is naturally awake."[16] Simply put, there's a little bit of "trying," especially in the beginning. Then there is the place of true resting, of letting go completely. At this point we're not looking anymore, we're not finding, we're not searching, we're not striving. That would be missing the point. We're resting back into our inherent self-arising nature, which is awareness itself. That's the doorway we mentioned earlier. And since the nature of mind is self-existing wakefulness, there's no zoning out at this point. Instead, one could say there's a subtle zing, a mild cognitive arousal[17] that takes place.

Let's use the metaphor of a surfer in the ocean to help us understand this paradox. Further out from the beach, the waves are just swells. Closer in, the swells stand up and peak into waves, eventually breaking into boisterous whitewater that ends up rolling out on the beach. In order to go catch a wave, a surfer has to first get through this turbulent surf. This physical exertion, the ducking and diving, could be compared to "tighten tight," to getting through the habitual busyness and distractions of our everyday dualistic mind in meditation. But once through, the water is suddenly calm. Deep in, one could lie on one's board and relax completely, not doing anything, enjoying the gentle sway of the swell.

Thus meditation is a tool for getting through the surf of dualistic fixation. When we find ourselves struggling in the surf of life, any advice to "just rest" or "just let go" may not seem very helpful at all. In fact, caught in the tumble of the breaking waves, it may seem profoundly unhelpful—even unkind. After all, hanging out where the big waves break is not an easeful thing to do. But when you're effortlessly floating on the backline beyond the surf and someone whispers, "Just relax; let it be as it is," you might welcome it in a different way. From that vast view, it is clear that the surf is also part of the ocean—the surf in itself is not a problem.

In the words of the great master Āryadeva the Brahmin, once we "look" and recognize, then

> With body and mind thus in their natural state,
> Without further intervention, a fresh awareness arises,
> Extending just as far as the reach of empty space,
> In the vast expanse remain absorbed without constraints or limits.
> At that time you will experience a state of consciousness
> Free from any support, from any sort of foundation,
> An awareness abiding nowhere,
> Not absorbed in either the five aggregates[18] or any outer object.[19]

Charlotte's Reflections from Solitary Retreat: On Our Mountain

Solitary retreat is an integral part of the traditional Vajrayana path. The great masters have generally all spent a significant portion of their lives in retreat, often in the wilderness, in total isolation. For those of us who live the householder life, solitary retreat can be a rare gem that offers us the opportunity to literally unplug and dive deeply into meditation practice. The following reflection was written during one of my solitary retreats:

Look in the way of not looking.
Your mind will not be seen by looking.
Not seeing in itself is the nature of phenomena.
If you see [something,] it is not the nature of
phenomena.[20]

It's been raining for much of the day, so I've been sitting and practicing in my abandoned little cabin that I just named "Yogini's Temple." It's on the edge of a hidden little meadow on the mountain behind our house. It's filled with old wasp nests, spiderwebs, and the droppings of years of rat and mouse wanderings, but the walls are sturdy and the roof doesn't leak—a perfect refuge from the sheeting rain. I sit by the open rickety door looking out at the sloping meadow with its vibrant May grasses. The branches of the little ponderosa by my hut peek past the door, and as I practice I watch silver drops of water form on the end of each pine needle. I've been doing a lot of looking, a lot of seeing. But I haven't been looking for anything, at least not outside my door.

It's a different story when it comes to my mind. I'm looking for all sorts of things—insights, moments of bliss, peace of mind, realizations, the occasional gift of a creative spark. It's great when these show up, some sense of satisfaction—*this meditation is really working for me.* What's so liberating about Machig's teaching here is the permission—no, actually, the *directive*—to stop looking. Whatever might be found in those *nyams*, those great meditational experiences,[21] are only that. They are the sea star floating by, the colorful parrotfish, the glistening silver eel, all of which are indicators that you are in the ocean. But if you want to be aware of the ocean, counting fish is not the way. You can't actually see the ocean because, Machig suggests, you are it. The harder you look for the essence of your being, your mind, the more mystified you will become.

One might come away from this teaching thinking it is better to turn away from the project of looking or meditating altogether, head downtown, and just eat ice cream all afternoon. And yes, that's certainly an option. The ultimate meditation involves no cushion or technique whatsoever. But within the context of practice, this is a beautiful meditation instruction: "Look in the way of not looking." We can look, we can see; we can wake up and become aware. The world can light up in spectacular shades of color when we sit in meditation. How wonderful! But there is nothing to hold on to. There is nothing to be caught with the hook of our looking.

The way of not looking is perhaps a way of total delight in the myriad forms that arise, pass by, and exit the stage, grasping at nothing. The way of not looking sees much, perhaps even more, because it looks for nothing. The way of not looking is like a mother lovingly watching her children play, hearing their laughter. It is enough. The way of not looking allows everything, dismisses no one. We can find incredible rest here in the way of not looking, much like being the ocean itself. We are already there.

The deer come down through the trees just as I finish my practice. I sit very still, watching them eat the fresh wet grass. A young buck kicks himself into a frenzy, chasing off two of his mates. A young doe looks on, as though wondering what to do. In the end she is the only one who sees me, yet she is still too young to be afraid. And then, after the others have strutted away, she gently turns as well. There's nothing left to see now, just the sloping meadow with its bright green grasses.

Loving Radiance

Another key aspect of meditation, and particularly of resting in open awareness, is what we call "loving radiance." The open space of awareness, that vast and unconstricted nature of wakefulness, is not inert; it is not a sterile void but rather imbued with luminosity and radiance. "Everything is rainbow-like," as Karma Chagme suggests.

Although totally beyond explanation or concept, the nature of mind is traditionally described as empty in its essence, radiant in its nature, and compassionate in its manifestation. This corresponds with the three inseparable "bodies" or dimensions of existence called *kayas*: the dharmakaya, sambhogakaya, and nirmanakaya. The empty essence, dharmakaya, refers to the formless, infinitely vast and open dimension of reality that fundamentally underlies everything absolutely. The radiant nature, sambhogakaya, alludes to the self-arising clarity and luminosity that imbues this vastness—the radiant energy body of reality. And nirmanakaya, the compassionate manifestation, refers to manifest reality as the dynamic and responsive expression of ultimate reality. In simplified terms, we might say that the world is made of compassion, the world is made of love. When truly resting in the nature of mind, we have an experience of the inseparability of all three. The spaciousness of Skymind is imbued with luminous radiance and the warmth of compassion. This is the loving radiance of Skymind.

In the quote at the beginning of this chapter, Machig notes that when we rest in our basic nature, we will encounter "the power and energy of blessing," which we might consider another way of describing loving radiance—a continuous glow of basic goodness, wholeness. This is not conditional or targeted love but more like the sun's effusion of infinite, warm light that unconditionally shines on all things.

One of our heart teachers was Lama Tharchin Rinpoche, who graced us with frequent visits to Naropa University. We received many powerful and insightful teachings from him, but perhaps the greatest gift he gave us was his loving presence. I (Charlotte) remember one of his first Dzogchen teachings, "View, Meditation, and Action," which I attended shortly after having completed my graduate studies. Like a good student, I came prepared with notebook and pen, and tried to take copious notes. But by the end of the retreat, I realized that I really had no conceptual understanding of what he had taught. My intellectual mind, which I had been training intensely for the last many years, was at a loss. But something else had moved in me, the deeper attunement to a wisdom that was far beyond conceptual mind. Over the years of ongoing study with Rinpoche, I began to realize that his very presence was a teaching; he was an embodiment of loving radiance. His entire being emanated unmitigated warmth, love, compassion. This loving radiance ignited my own being with an openness, heartfulness, and clarity that I had not experienced before.

How do we access the spacious, loving radiance of Skymind? At a basic level, we need to move beyond any idea that meditation is a purely mental activity. It is not. Rather, resting in the nature of mind is the awakening of the *totality* of being—a vibrant wakefulness that includes head, heart, and body. (We'll say more about this in chapter 9, which outlines the subtler aspects of resting in open awareness.) If we imagine, for example, that the seat of awareness is in our heart center rather than our head, we may tap into a sense of warm, radiant wakefulness that emanates through our entire body and extends effortlessly like rays of sun into the space around us. Then we might recognize that this radiance is not just "ours" but that the whole of reality is radiant, luminous. There's a point at dawn when the first light peers over the horizon. Suddenly, in one instant, the whole landscape lights up in pink, vibrant brilliance. Everything enlightens simultaneously. Just so, awareness awakens into infinite spaciousness, infused with luminosity, imbued with loving radiance.

ATTENTION AND AWARENESS — EXERCISES —

The following series of exercises invite you to work and play with your attention and awareness: focusing, honing, intensifying, releasing, expanding. We've gathered and developed these over our years of teaching meditation, and some are inspired by instructions and practices we have received from our teachers.

Because the visual sense is dominant for a lot of us, our attention tends to follow where we look. The next three exercises help us to decouple our attention from our visual field and introduce a sense of open awareness. These exercises could be combined as each naturally progresses into the next. You can do this anywhere, but it's written assuming you're inside a room. Please note that the Awareness of Awareness exercise below contains an invitation to let go of what we're holding. This may be easier for some and more challenging for others. Please be gentle and kind to yourself when you practice this.

Peripheral Vision Exercise

- ✧ Sit in a relaxed posture with open eyes gazing at the level of the horizon or a little bit above. Your gaze is open and not focused or fixated on any one object in your field of vision.
- ✧ Now extend your arms outward on both sides, with your index fingers pointing up. While continuing to look straight forward, position your fingers so that they are at the very edge of your peripheral vision on both sides.
- ✧ Now, *without moving your eyes*, move your attention within your visual field and place it on your left finger.
- ✧ Now, again without moving your eyes, sweep your attention across your visual field and place it on your right finger. You're simply becoming aware of what is on the extreme right-side periphery of your vision.
- ✧ Now, distribute your awareness evenly between the right and the left fingers. Just take in everything in your field of vision between your fingers, without focusing or fixating on any one thing. This is an example of how we can open or distribute our awareness without fixation.

360 Awareness Exercise

- ✧ Sit in a relaxed posture with open eyes gazing at the level of the horizon or a little bit above.

- ✧ Once you're settled and without moving your eyes, shift your attention to the wall or the part of the room that is behind you and become aware of the objects that are there. Just rest your attention on that lamp or bookcase or doorway or whatever it may be. So even though your eyes are open, your attention is not on what you see in front of you but on what is behind you.
- ✧ Now bring your attention to what is to the left of you in the room, again without looking at it. Rest your attention there for a short while.
- ✧ Now move your attention to what is to the right of you in the room, and rest there for a short while.
- ✧ Now become aware of all three of those sides—behind you, on the left, and on the right—all at the same time. Your awareness is evenly distributed, not fixated or jumping from one object to another.
- ✧ Now complete the circle by adding what's inside your visual field in front, becoming aware of the entire room all at the same time, and relax into that 360-degree awareness. Rest here for a good while. Rather than striving, relax more in order to perceive the entire room at the same time, letting your awareness simply be aware.
- ✧ Now proceed by placing your attention on a familiar object that you know is outside of the building you are in, like a tree in the garden, or a bus stop on the street, or a street corner nearby.
- ✧ Now linger at that place and take in the scene immediately around you, as if you are standing there, scanning it with your awareness.
- ✧ Then bring your awareness back to your body in the room.

- ✧ In the final step, let your awareness again expand 360 degrees, but this time keep gradually expanding outside the boundaries of the room, in concentric circles around where you are.
- ✧ If you're in an apartment or a house, your circles may include the entire building, then the entire block, then the entire town or city, and so on.
- ✧ Keep expanding your awareness as far as you are able to, finally into infinite space, and then let it go at that. Again, don't get caught up in trying to figure out the details. Just let your awareness rest in a larger area, being aware of all phenomena within that circle without attaching to any one thing.

Awareness of Awareness Exercise

- ✧ In the previous exercise you expanded your awareness into physical space. Now gently let go of the idea of physical space and release into all-inclusive spacious awareness.
- ✧ Now we are not so much focused on the objects of perception but on the experience of being aware itself. Awareness is self-arising and inherently awake, so let awareness rest in its own ground.
- ✧ Let go into all-encompassing awareness. This is awareness resting in awareness.
- ✧ Let go and rest as deeply as you can. There is nothing you need to hold on to. Just rest. Nothing to do. Surrender completely—and rest.
- ✧ Gently remember this place of rest so you can come back at will.

- ✧ When you're ready, gently come back to being aware of your body. Your body is imbued with awareness: radiant, at ease. Gently ground in your body, and close out the meditation.

The following two exercises help us to engage with our attention and awareness in increasingly conscious ways:

Bow and Arrow Exercise

- ✧ Imagine that your head is a bow, loaded with an arrow pointing out of your forehead. The arrow is your attention.
- ✧ Begin to pull the string of the bow back, drawing the arrow of your attention with it, out the back of your head. As you pull, you feel the tension of the bow steadily increasing.
- ✧ You need some effort, some force, to continue pulling the arrow back; your attention is intensified more and more as you pull it back.
- ✧ Draw the arrow of your attention back as far as you can and hold it there for a while, so your attention is completely focused, taut, acute.
- ✧ When I say "Now," let the arrow go all at once. Let your attention-arrow shoot out into the vast open space in front of you. When it reaches the farthest extent of its flight through space, let it explode into open, all-encompassing awareness.
- ✧ Now!
- ✧ Rest in this vast, open awareness. Just rest . . .
- ✧ Now gently ground your awareness in your body, and close out the meditation.

Slingshot Exercise

- ✧ Visualize a golden, luminous sphere in your heart center. Imagine this sphere is the locus of all your attention.
- ✧ The sphere is held against the elastic band of a slingshot, positioned vertically in the center of your body, aiming straight up to the sky.
- ✧ Now slowly and steadily begin to pull the elastic of the slingshot downward, along with the luminous sphere. Your attention, as the sphere, is being drawn down into the earth below; the tension gradually increases as the elastic stretches.
- ✧ Down goes your attention, deeper and deeper into the earth. Feel the increased resistance and tautness of the elastic as it stretches more and more.
- ✧ Pull your attention down as far as you possibly can, and hold it there, single-pointed and strained with total focus.
- ✧ When I say "Now," release the slingshot all at once. Let the golden sphere of your attention fly up through the center of your body, out the crown of your head, and up into the sky. Let it soar upward, higher and higher. At its apex, feel the golden sphere, and your awareness with it, explode like a firework into open, all-encompassing awareness.
- ✧ Now!
- ✧ Rest in this vast, open awareness . . .
- ✧ Now gently ground your awareness in your body, and close out the meditation.

8

The Skymind Meditation

All teaching of phenomena is mere symbols.
Do not dwell on books; do real practice.[1]

In chapter 7 we discussed two primary meditation techniques: meditation with an object, and meditation without an object. With an object we focus our attention on something, most often the breath, and without an object we rest in so-called open awareness.

The following Skymind meditation intends to bring together these two major techniques of meditation. This practice was inspired by our own experiences, primarily in Vajrayana practice, and does not include any elements that would normally require formal transmission and instruction. It is a simple, essentialized practice for honing attention and cultivating open awareness. The idea is that you can choose to emphasize aspects of the practice according to your own tendencies, level of progress, or state of mind on any particular day.

Posture

Body posture is very important in any meditation practice. It sets up the basis for your meditation and helps bring your attention into the present moment. After all, that's the only place where your body (and everything else for that matter) actually exists. It is also true that we each have a unique body, and a different relationship with our body.

So, these instructions are based on what has traditionally been presented in Buddhist texts as well as what we think would work for most people.

In Tibetan Buddhism, the optimum posture to facilitate calmness and concentration is known as the seven-point posture of Vairocana.[2] In brief, you want a stable base, either with legs crossed on the floor or sitting upright in a chair. Your back is straight; your shoulders are back so you're not slumping. Your hands rest on your knees or in your lap. Your head is upright with a straight neck. Your jaw is relaxed, and your mouth can be slightly open with the tongue lightly touching the tip of the palate.

In the seven points, the eyes are open but looking down. However, we strongly recommend keeping your eyes open but raised to a level above the horizon, in keeping with Vajrayana instructions. Open eyes are particularly conducive to open awareness practice, where the basic idea is to integrate the totality of our experience into our meditation—all at the same time. It also helps us to integrate inner and outer space (see chapter 9). With your gaze raised, make sure you are not tilting your head back. Even though your posture is upright and uplifted, you should not be straining, and you should be able to relax completely, with your skeleton supporting you almost effortlessly.

The practice is written without too much explanation so that it may be used as a guided meditation, adding natural pauses. Below we discuss further options and enhancements.

The Meditation

Sit in a meditation posture (described above) with open eyes gazing at a level above the horizon. Use relaxing outbreaths to gently release tension in your body. Bring your awareness into the present moment through this focus on relaxing your body. As best you can, let go of distractions or preoccupations, using the outbreath as support.

The Sphere

Bring your attention to a place four inches (ten centimeters) above the crown of your head. Imagine a small sphere there that is translucent and made of light: radiant, brilliant, golden-white light. Although this sphere is outside of your field of vision, you anchor your attention to remain focused on the sphere, without distraction. You may imagine that the sphere is a manifestation of the luminous essence of all things; it's imbued with potent benevolence. The radiance is that of ultimate wisdom and compassion, whatever that means to you, and you imagine it to be profoundly compelling.

Maintain your attention on the sphere without distraction. If and when your attention wanders, simply bring it back to the sphere, repeatedly. You may imagine that the sphere is powerfully magnetizing all your attention, and with it, all your thoughts, all your distractions, drawing in anything and everything that arises in your experience. You don't have to forcefully move your thoughts out of the way; whatever arises in the space of your mind is simply drawn to the sphere, resulting in a single-pointed focus on the sphere.

Keep bringing your attention back to the sphere until you are able to stably maintain your focus on it. There can be a sense of ease here, as attention simply rests on the sphere. If you are unable to maintain your focus, spend more time with this part of the practice until you are able to stabilize your attention on the sphere.

The Sphere Descends

Once your attention is stabilized, intensify your focus on this sphere and have it increase in brilliance. Now the sphere begins to slowly descend toward the top of your crown. As it enters your crown, feel the light of the sphere radiate throughout your entire body, lighting you up with ultimate benevolence and radiant compassion. The sphere continues to descend down the central channel[3] of your body until it comes to rest in your heart center. At this point you visualize your entire body suffused with the light of the sphere, and you may imagine this light to be profoundly purifying and healing. Rest in the feeling of loving radiance throughout your body.

Radiating Light

Next, imagine that the light radiates beyond the boundaries of your body, out into the surrounding environment, pervading all of space and all beings within it. Rest within this radiance—the loving radiance of the awakened heart.

Now let your awareness expand out with the light as it keeps expanding all around, up and down, 360 degrees, into infinite space. Don't force your awareness to expand. Just let it effortlessly fall open and radiate out like light.

Resting in Awareness

Once your awareness has expanded out with the light, let go of the visualization, just relax, and rest in vast open awareness. This is the main part of the practice. You're not focused on anything in particular, just resting in expanded awareness—360-degree all-encompassing awareness. Let everything be just as it is. Relinquish any trying or striving. You are not avoiding anything; all phenomena are included without exception. Yet you are not preoccupied with anything or fixated on anything either. You are simply letting your awareness rest in its own spacious ground, letting things take care of themselves. Surrender into what is already there. Just rest.

If thoughts or distractions arise, recognize them as arising within the space of awareness, like clouds moving through the sky; and rest back into awareness itself. Surrender anything you are holding or that you feel you should be holding. Keep relaxing and continue to rest in warmhearted, radiant wakefulness.

If you're able to stabilize your awareness, then thoughts, sensations, and perceptions will simply self-liberate in that space. If thoughts continue to arise and you find yourself becoming distracted, or if you find yourselves spacing out into a vacuous state of mind, you may bring your attention back to the sphere in your heart, restabilize your attention, and then expand out into open awareness again: spacious, wakeful, and present.

On the other hand, if you find an involuntary contraction against the space, that it is too vast or you encounter a boundary of fear or doubt, that's also okay. Just simply return to where you feel comfortable, and again relax and rest, gently exploring these boundaries.

Rest in this way for as long as you can remain in this experience or for the duration of your meditation session.

Dissolution

Now let your awareness, and with it the original light rays, gradually dissolve or retract back into your body. Then your body, with the light, dissolves into the sphere in your heart. Then the sphere dissolves completely, either instantaneously or gradually. Now rest in what remains. Rest in vast, luminous emptiness. Rest here for a short while or as long as the genuine experience endures.

Now become aware again of the ground beneath you, your body touching the seat. Become aware of your body and physical sensations, if that's comfortable to you. This concludes your meditation.

Carry the feeling of vastness with you throughout the day or into your dreams at night. Also during the day, whenever you remember, flash on the sphere above your head as a reminder to come into instantaneous presence.

Skymind Meditation: Refinements

It may be beneficial to keep the practice as simple as possible, at least in the beginning. But below are some refinements that may be added according to your preference or as you progress.

Open Eyes

Why do we recommend open eyes? It is common in the Tibetan tradition, and there are a variety of reasons for it. The most basic is integration: If all phenomena are a manifestation of the ground of being, then what we see is in fact that display. So, we are not trying to get away from anything or go someplace else. We are very much sitting with things just as they are, hence we don't close our eyes. At a subtler level, there are energy channels connecting the eyes with the heart center, which comes into play at the highest levels of Dzogchen practice.[4]

Depending on what you're used to, meditation with open eyes may feel uncomfortable at first, but one becomes accustomed to it with practice. As an option, you could close your eyes during the visualization of the sphere but open them again as soon as the sphere has reached the heart center and you expand your awareness to rest.

Options for the Sphere

Establishing the Sphere

When first visualizing the sphere, imagine that it is established and present above your crown, whether your attention is with it or not. That way, you can simply bring your attention back to the sphere rather than regenerating it each time. This is a subtle point but can be very helpful when you're working on stabilizing your attention.

Enhancements of the Sphere

By focusing on the sphere, we are practicing honing our attention and bringing about a sense of loving radiance. In order for the sphere to be more compelling to us, we may find benefit from applying one of the following enhancements:

- **Teacher or Deity:** If you have a spiritual teacher or a deity you feel very close to, someone whose wisdom and compassion is apparent and who effortlessly inspires devotion in you, visualize their image inside the sphere. Imagine that the sphere is resplendent with their pure essence. You may imagine that the wisdom of the teacher or deity ultimately calls forth your own inherent wisdom.
- **Sacred Symbol:** Visualize an object or symbol that is particularly meaningful or inspiring to you inside the sphere. Something that evokes a sense of wakefulness and reminds you of the loving radiance within you. An example from the Vajrayana tradition is a double vajra.[5]

Options for Radiating Light

When visualizing the light radiating out from the sphere in your heart center: Since all phenomena are a manifestation of the radiance of the ground, you may imagine that the light that goes out paints everything around you, all phenomena, into their rainbow light essence. You—and the world around you—don't disappear into some kind of empty vacant space. No, you are sitting surrounded by books, chairs, windows, trees, clouds, buildings . . . yet you see the essence of everything; you see it as the radiant display of the ground of being. You're made of light, and everything around you is made of light. Don't force this. Don't become overly preoccupied with this. Maybe just flash on the idea that everything is radiating from the ground of being in this moment, inseparably. See it as such, then let the thought go and just rest.

9

A Deeper Look at Open Awareness

Reducing our obscurations bit by bit through the practice of meditation can be viewed as a progressive approach to finally being able to rest in the vast expanse of our uncontrived nondual mind, or Skymind. But from a more absolute point of view, since the luminous ground is always already our true nature—with zero possibility of actual separation from it—one could ask why anything has to be "done to attain what is already reality."[1] Aiming to attain a goal in the future implies that we are not there now, in effect postponing the recognition of our true condition. This is why Machig says,

> *Don't search, don't practice; rest in your nature.*[2]

We explore the *meditation of non-meditation* and other related topics in the Fruition section below. But for now, let's focus on some of the finer points that may help to deepen the practice of the Skymind meditation or open awareness meditation in general.

The Importance of Relaxation

Years ago, we invited a young Tibetan rinpoche (literally "precious one," an honorary title for a teacher) to Naropa University to teach a weekend retreat. He was still learning English, but he did not request a translator. His primary message was simple and clear: Just relax! He would expound on this with more complex concepts—and we would all watch him expectantly—but then it would be as if he just realized he was trying to say the same thing but in different, difficult English words. So, he would break it off and with a huge smile tell us once again to "just relax." We have attended countless teachings in the ensuing years, but that one still sticks with us for the sheer simplicity and joy we all experienced together.

Almost all meditation techniques emphasize relaxation, both physical and mental. Thus a good way to start any meditation session is to bring our awareness into our body and to relax physically as completely as possible. Relaxing our physical body tends to also help slow down our thought cycle and relax the mind, with the additional benefit of bringing our attention into the present moment.

There can be a tendency to locate the center of our perception, the locus of our awareness, in our head. As a result, we may have a subtle experience, especially early on, of meditating *from our head*. Conversely, in the Tibetan tradition, the heart center is associated with the mind. When we relax and bring our awareness into our body, and particularly to our heart center, as we do in the Skymind meditation, we may experience our meditation as being less heady, more embodied, and coming *from the heart*, so to speak.

A further benefit here, especially as we're developing our practice, is that we are reminded of and can more easily experience the loving radiance and inherent compassion of the nature of our mind. In addition, our body and body awareness may also serve as a welcome refuge in more extreme cases of experiencing dissolution, such as in psychedelic therapy or to counter dissociation.

However, depending on our past experiences, traumas, conditioning, and individual tendencies, it may not be so easy for us to relax or bring our awareness into our body. Learning to relax is in itself a whole path, and it may take time. Some of us may even experience increased anxiety when we try to relax, at least initially. It is thus important to work with relaxation within the arena of our personal context and to be gentle with ourselves. Yet working in this way with embodiment can be a powerful way of encountering, processing, integrating, and sometimes releasing patterns of trauma and other contractions that may be held in the body.

Let's return to Machig's verse, discussed previously:

While concentrated by concentration, relax by relaxing.
Released by release, let go freely.
Freed by freedom, rest by resting.
That's the resting place of meditation.[3]

"Let go freely." When we relax, there's an element of surrender. Ultimately we surrender into all-pervasive awareness, our all-good wakeful nature that is always present. In order to do that during meditation, we have to initially let go of the powerful urge to make meaning and tell stories about everything we perceive and ultimately of our deeply conditioned patterns of contraction, and this is usually not so easy. As soon as you find yourself going into storytelling or meaning-making, relinquish that, let it go, and just come back to purely perceiving. Then stabilize your attention, and rest there. (Remember Machig's verse "Rest like a corpse" and our discussion of the art of letting go in chapter 3.)

Expanding Awareness

When we rest in the Skymind meditation, we are practicing open awareness meditation. But how do we do that? Open awareness is really nonconceptual, but let's see if we can point to it with words. When we let awareness rest in its own ground, our experience is transpersonal, spacious, and vast. On a day-to-day basis, however, our experience of ourselves is usually one of being "localized" in a specific place, and our awareness usually hovers close around our body. This close-in field of awareness is a foundational aspect of experiencing ourselves as a "self."

In open awareness meditation, it may be helpful to think of "expanding" our awareness beyond these habitual boundaries of the self. To revisit our ocean and wave metaphor: Expanding our awareness is not like the small wave trying to explore the scary, deep ocean. It is more like the wave realizing that it is in fact also ocean and thus expanding its awareness to encompass its oceanness. So it becomes not the wave trying to rest as ocean but the ocean resting as ocean. Again, it is not the "small" self becoming aware of the larger world "out there" but rather awareness resting as awareness, resting in its own ground, which is naturally expansive and all-encompassing. This may sound like just another pointer, but it can be a key distinction in terms of how we rest.

An important metaphor here is space. In open awareness meditation we can be said to focus on "mixing space and awareness." Aryadeva explains it thus:

If looking for a simile, one could say [mind] is like space.
The supreme method here [to realize the nature of mind]
Is to unite space and awareness.
When thus mixing space and awareness,
You spontaneously purify all fixed notions
Such as reality and characteristics, negating and establishing,
And you abide in the truth of suchness, dharmatā,
Free from dualistic subject-object cognition.[4]

Recall the awareness exercises at the end of chapter 7. We begin by expanding our awareness from the internal space of our body, into the physical space around us, into expanding circles of 360-degree awareness. Our awareness is relaxed and open. Finally we expand beyond any notion of physical space whatsoever and rest in open awareness.

Remember also that the space of awareness is not nihilistically empty, neutral, or sterile. Although beyond concept, it is more helpful to think of it as imbued with luminosity, with self-arising compassion, the awakened heart of bodhicitta, what we have termed loving radiance. In other words, our open awareness meditation tends to be a more warmhearted affair.

Another tendency is that we are so deeply conditioned by our dualistic experience that when attempting to "rest in the nature of mind," our overactive minds end up creating an experience that matches what we think that means. This conceptual meditation space may be sterile, empty, and cold; filled with colorful light and radiance; or blissfully warm and fuzzy, depending on our proclivities. A common characteristic of these meditation spaces is that they tend to be insulated from everyday reality. This would be a misunderstanding of the all-encompassing nature of basic space and being with everything just as it is. Remember Machig's instructions from previous chapters:

[T]he realization of the nature of mind
Includes all phenomena without exception.

and

So then, rest relaxed . . .
Rest just so with everything.

However, even if we managed to create such a space, it's not the end of the world. Once we realize it and are able to relinquish it, it can be viewed as progress on the path of meditation.

Awareness of Awareness

Once our attention is stabilized, the meditation instruction is to "let awareness rest in its own ground" or to "let awareness become aware of itself." (Please refer to the Awareness of Awareness Exercise in chapter 7.) Related to this, one might also say "Let mind look at mind." Karma Chagme describes it as follows:

> Right now, look! Look inside. Look into your own mind.
> By looking into your mind, you'll not see it, for it's not a thing.
> Dharma is this very emptiness, true nature of your own mind.
> Mind is not nonexistent; it is whatever appears.
> Dharma is the wisdom of awareness, your very mind itself.[5]

In normal everyday life, our attention tends to go outward, and our thoughts might feel like they issue forth from a central point or central self. According to Lama Tsultrim's instructions, in meditation, the invitation is to turn that outgoing attention around and have it look at itself, look at its own source. This should be done as a practical exercise, but Karma Chagme tells us what we're going to find: nothing, "not a thing." If there is anything there to find, it is just pure awareness itself. Once we find that, the invitation is to simply rest in it:

In the same way, mind itself,
Has no support, has no object:
Let it rest in its natural expanse without any fabrication.[6]

Since awareness is inherently expansive and all-encompassing, when our "awareness rests in its own ground," we are in fact experiencing Aryadeva's mixing of space and awareness.

Uniting Inner and Outer Space

Space does not disturb space.
Outer space does not disturb inner space.
Inner space does not disturb outer space.[7]

The following is a subtle refinement that may be helpful when practicing open awareness as in the Skymind meditation. Let's make a distinction between "outer space" and "inner space," where outer space is the physical space around us that we experience through our sense perceptions, and inner space is our psychological or mind space.

As an example, you might experience inner or mind space when you go to bed at night, right before you fall asleep. You're aware of being conscious but without focusing on any one sense perception. Or if you've ever taken almost any psychedelic in a sufficient dose and closed your eyes, you might have experienced a vivid introduction to this inner space. In that context, it is a world of form and light that does not resemble the outer world we perceive with our senses. The shapes tend to be translucent, fluid, and dynamic, with patterned matrixes hinting at a much more vast and transpersonal underlying intelligence.

Yet our experience of this inner space is still that of a point of view (i.e., dualistic), thus creating an experience of self as perceiver. In working with awareness, or in open awareness practice like Skymind, the "expanding awareness" or "adding space" techniques should also be applied to this inner space. In other words, expand and "become" that inner space being aware of itself rather than identifying as a point of view that is aware of the space. With the proliferation of psychedelic-assisted therapy, this may serve as a helpful technique in the progression from more dualistically oriented transpersonal experiences to a more nondual experience.

~ EXERCISE ~

Uniting Inner and Outer Space

- ✧ Bring your attention into the present moment..
- ✧ Close your eyes and relax completely.
- ✧ Become aware of inner space.
- ✧ Imagine this space to be vast, then expand your awareness into this inner space, and "become" the space.
- ✧ While maintaining the awareness of infinite inner space, gently open your eyes.
- ✧ Expand your awareness into infinite outer, physical space, and "become" that space.
- ✧ Unite the awareness of inner and outer space, relax, and rest.

As a way of integrating one's meditation practice with everyday life, there are two traditional techniques that we would like to emphasize: taking short moments, and seeing the world as a dream.

Taking Short Moments

The great fourteenth-century Nyingma master Longchenpa suggested we practice

> Short moments, many times;
> Like collecting water from the eaves of the roof.[8]

Tulku Urgyen Rinpoche encourages us to do the same, until the short moments of recognition become continuous.[9] Pause. Drop into Skymind. Let go completely. Add space. Rest. You can do this at any moment in the day, as often as you remember, or even in the midst of doing something like washing the dishes or driving. Especially when you feel particularly contracted, afflicted, or encumbered, try to remember to let go and add space—to take a short moment. Eventually we want to cultivate the ability to rest in the view not just when we are meditating but throughout all the activities of the day—when sitting, when walking, and even when talking.

Seeing the World as a Dream

Another common practice is to view the world as a dream. Longchenpa says,

> Then as the main praxis meditate like this:
> The outer world, its mountains and valleys . . .
> and the internal world of body-mind . . .
> all experience, should be attended to incessantly as dream . . .
> Moving or sitting, eating, walking or talking,
> with constant attention sustain dream-consciousness.[10]

This does not mean the whole of manifest reality is *just* a dream, that it is nonexistent. The dualistic display of all phenomena arises out of the ground, a "space of unstructured brilliance and emptiness,"[11] and is not separate from it. That's why Longchenpa continues,

> Yet delving deeply we find neither truth nor falsehood,
> for neither present nor absent, it is beyond all conception;
> we know it like the sky, inexpressible, unimaginable,
> fundamentally ever fresh and pristine.[12]

And so we train to see the world like that, to remind ourselves that everything is profoundly interconnected. We relax and see the world as slightly less solid. We see the rainbow light that shimmers underneath the dense physical manifestation of phenomena—the underlying radiant, energetic matrix.

The culmination of our meditation practice is the complete integration of our meditative view and everyday view. At that point we see everything as already integrated, and there's nothing more to do to realize it. We are resting easefully and effortlessly in naturally arising awareness.

Charlotte's Reflections: Solitary Retreat at Dragon's Nest

My final morning in my retreat cabin at Tara Mandala, the last day of my monthlong solitary retreat. I'm in Dragon's Nest, a small but glorious cabin built into a lofty rocky ridge overlooking the wilderness of southern Colorado. The mama bear was back in the meadow during my morning practice. Later, a wild horse with her foal came grazing in a lower patch of open grass. I've had to move inside from my lofty outside perch that I love so much because the gnats are out on their morning feeding spree. The cabin is quiet except for a few creaks in the roof as it adjusts to the rising temperature.

In these last hours of my retreat, I contemplate Machig's verse:

> *At first, you came alone. In the end, you will go alone.*
> *So now also you must train alone.*[13]

In many ways, what Machig is offering in this verse is supremely evident to all of us. We were born alone, and we will die alone. It doesn't seem like a particularly joyous or inspiring verse to end my retreat on; yet also, appropriate. We *do* train alone. It's what retreat is all about: to slowly reel in all the projections on a world-out-there and bring them back home to their origin. To be for a while with yourself and notice and work with all that arises. To recognize, to see, to become aware; sometimes to struggle, to fight, to defend; and also to let go, release, settle back, settle in. It's a whole carnival right in your own mind-body-heart, a whole universe unfolding with its tricks and shows, its sorrows and joys, its insights and its melancholy—all in a twelve-by-twelve-foot cabin.

To train alone means we have to do the practice ourselves, we have to come to know our own mind. But the exquisite beauty is that you can, and you will. Because what is to be found is the nature of your mind; what is recognized is the nature of reality right in your twelve-by-twelve pocket of the universe. The brilliance is that in this deep dive into the itsy-bitsy particularity of how you are in this moment, the entire, vast, all-encompassing expanse of being is accessed. It's the little mountain stream that takes you to the open ocean.

Since you've trained alone, no one can take it from you—even though no one could anyway. It's like once you've tasted something yourself, no one can tell you otherwise. So it is good we must train alone. It's actually a blessing that we can, that we must.

10

The Liberation of Morality

Padmasambhava, also known as Guru Rinpoche, the beloved eighth-century master acknowledged for establishing Buddhism in Tibet, is often quoted as saying, "Though my view is as vast as the sky, my action is as fine as barley flour."[1] In its expansive embrace, the view of Skymind offers a profound refuge. Then there are the very real decisions and choices of everyday life. The suggestion here is that we bring the same imperturbable clarity of vast view to bear on the details of how we engage, speak, and relate, even at the minutest level of our actions.

Machig's teaching is similar:

If you don't know occurring circumstances as supports,
even with a lofty view, you will lose your way.[2]

This is Machig's version of "where the rubber meets the road": Embodying the big view of Skymind in the grit of mundane existence marks the journey of authentic living. We may tend to blame and bemoan challenging circumstances in our life, but as Machig notes, if we don't appreciate, lean into, and learn from the rub of "occurring circumstances," our view alone will lead us nowhere.

In the tripartite path of view, meditation, and action, this points to the importance of action: the behavior that follows from, aligns with, and ultimately is a tangible application of the view. It is the integration of wisdom and awareness into every aspect of our lives.

Morality and Ethics

Right action or right conduct opens us to an investigation of morality and ethical behavior. It can be easy to think of ethics as heavy-handed, a set of rules and commandments: Don't kill. Don't steal. Don't lie. But there is a reason ethics are part of all religions. On a collective level, ethics are essential for a society to function and prosper. On a personal level, morality allows us to recognize the chaos and drama we create in our life and clean it up. The liberation of living a moral life is bringing order to our external life as well as our inner landscape so that we have a platform from which we can realize and grow into integrity, authenticity, and wisdom.

The very earliest teachings of the Buddha include *shila* (Skt.; Tib. *tsultrim*) or ethical conduct, which, along with wisdom and mental discipline, outline three parts of the Eightfold Path that leads to the relief of suffering and ultimate liberation. Further categorized as right speech, right action, and right livelihood, these guidelines offer the opportunity to embody mindfulness and compassion in the seamless continuum of a wakeful life.

Many of us may have the good fortune of taking basic moral behavior for granted—*not* being preoccupied with whether or not we should steal, for example. But even then it doesn't mean that morality is not important. There are all sorts of subtler forms of denial and dishonesty—with ourselves and with others—that we can get caught in. What's the use of sitting and meditating while we're unkind and unskillful in our everyday interactions? Can we even begin to practice the subtle art of liberation when our life is filled with lies, drama, or subterfuge?

What even is a *clean and moral life*? What are the rules? Here, as elsewhere in this book, it depends on one's life circumstances and level of development. Traditionally in Buddhism there are three levels of moral development. The most basic level is a commitment to not harm others. This is the realm of externally imposed codes of conduct such as national penal codes and the fire-and-brimstone departments of almost all religions. This level is the bare minimum for a functioning and safe society, let alone an enlightened society. It is also where basic kindness and compassion begin.

The next level of morality is to strive to actively benefit others. Here the guidelines shift from injunctions against harming to encouragements to actually help and heal, from not stealing to practicing generosity, from not lying to speaking with truth and love. In Buddhism this is the bodhisattva level, referring to the being who has dedicated themselves completely to benefiting others. When we are embedded in dishonesty, contrivance, and conning our way through relationships, we don't have the bandwidth to extend compassion to others. Basic morality creates some order in this landscape: You finally lift your head out of the drama of self-involvement and have the energy and wherewithal to become curious about others and to want to benefit them. There's some space for naturally self-arising altruism to occur.

At the third and subtlest level, there's a promise of liberation in morality. Here morality is not rooted in an externally imposed code of conduct but rather a compassionate attunement based on our lived experience of inextricable interconnectedness. Relaxing into Skymind, we extend into the nature of everything, inseparablly. We arrive into effortless spontaneous presence, which is not preoccupied with figuring out what we should or should not do. Action arises as a natural mindful and heartful response to the situation we find ourselves in. We can trust ourselves and our ability to be present to meet the moment with responsiveness rather than reactivity.

The ultimate morality arises not from a memorized book of rules nor from an externally imposed imperative but from directly accessing the self-arising awakened heart of our innate wakefulness, bodhicitta.

Machig suggests that

> *[Not to dwell in the space of the Great Mother,]*
> *although performing characterized virtuous acts,*
> *is to remain a long time in cyclic existence . . .*[3]

The awakened moral life is not about tallying up as many "good deeds" as we can, however beneficial those may be. The point really is that our "goodness" arises from the realization of our true nature—Buddha Nature—which is not different from the true nature of all beings. To "dwell in the space of the Great Mother"[4]—that is, to dwell in Skymind—means that our actions are inspired by this realization and the compassionate awareness of fundamental inseparability.

This is where meditation, and specifically the Skymind meditation, becomes particularly relevant. When we rest in open awareness and loving radiance, we are cultivating a familiarity with our true nature. Our embodied awareness of inseparability becomes the default setting from which we move into our everyday lives.

Thus morality is about manifesting an environment of clarity, insight, and kindness in which wisdom and compassion naturally arise. But it's hard, if not impossible, to relax into this spontaneous presence if we're dealing with the turbulence that comes from not living a life of integrity. We can't actually relax because our energy is tied up in upheaval and drama. Which brings us back to the importance of basic morality. The ongoing practice of morality, then, is about waking up at every level of our life to the patterns that drive us, to the impact our behavior has, and discovering the ways we can meet each moment with authentic, compassionate wakefulness.

Karma

The traditional teachings on karma similarly highlight the acute relevance and impact of conduct. Literally meaning "action," karma refers to the natural current of cause and effect. Everything manifests in response to causes and conditions, and itself sows the seeds for future manifestation. Whatever we do is conditioned by previous experiences, thoughts, and circumstances, and what we do now sets up ripples that predispose our future.

One way of understanding the principle of karma is simply that everything impacts everything else, or even more succinctly: Everything matters. It also means there is no external arbiter or scorekeeper monitoring our or anyone else's action and conduct. In a profoundly responsive and interconnected world, we are ultimately all co-creators of our reality.

From this vantage point, we can also understand the liberating nature of karma. From a purely superficial perspective, karma may be misinterpreted as a heavy chain, an impersonal and inescapable process of judgment tallying our good and bad deeds, and meting out instant and long-term retribution. But really karma points to the profound interdependence of all things. Everything arising as a result of causes and conditions, and itself giving rise to further causes and conditions, paints the picture of an intricately interlaced fabric that is constantly in flux.

Everything is influencing everything else in a beautiful display of tremendous energy. This is referred to as *pratītyasamutpāda* (Skt.), dependent co-origination, in traditional teachings. This interdependence is true not only of external phenomena but also of our inner life, our psyche. Our energetic disposition is constantly influenced by what's going on around us. The liberation in understanding karma is that rather than contracting in fear around the potential repercussions of anything we do or say, we instead open into the view of profound interconnectedness and the resultant arising of compassion free of judgment. Karma is the lived experience of interdependence.

At the personal level, karma invites us to bring mindfulness and honesty to our thoughts, speech, and actions. Because of karma, we receive continuous reflections and ongoing feedback on our behavior. And because of karma, we can continuously adjust, realign, or radically change how we show up. A sense of agency and empowerment dawns in the realization that we can and do continuously make a difference. Becoming conscious participants in the dynamic of karma, we can elevate our life to greater integrity and authenticity.

At the collective level, karma inspires us to tap into compassion. We're not going around telling others to clean up their act because karma will come to bite them. Rather, the truth of karma helps us understand that everybody (including ourselves) is a product of their circumstances, influenced by a tremendous, incalculable number of factors and conditions that have brought them to where they are. Instead of blame, there is compassionate understanding. We are all, all together, swimming in this ocean of totality. Everybody is affected by everything else. The conditions and particular contexts of others have them show up in certain ways, act in certain ways, as is true for us.

No blame does not mean no justice. In fact, it's from this place of big view and compassion that we engage in the work of cultivating social justice and collective well-being. We're not working from a basis of solidified judgment, standing on a wobbly platform of moral superiority. Rather, we work toward a more just, equitable, and peaceful world by tapping into the understanding and insight that arise in the lived experience of interdependence.

Machig's synthesis of these teachings is pretty straightforward:

People who engage in negative actions
are like little kids clutching fire . . .
It produces your own sorrow. . . .
. . . [T]o commit negative actions
is exceedingly stupid.[5]

Aside from the consequences of negative actions, Machig is saying that harmful actions themselves create unhappiness. It doesn't really matter whether or not we "get away" with anything but rather about realizing that negativity—whether in action, speech, or mind—creates its own unease, turbulence, and discontent. With so much intrigue already in life, why create more? Like clutching fire, you burn your own hand.

This teaching is illustrated in a story from one of the Buddha's previous lives, collected in the Jataka tales. In this particular former life, the Buddha had lived as the young student of a great spiritual master. One day, the master, who had up until then been known for his great moral virtue, sent all his students out into the town to steal something. "But," he warned them, "you must steal in such a way that no one sees you." Hesitatingly the students filed out to perform this strange task, until only the young student, the future Buddha, remained. "I cannot go," he asserted, "for I will see myself."

There is no great judge watching us. You are the one that sees; you are the one that knows, from the loudest dramas to the innermost secrets. This beautiful little story highlights the straightforward simplicity and ease of the moral life, marked by clarity and transparency, with nothing to hide. True honesty, to ourselves and to others, creates a lighter, less weighted, and more liberated life. A life of radical authenticity, seamlessly aligned from our innermost heart to the details of our every action. A life with a view as vast as the sky and conduct as fine as a grain of barley.

Morality in Action: The Practice of Right Speech

Let's take a closer look at one aspect of morality: speech, or right speech as it is called in the Buddhist tradition. This is a particularly germane topic given the central and pervasive role that speech—spoken and written—plays in our modern society.

One may easily consider speech a free commodity: We can say as much or as little as we like; we can proclaim, explain, and rant, then retract, delete, and undo to our heart's content. But words, as we realize upon some examination, have incredible power—to create and destroy, to soothe and harm.

In traditional Buddhist teachings, the most basic level of right speech outlines injunctions: not to engage in lying, divisive speech, harsh words, or idle chatter. It is clear how these forms of negative speech harm others. But as Machig's verse highlights, they equally contribute to our own suffering, akin to a child "clutching fire." Like an iceberg that reaches far deeper into the ocean depths than above the surface, outward expressions of negative speech suggest an equal or perhaps even greater unrest and unease within.

Lying to others reflects dishonesty and disharmony within ourselves; what we project outward is not congruent with what is taking place inside. Not lying is an ongoing practice of radical honesty with ourselves, and a courageous and uncompromising alignment with reality. Honesty is not just about speech. It is a stance that we take toward our entire life. We become transparent with ourselves, about what we avoid or ignore, what we cling to, what we judge. We recognize our patterns. This is not about being hard on ourselves but rather cultivating curiosity, clear seeing, and compassionate openness with ourselves and thus ultimately with others. This kind of radical honesty is a complete path in itself. It heads us toward liberation.

Divisive speech and harsh words reveal the seduction of negative speech. One of the quickest ways to bond can be through shared negativity, like becoming friends through a common enemy. Negativity has a quick-moving, magnetic charge; it's probably why bad news makes far more headlines than good news. But it's also a short-lived saccharine high, leaving us with an empty feeling afterward, or the constant need to keep refueling—like a cheap addiction. More often than not, divisive speech and harsh words arise from a wobbly ground of insecurity, self-critique, and self-doubt rather than a solid foundation of genuine self-honesty.

The teachings on right speech create a platform for contemplating speech as a form of ongoing contemplative practice. What is true to say? What is necessary? What is kind? When and why do I engage in negative speech? What would I say if everything I said could be heard?

When we begin to bring mindful attention to our use of speech, we also develop the capacity to use speech as a skillful means of relating, connecting, soothing, healing. In this deeper level of right speech, we can engage in the practice of conscious speech as a form of active compassion. We (Pieter and Charlotte) have regular "clearings" in which we create intentional space and time to speak truthfully and openly while being heard by the other. Clearings have become a cornerstone of our relationship, inviting us into an ongoing practice of self-honesty explored and expressed in the context of partnership.

There's a third and subtler level of speech that we can access once we bring awareness to our words. In Buddhist teachings—and interestingly shared by other traditions[6]—the vast, empty potentiality of the ground of being comes into manifestation first through sound, then transforms into light, and finally densifies into form. The idea here is that sound creates reality. When we speak, we are manifesting. Words are not empty but rather carry generative potency.

Speech can, for example, open into the creative flow of poetry as an expression of ineffable, ultimate reality. Refusing the bondage of conceptuality, the *mahasiddhas*, the great Tantric masters,[7] offered their songs of realization (*dohas*) in place of treatises or sermons. Their poetry, like that of so many other spiritual traditions, recognizes within its own fleeting, ungraspable form the evanescent, numinous nature of absolute truth. For the rest of us, we might consider that some of our deepest truths are revealed in the spontaneous love poem we whisper in our beloved's ear or the song of joy we sing to the first spring flower that soon dissolves into the morning breeze.

In everyday life, we can proceed with the view that our words have impact, that speech is not "free," and that indeed, when used mindfully, it can be a potent form of creativity. This realization need not be heavy-handed. It can serve as an invitation to step into the empowered agency of our speech. In the biggest view, we could say that when we truly relax into our nature, as Machig has been suggesting all along, speech becomes an expression of direct insight and uncontrived wisdom, simultaneously offered and released in the perfection of the moment. The weighted decision of what to say or not to say is liberated into the self-arising heartfelt expression of love, care, and fierce clarity.

The vast view of Skymind entails a profound commitment to showing up with honesty, clarity, and integrity in our everyday lives. Because we recognize our inescapable interconnectedness with everything, Skymind means that everything we do, say, even think matters. We invite you to bring attention to this recognition of inseparability in your Skymind meditation practice—at the physical, emotional, and mental levels. Take note of the feeling and awareness of nonseparation—how could your actions not have impact? Thus traditional ethical guidelines may be helpful initially, but ultimately we are invited to embody integrity and authentic, spontaneous presence in every moment and aspect of our lives: relationships, work, speech, actions. This invitation is not a burden but rather a call to a liberated life of transparent, open, and profound goodness.

11

The Path of Radical Responsibility

Born into a well-to-do family, Machig Labdrön lived a comfortable life for much of her youth. She became well respected for her ability to read the *Prajñāpāramitā Sūtra* with ease and speed, and she spent her young adult years in high-class social and religious circles. Machig's life took a radical turn, however, after an encounter with Kyotön Sönam Lama, a teacher who would have great significance for her. Impressed by her skilled recitation, Sönam Lama asked whether she truly understood the *Prajñāpāramitā Sūtra.* Machig responded with intellectual correctness. But Sönam Lama suggested she find a deeper understanding "beyond all conceptions,"[1] arising in her "innermost being."[2] Taking his teaching to heart, Machig reread the texts and, so the story goes, in contemplating the chapter on demons, came to a true realization of no-self.

To reflect her release of self-cherishing, Machig discarded her beautiful clothes, wearing instead the clothes of a beggar. Leaving the company of nobles and the comforts of monasteries, she lived with lepers, giving up her fine food and luxuries. She came to live without preference for praise or blame, pleasure or pain, resting within the "equanimity of the expanse of *dharmata,*" the essence of reality, suchness.[3]

We have always found it particularly interesting that Machig's deeper comprehension arose from reading the chapter on demons. As her subsequent decision to radically change her life highlights, there is a teaching here on bringing awareness to and engaging with whatever arises, particularly that which is most challenging, as a way to live into the fearlessness and liberation of vast view.

This story of Machig's life is powerful because it exhibits the courage to turn toward rather than avoid difficulty. Since from an absolute point of view, everything is included, we cannot actually avoid anything. Machig puts it this way:

Carry the load of appearing conditions. . . .
If you don't carry the load of all phenomena,
the remedy of peace and happiness can't liberate you.[4]

In our own words: Be with experience *as it is, whatever it is.*

At an everyday level, to "carry the load" means that we engage with the circumstances of our life head-on. We're not continuously avoiding or ducking from difficulties but meeting whatever happens as an integral part of the journey of awakening. Resting in the nature of mind is often described as being with things as they are. Similarly, Machig's instruction here is to be with our experience *as it is.*

"To carry the load" means to take on the whole package of pains and joys. It means not to turn away from ourselves or from others in all their beauty and ugliness. At times, the "appearing conditions" will be the nurturing touch of a loved one, the well-deserved satisfaction of an accomplishment, the beauty of a late summer sunset. Do not turn away. At other times, the conditions that appear will break our heart—the final words of a dying friend, the unresolved conflict with a loved one, the brutal memories of history, the burning hatred of political vitriol, the heart-wrenching images of suffering. Do not turn away. In the view of radical inclusivity, in the reality of interdependence—the lived experience of Skymind—we must hold it all, without hesitation. To "carry the load" means to see ourselves as always inevitably involved, as oppressors and as oppressed in the ongoing dynamics of justice and injustice, freedom and suffering. It means to take radical responsibility, not just for what we've personally done or not done but for the whole catastrophe and brilliance of beingness.

But there are many ways we can carry the load. Growing up in New York City, I (Charlotte) remember looking at the massive metal statue of the Greek god Atlas on Fifth Avenue, carrying the globe on his shoulders; his head heavy, back bent, his mighty arms holding aloft a world that would crush him. We often move through our lives like this, continuously burdened by the real or imagined baggage of our destiny, responsibilities imposed by ourselves or others. The chore of life; the weight of the world. This is one way of carrying the load of all phenomena.

Buddhism offers us an alternate image, that of Prajñāpāramitā, the Great Mother, who births all things in her womb of totality, holds all beings in her arms—boundless, nurturing, ever-present. Prajñāpāramitā is fundamentally another name for the ground of being. And like the ground, she is described through the metaphor of space, a vastness that can hold everything because it itself is nothing. Space holds every star system, every galaxy, every planet, every building, chair, fork, every speck of dust. Is space burdened, like Atlas, by carrying the load of all phenomena? No. Space carries totality in a vast immeasurable embrace.

We can recognize and practice abiding in this all-embracing space in our Skymind meditation practice. When we rest in open awareness, we are indeed resting our awareness as space—open, boundless, all-inclusive. Whatever "appears" during our meditation—thoughts, sensations, emotions—is simply held in the vast expanse of awareness itself. We don't have to strive to get rid of anything or to grasp anything; we practice resting into awareness itself, which effortlessly holds everything. You may notice that a pervasive quality of ease arises in this spaciousness of practice.

From this perspective, to carry does not mean to strain harder, to brace ourselves against the weight of existence, but rather to rest back into the totality of all, the very ground of being, all at the same time. To "carry the load of appearing conditions" as Prajñāpāramitā is to recognize ourselves in the infinite space of interconnectedness with all beings. This interdependence is empowering, enlivening. In Skymind we hold all things and know we are profoundly held. It's not the small self that is carrying the big load; it's not "me" taking it all on. That is absolutely overwhelming. The profound resource is the fact that you yourself are part of all phenomena; you, like all manifestation, are arising from the ground of being. To carry the load is an invitation to relax into our transpersonal, vast, resourced self, our true nature—

Skymind. And from here we cannot *but* meet all appearing conditions with tremendous resourced agency. Perhaps even with delight!

Machig concludes this verse by suggesting that "if you don't carry the load of all phenomena, the remedy of peace and happiness can't liberate you." The implication is that liberation is found only *in* taking it all on, a total embrace of all appearing conditions. Deliverance, ultimate peace, and happiness are not separate from all that surrounds us, after all. We just have to realize this.

The "remedies" Machig is referring to are all the strategies we've developed in a lifetime to avoid the unpleasant, even at an everyday level. I, for one, do the dishes when conflict arises; it's my little escape into the remedy of activity. Others may turn to a drink, sidestep into flippant humor, or storm out of the room. Then there are the more positive remedies like exercise, nature, travel. Even spirituality can at times become a "remedy of peace and happiness." Machig is suggesting that we examine how and when even our most well-intentioned and best-serving practices of finding solace become a way of escaping the crunch of life. Ultimately, Machig is saying, these will not liberate you. They can't because if they serve as an escape, then sooner or later you'll end up back where you started—with the unresolved issue, the unacknowledged longing, the aching heart. These remedies of peace and happiness are like a vacation; they give us a break but they do not liberate us.

Spiritual life is not a remedy against ordinary life; the point is not to get away from anything. The radical truth is that we can't actually get away from anything. It is actually our avoidance that creates the false impression of separateness, otherness, duality. Thus to embrace all things brings us back in touch with the wholeness, the totality that we—and all things—truly are.

Machig's unequivocal statement that there is no ultimate peace and happiness without carrying everything may sound like we have to first do *this* thing before we can have *that* thing. Convenient for our *always-have-to-be-doing*, *have-to-earn-it* conditioned selves. But that's not what she's encouraging here. The reason she can be so unequivocal about this is that absolutely all phenomena are a manifestation of the all-encompassing ground of being. When we realize that, when we integrate and rest in that, we are indeed carrying the load of all appearing conditions, but effortlessly!

The beauty of these teachings is that in carrying the load we are invited into a lived experience of our vastness, into absolute bodhicitta, the awakened heart. Leaning into all phenomena opens into wakeful presence and fearlessness. Imagine the feeling of knowing that whatever comes across your path is workable in some way. That is true peace; that is true happiness. We haven't turned away from anything. Thus we find that we can, in some radical and immeasurable way, relate to and perhaps even discover love in everything.

12

Non-Avoidance and the Path of Radical Acceptance

When we teach on the topic of avoidance at retreats or workshops, to demonstrate our point we'll sometimes lean sideways, turn our head away, and bring our hands up to the side, as though shielding from something ugly or terrifying—a literal posture of avoidance. The gesture shifts our whole body into an uncentered, contorted posture, tense and strained. We'll ask students, "Imagine you had to go through your day like this?" Our neck and arms begin to ache at the very thought.

As humans we are deeply conditioned to avoid discomfort. We turn away from what we perceive as unpleasant, negative, uncomfortable, or painful almost automatically, subconsciously. Most of us have developed powerful mechanisms to ignore, avoid, or suppress our feelings. These mechanisms may take the form of distraction, like preoccupying ourselves with looking at our phones, watching TV, doing busywork, or whatever our favorite avoidance mechanism is. Even when we do pay attention to the unpleasant emotions, we tend to immediately develop a narrative about them and strategize about how to fix them rather than just feeling what we're feeling.

Physiologically, of course, this fulfills an important and necessary survival function, like jerking your hand away from an open flame. And psychologically there's wisdom and good sense in avoiding harmful environments and relationships. But there are many downsides to avoiding or ignoring every unpleasant feeling on a day-to-day basis. Constantly avoiding the reality of our own negative emotions, anxieties, and bad moods may lead us away from a courageous, openhearted, and authentic life. Furthermore, we start to project that attitude onto our external world and relationships, resulting in subtle but persistent denial. We are out of alignment because we are subconsciously insisting on seeing life the way we would like it to be rather than the way it actually is.

Avoidance itself is a kind of suffering. We get locked in a posture of turning away, thinking that it's better than actually just being with what we are avoiding. "I just don't want to go there" is a way of closing ourselves off from parts of our experience. This reflex often has more to do with an anticipation of discomfort rather than with the affliction itself. In other words, we turn away before we actually experience the emotion itself. Sometimes this avoidance itself becomes more uncomfortable than the thing we are avoiding, especially over time. Eventually we end up boxing ourselves into an extremely limited experience of life. This kind of avoidance is strenuous, draining, and ultimately unsustainable, like the physical posture we described above. It is suffering in itself, the suffering of avoidance.

When we avoid, we end up splitting our reality. Good feelings and bad feelings. Comfort and discomfort. Hope and fear. Cultivating an attitude of constant avoidance is like building a walled garden. We try to make everything "inside" perfect and beautiful, and keep the "ugly" out at all costs. But we don't have to think too hard to realize this is a fear-based lifestyle. We're spending so much energy on building and maintaining our walls. What's liberating about that?

If there really is a nondual awareness beyond the daily experience, simple alchemical logic will have us commingle equal parts of light and dark and embrace the entire mandala of manifestation—no preference—in order to transcend the limitations of each. Yet we avoid contact with the dark at all costs.

From the view of Skymind, the practice of non-avoidance is hardly a choice but rather an expression of our fundamental understanding that everything belongs, everything has its place. We have the capacity to work with whatever we meet on the path of life.

The Practice of Non-Avoidance

So how to deal with this? The advice here is to turn toward our shadow, to turn into the unpleasant, to "feed our demons."[1] Machig encourages us:

At the time that adverse conditions occur,
it is crucial to know the vital point of taking it on.[2]

What Machig is saying here is that when the going gets tough, when we encounter "adverse conditions," the key instruction is to actually be with what is occurring, to meet the difficulty, to engage the challenge. "Taking it on" reflects the wisdom of non-avoidance and an attitude of radical acceptance, even and particularly in the face of adversity.

The beautiful jewel here is that we don't have to try to sidestep or reject our afflictions: our experiences of disappointment, loss, discouragement, sadness, grief, anger, resentment, despair. We welcome them, feel into them, and work directly with them. We turn into discomfort and affliction, not just as an unavoidable part of life but as a key part of our liberation. We don't have to find a high-enough mountain to access the nature of mind and finally be free. No, we find liberation in the "smelly nest of the ego," a phrase attributed to Chögyam Trungpa. We find liberation *within* our circumstances. That's the good news.

So we bring our challenges onto the path of waking up. We begin by bringing mindfulness to the avoidance impulse itself, whenever it surfaces. Avoidance can serve as a red flag, a helpful marker to call our attention to a previously unconscious evasive maneuver in progress. Transactionally, the payback is much higher in turning toward what is actually arising rather than turning away. The primary benefit of suppression is expediency, like when we push emotions aside in order to efficiently deal with a crisis. But when it becomes a habit, the benefits decline precipitously. On the other hand, turning toward whatever emotion is arising has many potential benefits.

So how do we do this? We intentionally turn to face the full experience of the emotion we were trying to avoid in the first place. We literally feel the affliction and the tension of avoidance and turn toward it. We embrace the fear and resistance around the feeling. We let go of the narrative we've built up around it and focus on the actual felt sense of it, which begins with how it feels in our body. We fully open to it, we accept it. It is valid and real inasmuch as it has arisen. Suppressing it would not make it less real. Or more precisely, suppressing it would make suppression and avoidance real for us, which is arguably even worse.

In facing our experience, the affliction may even persist. We're not in the business of "fixing" everything. We are in the business of accepting things and integrating them into a vaster view. We're not going out to hunt all the sharks in the ocean and turn them into vegetarians. No, we are resting in the ocean with the sharks and their sharp teeth, but there's a deep sense of workability that arises in this process.

But we must also be mindful. Sometimes even when we do try to turn to face our demons, we still tend to approach them from the side of the "light": from a base assumption that our disposition should fundamentally be happy and light. So we hold our nose and deal with the repugnant shadow just in order to "process" it, "work through" it, or transform it and come back to our rightful place in the sun. In this regard, the psychologist Carl Jung says,

> Filling the mind with ideal conceptions is a characteristic of Western theosophy, but not the confrontation with the shadow and the world of darkness. One does not become enlightened by imagining figures of light, but by making the darkness conscious.[3]

On the path of non-avoidance we rest within—not outside—our direct experience. There's a profound, delicious honesty in the courage of turning into rather than away from our situation, a gift of strength and agency. A quality of fearlessness arises as we recognize our capacity to be with whatever arises; perhaps even the pain, challenges, and difficulties are fundamentally workable. It doesn't mean that we should feel bad all the time, but we encounter a basic okayness that underlies the seesaw of our emotions. There's openness and spaciousness. We tap into a bigger view without withdrawing or denying anything. Complete, wakeful presence.

As you practice Skymind meditation, you might notice where your edges are. Within the open space of awareness, are there thoughts, emotions, or sensations that you want to avoid or push away? Even as you notice this reaction, can you glimpse a bit of sky behind the dark clouds of thought? Is there a broader, more expansive awareness that embraces even the difficult sensations? Our Leaning into Darkness practice below may support you in working directly with these challenges as well.

Radical Acceptance

The wisdom of non-avoidance naturally leads us onto a path of radical acceptance where the vast view and the detail of everyday life meet. If we can bring attentive, clear-seeing mindfulness and acceptance to what's happening in the "right now," we begin to see and engage with reality just as it is. That acceptance in each moment connects us with the vast acceptance of everything as it arises out of the ocean of awareness.

Machig invites us to start seeing whatever is happening as an opportunity to expand our minds and hearts:

> *No matter what sickness occurs in the manifesting circumstances, know that each one is a training exercise.*[4]

Acceptance is a training exercise in expanding the borders of our personal territory. It's an invitation to say "This too, and yes, this too" until we actually can rest in the lived experience of Skymind. We're not making an enemy of the "sickness" but rather training in complete, radical acceptance.

The path begins with self-acceptance, a courageous and compassionate willingness to include any and all aspects of ourselves that we might want to discard, ignore, destroy. We make peace with ourselves. That doesn't mean simply to give in or to give up. Sometimes we fear that if we accept our afflictions, we may end up strengthening or perpetuating them. But that's only true if we obsess or think about them. Here we are simply turning to that affliction with an open heart, with mindfulness and a compassionate attitude, rather than fighting or avoiding it. In self-acceptance there's more bandwidth; we're less preoccupied with fixing ourselves and more curious about the world around us, about others. Interestingly, when there's genuine self-acceptance, the tightness of self-involvement relaxes; our acceptance of others expands as well and natural compassion arises.

I (Charlotte) remember cooking a pot of soup and contemplating the fact that the carrots, onions, and spices that were inside the pot were considered part of the soup, whereas the odd piece of vegetable that had fallen outside the pot was considered a mess. The only thing that truly distinguished one from the other was which side of the rim of the pot it was on. If the pot were only a bit larger, the "messy" parts would be inside the soup. Our "self" is much like this. We create the edge of our pot of self through our identity—our ideas of who we think we are, should be, or want to be. The parts of ourselves that fall inside this boundary are accepted; those that fall outside are considered faulty, problematic, unworthy. We spend a lot of time and energy trying to clean up the messy parts of ourselves. But what if rather than trying to wipe these parts away, we were to expand the rim of our pot, widen our notion of self to include even those ornery fragments of an imperfect self? What if we kept expanding until our pot was so big it included all things, until in fact there was no rim at all?

This path of radical acceptance is about falling in love with the zing of reality itself. Whatever is going on in reality can only be found in the moment. When you show up in the moment, leave your preferences at the door. Strong preferences overshadow the freshness of the experience. We tend to do this all the time. We miss the raw truth and magic of the moment, instead projecting a story onto it, a preference based on preexisting beliefs, hopes, fears, or resistance.

You may remember Machig's suggestion, discussed earlier:

> *Know occurring circumstances as supports.*[5]

Radical acceptance of "occurring circumstances," however they appear, supports our ability to love the totality of reality. The vast view calls forth nondiscriminatory compassion for the brilliance and pain of everything in the world. This could be difficult since it means accepting the reality of injustice, for example. But we accept without condoning, and this becomes the raw, awakened ground of our compassionate engagement to relieve the suffering of injustice. In the spaciousness created by acceptance we develop the ability to respond ("response-ability") rather than simply react or ignore. We're not continuously defending the borders of our territory, building the walls around our garden, or safeguarding the edges of our pot. No, we are fully engaged and present in the realities of our life and our world, grounded in the wisdom of our vaster, true nature.

Let's step back for a moment to review the trajectory of the Skymind journey so far: In recognizing the vast view, our inseparability from the ground of being and the innate spaciousness of our awareness, we realize that we can indeed rest in the embrace of totality, the Great Mother, the groundless ground itself. We are held unconditionally. We are whole, brilliant, complete. But this uncompromising embrace also means that *everything* is included, nothing is fundamentally rejected. And so we step into the awareness of primordial responsibility, an awakening to the simple fact that everything does indeed matter. Thus our lives become a journey of meeting with radical acceptance, rather than avoiding, whatever we encounter. This need not be a burden but rather an invitation to expand our mind and heart into the vast compassionate nature that is our true nature. In the next chapters we explore what it means to awaken the heart into the uncompromising compassion of Skymind.

~ EXERCISE ~

Leaning into Darkness

Let's draw on a particular affliction—feeling anxious—and use these teachings on non-avoidance and radical acceptance to see how we might work with it. You can follow the same steps with any difficult emotion that is particularly alive for you.

- ✧ **Getting Triggered:** Something happens or you imagine something happening that elicits a feeling of subtle anxiety in you. (Machig calls these "inner demons," the afflictive emotions that "run on and on." Though we may point to an external cause, what we work with are our internal reactions.)

- ✧ **Be Mindful:** Notice the feeling of anxiousness as it arises, and catch yourself at that point where you want to "do" something with it, like ignore it (distract yourself), indulge it (get more and more worked up, or feel sorry for yourself), or fight it (project blame and aggression on others or yourself).

- ✧ **Don't Avoid:** Non-avoidance begins by noticing what's happening and then reversing the ingrained tendency to ignore, indulge, or fight it. Notice the tension of avoidance and instead say, *Ha, wait, let me turn toward this anxiousness.* Turn your awareness in toward the feeling of anxiousness, gently and self-compassionately. Surrender to it for the moment.

- ✧ **Accept:** You probably don't like feeling anxious. In acceptance, there's a courageous reckoning, a radical honesty with yourself: "I'm feeling anxious, and that's okay." Acceptance has simplicity, just being with what *is* in its rawness. So you have to be okay with feeling something you don't like to or don't want to admit to.

- ✧ **Drop the Storyline:** When triggered, we jump very quickly to an internal narrative of conjecture, justification, or defense: "What if that happens?" "If only I had . . ." "If only they had . . ." "Why is this happening?" Or fixing: "What can I *do* about it?" When we go into story, we might think we're engaging with the issue, but we've left the vibrant presence of reality for a mental landscape of figments. Acceptance means letting the story go. Drop the commentary about your anxiety. Instead, stay with the feeling of anxiousness just as it is.

- ✧ **Access the Felt Experience:** Turn toward the anxiousness as an embodied experience, before words, ideas, or concepts. What does it actually feel like in your body? Before you name it *anxiety*? Is there tightness in your chest, numbness in your hands, tension in your belly? Psychologists have mapped emotions to distinct physiological responses and particular parts of the human body. We feel with our body. The practice of "taking on" our emotions uses our embodied, felt experience as a gateway for gaining access to the deeper intelligence of any emotion, however challenging that emotion may initially seem.

✧ **Be the Feeling:** As you let yourself simply feel the feeling of anxiousness, relax into the underlying energy. There may be tenderness or fierceness here, intensity or calm, or any number of other feelings. Without any story, ride the waves of emotion without needing to make anything specific happen. You're not trying to figure anything out. Relax more and more into feeling itself.

✧ **Rest:** Once you're able to rest in the feeling, then let yourself open into expansive, embodied awareness. The psychologist John Welwood calls this "basic aliveness," which underlies all feelings and emotions. Rest, just rest.

This process may take some time and need to be repeated again and again, or you may find that you can move through these steps quite quickly. The point is to engage with the emotion so directly that you gain access to the deeper, heartful wakefulness out of which it arises, and thus relate to yourself and the situation with greater clarity, openness, and compassion.

13

Go to the Places That Scare You

Machig Labdrön was revolutionary in being the first Tibetan—and a woman, no less—to establish a Buddhist practice and lineage outside of the tradition's native land of India. Her extraordinary brilliance was honored in her first meeting with Padampa Sangye (the more familiar "fatherly" name often used for Dampa Sangye), the esteemed Indian teacher who, so the story goes, had a vision of Machig and searched her out on one of his trips to Tibet. Upon meeting, Machig bows to Padampa, who stops her and acknowledges his high esteem of her. Instead, they touch foreheads in a gesture of mutual respect. Padampa was the founder of the lineage called Zhijé, the Pacification of Suffering, and played a key role in Machig's life and her development of Chöd.[1]

In the course of their exchange, Machig asks, "How can I help sentient beings?" His response has become a famous teaching in its own right, expressing key elements of the Chöd view:

> Confess all your hidden faults,
> Approach all that you find repulsive!
> Whoever you think you cannot help, help them!
> Anything you are attached to, let go of it!
> Go to the places that scare you, like cemeteries!
> Sentient beings are as limitless as the sky,
> Be aware!
> Find the Buddha inside yourself![2]

Dampa Sangye, also referred to as “Padampa” or “Father Dampa”

Confess all your hidden faults.

Religions worldwide have a long tradition of confession. While some of us may initially recoil from the notion of confession with its connotations of sinfulness, the practice of confessing is ultimately one of radical honesty with ourselves and with others. Admittedly we all have faults. But we all probably also have hidden faults—those patterns of thought, reactivity, or behavior that we consider less than noble and that we might not even admit to ourselves: jealousy, envy, arrogance, greed, aggression; our particular dislikes and irritations that make us critical, judgmental, ornery; our uniquely crafted secret desires and temptations. To inquire into our hidden faults is to open the cellar door to the shadows of our identity, usually draped in cobwebs of shame. To confess is to lay bare, to reveal to the light of awareness. When I confess, I crack open the neatly manufactured persona I have made of myself, in my own eyes and those of others—that I'm kind or wise or successful, that "I have it all together."

Becoming a mother has given me (Charlotte) ample opportunity to explore and reveal the shadowy vaults of my psyche. My first son became my foremost teacher in revealing my capacity for anger, an emotion I had kept well hidden for the thirty-five years before he was born. How could a small being, not even half my height, evoke such frustration, such intense irritation, such heated temptation to aggression? It was always something quite small that got me going—his refusal to do what I asked, his willful determination, his stubborn solidity. Wasn't I the one directing the show or at least directing the trip to the grocery store? Even as my boys got older, and even with all the love I had for them, I will admit there were times I wondered if I could find some way to escape parenting. Over the years I've had to confess the potential for rage that lies within me, the desire at times to simply run away. I am not the saintly Mother Mary I played in my eighth-grade school play, nor am I the "good mother" that I imagined one should be, the one who is always, without doubt or hesitation, gentle, kind, understanding, warm. I too am the "bad mother" at times, the bad mother I had previously conveniently considered "other" than me, someone else easy to judge from afar.

My confession began in relation to myself, recognizing that there were parts of myself—angry, rageful—I had not dared meet and thus had no fluency with, no capacity to navigate with mindful or compassionate skill. My confession extended to my boys so that I could begin to warn them about "monster mama" who was quickly approaching from behind the curtain. Even as I write now, my boys well into their young adulthood, I confess that the seed of rage and aggression lies within me. This path of motherhood, like the path of this being human, is quite messy at times. But I will say that in confessing my shadows of motherhood, in opening to the unwanted, I can also let myself relax more deeply into the immense, unspeakable blessings of motherhood, the depth of love that is beyond any conceptions whatsoever. In confessing, I let my heart break open in its rawness, its sadness, even its regret, and thus I come into contact with the immeasurable generosity of the heart, its irrepressible loving radiance. When we release the tight fist around what we *should* be, we open ourselves to the infinite blessing that is the nature of life itself, in all its messiness. This is the alchemical nature of confession.

We may begin to understand why Padampa's invitation might actually be of benefit to others. Confessing our hidden faults opens us humbly to ourselves and tenderly to the faults of others. We are less likely to fall into self-righteous judgment. Recognizing the ways we falter, we are possibly able to relate with compassion rather than indignation. As a human being, we share in the potential for doing great good but also for enacting harm and aggression.

Fundamentally we cannot benefit others when we function from a place of shame or insecurity, which puts us on an unsteady, wobbly footing. It is our unexamined wounds that elicit the most unskillful and often hurtful behavior that harms others. In confessing, we undercut the root of pretense. We bring light to our shadows, the hidden becomes seen, and thus their grip on us is loosened. This is some of the subtler, more tender work of Skymind: bringing into sky-like awareness the dark clouds that are as much part of the sky as the brilliant sun.

You might consider taking a moment right now to put down the book, consider a hidden fault of your own—however small or large it may be—and simply speak it to the silent space before you. Notice: What cracks open in the naming of it? How does your relationship to that fault change as you bring it to the light of day?

Approach all that you find repulsive!

Suffering is not pretty. However, if we want to benefit others—and ourselves, for that matter—we need to be willing to turn toward the wound: pain, ugliness, grief, loss. The sky, after all, sees everything, denies nothing. It is instinctive to turn away from what is repulsive. Even as a child, when I fell with my bare knees on the concrete sidewalk, I'd just hold my hands to the wound and not want to look. But a wound cannot be cleaned if it is not uncovered.

Sterilized Western culture hides the messier aspects of human life behind the walls of hospitals, prisons, assisted living facilities, mortuaries. Those of us living in this culture tend not to come in contact with the sick and the dying on a regular basis, unless a close friend or loved one is ill or it's part of our work. And what of the beggar or the person living on the street? Do you look them in the eye? Do you give them something? What does it mean to turn toward that which is painful and uncomfortable to see?

Padampa is not offering concrete answers to these questions, but he is suggesting that we turn toward and acknowledge the unease that may arise in these encounters. Once again, when we move in the opposite direction of our default tendency, we are forced to sit on the threshold—between beautiful and ugly, pleasant and unpleasant, acceptable and unacceptable, health and disease, right and wrong, me and you. Here in the liminality of not-knowing, the heart opens a crack wider in humility, tenderness.

Being with someone in their grief over loss, for example, can be a profound practice of *being with*. We can't make the departed return, nor should or can we fix the grief, sadness, and pain. Too often, we may find ourselves trying to make someone feel better, cheer them up, remind them that this too shall pass. And it will. But the journey of grief is grieving, not getting over it. There is a raw, gentle silence that dawns in this irreparable brokenheartedness.

Whoever you think you cannot help, help them!

In a world of ceaseless information about the ills of humanity and the environment, it can be easy to feel defeated, powerless, overwhelmed.

What could I possibly do in the face of the immensity of poverty, war, environmental degradation, global warming? Padampa says be bold. Don't hide behind excuses that you can't help, that you don't make a difference. The bodhisattva—the one who walks through life with the awakened heart of compassion—makes the absolutely irrational vow to "single-handedly" relieve the suffering of all beings, not in some delusion of grandeur but because this attitude of never-ending commitment to help is itself the source of benefit, the wellspring of goodness.

When you look at the world from the point of view of how you *can* help, a lot changes. Children and young people are such phenomenally inspiring teachers as they have not yet convinced themselves that they cannot help. I remember my eleven-year-old son doing research and switching the family to pellet toothpaste so we would no longer contribute to the consumption of plastic toothpaste tubes. Over the years, I've been moved again and again by the young people who come through my Naropa University classrooms, unwaveringly committed to contributing to and manifesting a healthy, just, and peaceful world for all. Padampa's invitation is to override our doubt and hesitation that indeed we can help.

From another angle, we might consider Padampa's statement in this light: Who do you think is beyond help? Who is so bad that they should not be helped? Whom are you willing to cut out of your world? And of course, there is an inner aspect to this: What part of yourself is so bad that it is beyond repair, beyond hope? Perhaps that hidden fault? *That* one, *that* part of yourself—that's the one to help.

Chögyam Trungpa taught that the spiritual warrior "[refuses] to give up on anyone or anything."[3] It's pretty radical, no? That's basically what Padampa is suggesting here. Consider what you've given up on, written off, within yourself, your relationships, your work; within human society or the world more generally. Go there, says Padampa, where the warm light of compassion seems to have the least reason to shine.

When you practice Skymind meditation, you might consider these teachings during the radiance portion of the practice. You are radiating light in all directions, pervading everything equally. There's an aspect of extending this loving radiance intentionally but also of resting in the awareness of the vibrant self-arising luminosity of all things.

You might notice where you hesitate to extend this radiance and then gently lean in to see where and how you might feel the vibrant aliveness of even these more challenging areas.

Anything you are attached to, let go of it!

Initially we may read "Anything you are attached to, let go of it!" as a directive to get rid of everything we have, whether outer possessions or more internal aspects of our identity. The practice of living in utter simplicity is practiced in countless traditions. The point here is not just to let go of things, however, but actually to work with our attachment. We can experience attachment whether or not we actually own something. The invitation is to work with the feeling of attachment—that clingy stickiness that keeps us bound in a relationship of neediness to the object of our attachment. When we're attached to something, there's often an underlying feeling of not being complete or whole without it.

So, as an initial practice, Padampa suggests letting go of whatever it is we are attached to. What possessions or accomplishments; what goodness, beauty, wellness do I cling to, do I consider mine, do I consider necessary to be fundamentally okay? What happens when I let them go? Who am I then? We can start by imagining something quite simple. I (Charlotte) think of shaving off all my hair, which offers me a wonderful combination of adornment, protection, warmth, and shielding. Think of something ordinary that you're attached to—something you like about yourself, that makes you feel comfortable. It's wonderful to like things about ourselves. But what happens when we imagine letting those things go? I feel exposed, naked, vulnerable, literally and figuratively. There's nowhere to hide, nowhere to pull back into my shell of comfort. It's also a call to show up more fully, not behind anything but in the nakedness of just being as I am.

We can work gently with letting go of things we are attached to, like giving a piece of jewelry that you like to a good friend. Notice where you want to hold on to it, and notice whether there's a way to both appreciate it and extend that appreciation into the generosity of a gift. This has to be genuine. You might decide you're not ready to part with it. In any case, you can work mindfully with the feeling of attachment, slowly stretching and drawing back.

There's also a sense of freedom that can arise as we let go of what we are attached to. I remember going over to a friend's house during a massive flood we were experiencing in Boulder. We happened to arrive just as they were packing things up in order to evacuate. The stream by their house had already swelled to such an extent that it had pulled down massive cottonwood trees and was busy undercutting the foundation of their house. I walked through the house with my friend to gather things up, and as she came to the room with her shrine and many prized possessions, she looked at me and remarked how actually, she could let them all go. I don't think it was because she didn't care for them but because the intensity of the situation catapulted her into an experience of true emptiness, an embodied realization that even the most beautiful, sacred item on her shrine was a symbol pointing beyond itself to something that could ultimately not be taken away, could not be lost.

Go to the places that scare you, like cemeteries!

And then Padampa goes on to say, "Go to the places that scare you, like cemeteries!" The Chöd tradition includes ongoing pilgrimage to haunted grounds (*nyensa*)—places of disease, decay, death. The practitioner meets that which is most frightening (and repulsive!) and thus directly encounters their own fears of illness, impermanence, loss. The traditional charnel grounds were littered with half-eaten, rotting corpses with wild animals prowling for a meal. More modern versions might be closer to a landfill, mass grave, or clear-cut forest than the finely manicured cemeteries Western societies have created for peaceful contemplation. The point is to enter a space where our constructs of normalcy, safety, and comfort are upset and we are brought face to face with disruption, uncertainty, and the tenuousness of life itself.

Rites of passage in cultures throughout time have celebrated the power of going to the places that scare us. The ethnographer Arnold van Gennep and many sociologists since him identify three key stages of a rite of passage: separation from the familiar, abiding in the liminal, return and integration. The liminal is the threshold, the space betwixt and between where what and who we were no longer applies. This may mean spending days alone in the wilderness, perhaps without food or water. It may mean ingesting plant medicines that lift the veils of habitual thinking and perception. We find ourselves in the unknown, radically awake to all that we encounter without expectation, façade, or formulas. It is terrifying, on one hand, because all our normal handles on reality have fallen away. It's profoundly liberating, on the other, because we can rediscover ourselves, our relationships, and the environment around us in totally new ways. Returning and integrating with their community, the journeyer offers insight and presence gleaned from a transpersonal experience stripped of any pretense. The Chödpa, a practitioner of Chöd, goes to haunted grounds as a repeated encounter with the liminal where identity and comfort are replaced with vulnerable courage, selflessness, and fierce compassion.

We don't have to travel far to meet the scary places within us—anger, sadness, insecurity, grief, loneliness, doubt, unfulfilled desires. Within this inner landscape, difficult memories, thoughts, and emotions become like dark alleyways we avoid in a city. At first, there are only a few parts of town we steer clear of, but over time more and more streets become off-limits—echoes of broken relationships, missed opportunities, regrets, losses, shame. We become prisoners in our own mind. To go to the places that scare us is to turn toward the walled passages and bad neighborhoods within, to bring the light of awareness and kindness to them so that they may once again be integrated into the full landscape of our being. This is liberation—not because we have not experienced darkness but because we have learned to open to it and integrate it into us rather than let it shut us down and close us off.

This is probably one of our favorite verses, one that is worth carrying in a pocket of your memory wherever you go. If there are any instructions for life, this is a good one to carry along. "Go to the places that scare you"—with awareness and an open, tender heart.

If you are moved to learn the traditional Chöd practice with its beautiful melodies, instruments, and visualizations, we recommend it as a potent practice. Other modalities that may be more accessible within a modern secular context are Lama Tsultrim Allione's Feeding Your Demons process (see her book by the same name).[4] Our practice Leaning into Darkness, described in the previous chapter, is a brief and simple experiential way to work with some of these ideas. (Also see chapter 5 for our model of applying different remedies for varying levels of affliction.)

Sentient beings are limitless as the sky, be aware!

We've always been struck by the strong exclamation here at the end of Padampa's teaching. Once we open our hearts to others and to ourselves, once we engage on this radical Skymind path of awakened compassion, there is no end. It's not an engagement with a closing date, a task we can check off a to-do list. It's a lifelong commitment to intelligent openness, honesty, presence, inextricable relationality with everyone and all things. But how else would we want to live, actually?

It's important to note that although Machig has asked Padampa how to best help sentient beings, he has not told her at all *what* to do. He offers no formulas or recipes for what we can do to be of benefit. What he does tell Machig is how to open our hearts, how to be in a way that allows our inherent compassion to arise of its own accord. What happens when we go to the places that scare us? What happens when we turn toward those we think we cannot help? For one, it is incredibly humbling. We become painfully aware of our armor of fear. If we keep looking, we become aware of what lies beneath our armor—incredible vulnerability, rawness, tenderness. Our heart cracks open in the experience of not having it all together, in not knowing yet being completely present with the intensity of what is. We are awake to everything. We let the world touch us deeply, poignantly, right at our "soft spot,"[5] as Chögyam Trungpa called it. We actually allow ourselves to feel so much, to be touched by everything. This is the awakened heart, bodhicitta—the experience of our innate compassionate nature. It is the inner warmth, the loving radiance of Skymind.

In the Skymind meditation practice, you can tap into this cracked-open heart as the light extends from your heart center. This can be a deeply embodied experience. We invite you to feel the intensity of vibrant luminosity permeating your entire body, as though every cell of your body were humming with aliveness, and radiating like rays of clear, warm sunlight pervading the space all around you.

Find the Buddha inside yourself!

This is Padampa's final directive. We may remember Machig's invitation: "Don't search, don't practice; rest in your nature." The Buddha is not outside yourself. The way to find the Buddha within is to confess your hidden faults, approach that which you find repulsive, let go of what you are attached to . . . When we have dropped the guises and crumbled the walls, when we have let our heart crack open, then our true nature, the precious jewel of our Buddha Nature, is revealed. And it is from this place that we are most able to help sentient beings.

Padampa's verses suggest that the path of Skymind means to examine, meet, and become intimate with all that the sky holds—the dark clouds of shame, the storms of anger, the freezing rain of fear. In this courageous and tender practice, our sky-like nature, our Buddha Nature, comes to shine in its immensely loving, warm, and compassionate brilliance.

14

Skymind Compassion

Avalokiteśvara, "the lord who gazes upon the world," the awakened being or bodhisattva of compassion, sees into all realms, the darkest and lightest, hearing the calls of those in need. For eons upon eons, Avalokiteśvara has worked to relieve the suffering of beings, tirelessly efforting to heal the ill, mend the brokenhearted, soothe the fearful. And so, as the story goes, Avalokiteśvara rises one morning to look upon the universe, and sees—despite countless ages of benevolent activity—that beings are suffering nonetheless, struggling in conflict, pain, and turmoil. Crushed by this realization, Avalokiteśvara shatters into a thousand pieces. In his great kindness, Amitābha, the Buddha of Compassion, reassembles Avalokiteśvara, now with eleven heads and one thousand arms, an eye on each of the thousand hands. Thus Avalokiteśvara returns, working ceaselessly to relieve the suffering of all.

Compassion is our capacity to see suffering, to be moved by it, and to respond to relieve it. It is the profoundly courageous willingness to be awake in our lives and in the world; to let ourselves be touched deeply by what we encounter; and to engage however we are able—with aspiration and action—to assuage suffering. The lived experience of Skymind is a path of awakened compassion that, like Avalokiteśvara's, is one of becoming ever more aware—seeing more, witnessing more, engaging more—to benefit others.

At the heart of compassion lies not one answer or one guideline. At the heart of compassion lies instead the willingness and courage to stay present and awake in the face of suffering, our own and that of others, with the wakeful intelligence of compassionate response. Heart open, mind open—this is bodhicitta.

Machig describes it in this way:

> *Buddha enacts the welfare of sentient beings*
> *as in the example of the precious jewel:*
> *through altruism that arises without concept.*[1]

The precious jewel is often used as a metaphor for our innate nature, bodhicitta, the awakened heart. It is the very essence of our being—vast, luminous, awake—that expresses itself as the tenderness of care and the irrepressible strength of love.[2] Chögyam Trungpa described it as the "soft spot" because it is where the world touches us and through which we touch the world. It is our profound intimacy with all things, meeting ourselves, others, the wind, the trees, the whole mess of humanity skin to skin. Bodhicitta is why we are moved by the pain of others, the stories of suffering halfway across the world, the fragile beauty of existence.

The blossoming of bodhicitta, the heart cracking open, may be experienced as a tremor of vulnerability because we realize we actually care; we care deeply. Trungpa noted that even the worst monster loves something, cares for something, however small;[3] that's the doorway in. Bodhicitta is a jewel because it is the most precious thing we have as humans, our inherent luminous and awakened nature that expresses itself in our capacity to connect and love. If you ask how to tap into bodhicitta, I might ask you, "What do you love?" Start there. See what happens when you simply love what you love. When we touch into raw openheartedness, we realize that our capacity to love is immense. We could actually love the whole world. The essence of our love is beyond measure, transcending whom or what we like or dislike, favor or disfavor. This is why bodhicitta is considered diamond-like, the unbreakable jewel. Even as it exposes us, it is also our greatest, unconquerable strength and the source of our deepest happiness.

In this verse, Machig is saying that altruism actually arises from our basic nature of its own accord. Compassion is the very expression of our awakened heart, who we truly are. This is why resting in our nature, as Machig has been teaching us from the very beginning, is training in compassion. When we connect with that wholeness, the ground of our being, our love of all beings emerges naturally. Remember Padampa's response to Machig on how to be of greatest benefit: "Find the Buddha inside yourself!" Discover the precious jewel. Live from that place.

Sometimes, in order to do this, we have to get out of our own way. We have to open beyond our persistent preoccupation with ourselves, beyond our claustrophobic self-entanglement. This, again, is why Machig emphasizes severance: cutting through our self-fixation. When we get beyond ego-clinging and rest in the ground of being. We find space and agency. We suddenly have the bandwidth to become present and curious about others and the world around us. This space is again the source of natural self-arising compassion.

The Skymind meditation is an opportunity to connect with the direct experience of both the openness of awareness and the radiant warmth of self-arising compassion. In our practice we don't necessarily direct compassion to someone, though we may be aware that our loving radiance extends to the people and places most in need of support. But as we meditate, we can attune ourselves to the embodied experience of the heart thrown open, without any object whatsoever. Notice how it feels to abide in wakeful, expansive, openheartedness. Tender, raw, vulnerable? Expansive, liberating, empowering? We can experience the vibrancy of bodhicitta in so many different ways. In our meditation practice, we learn to attune to bodhicitta as the essential energy of life itself.

There are countless stories of human compassion welling up in the most unlikely, even violent circumstances. One that has stuck with us took place during the Second World War in a forest in western Germany. It's Christmas Eve and a mother is preparing for a lonely dinner with her only son, a twelve-year-old boy, who shares this experience later in life. A knock comes at the door, and three lost American soldiers stand outside, looking for refuge from the cold night, their comrade bleeding from a gunshot wound in his leg. The woman knows that harboring the enemy could mean death for her and her son, but she invites them in, makes a bed for the wounded man, and draws on her meager food reserves to cook a larger meal. Not long after, another knock comes at the door. This time, two German soldiers request entry. She hesitates just briefly, then invites them in, revealing to them that she has just offered haven to the Americans. In no uncertain terms, she announces to all the gathered men that tonight, there will be no fighting. They will all leave their guns at the door. The fierce, compassionate mother speaks. They sit down together, eat, care for the wounded, get a night's rest; at daybreak, the German commander points the lost Americans in the direction of their troops and turns to walk toward his own. It is only one night, one meal. The war, critical for all of humanity, continued. But there in that little kitchen in the cold, snowy forest, a spark of bodhicitta glowed in the hearts and minds of enemies.[4]

We all have this capacity, perhaps brought on more clearly when the need is dire. We *can* love; we can love with courage, generosity, kindness, and a healthy dose of tenacity, beyond friend and foe. Skymind is vast in its loving embrace and thus radical in its compassion.

Compassion Beyond Measure

In traditional Buddhist teachings, the wisdom of emptiness and the skillful means of compassion are considered to be like the two wings of a bird. The understanding of unbounded inseparability (emptiness) is expressed through immeasurable compassion—limitless, unending, and unconditional. Both vast in scope and specific in focus, compassion includes all beings without exception, and each one in particular.[5] The practice is to extend our care beyond the picket fence embracing our loved and dear ones. And then too, it suggests that in those graced moments when we feel a love for all beings, we not forget to attend to the particular. Can we then also love our difficult neighbor?

In the lived experience of interconnectedness, the recognition that we are inextricably in and of this world together with all beings, compassion is choiceless. The Buddha's first teaching, the first of the Four Noble Truths, was just this: Suffering is. Compassion is that loving response that meets the suffering that is. Compassion does not delineate "my" suffering from "your" suffering, "our" suffering from "their" suffering. Compassion meets suffering in any and all of its forms, transcending all dualistic notions of sides. Like the sun, like Avalokiteśvara's thousand-eyed gaze, Skymind compassion shines equally on all.

This compassion does not arise from counting up each and every being and attempting to cultivate compassion for them. It is about resting back into the vast ground from which all of us manifest in the first place. Altruism that arises "without concept," as Machig calls it, is not generated altruism or manufactured compassion. It is not, as the teachings often say, adventitious, meaning an overlay or superimposed from outside. It is self-arising, the upwelling of what is already innate. It arises spontaneously as an expression of our inextricable interconnectedness. This living, active, and vibrant nature of compassion is understood as the luminosity or dynamic radiance of the ground of being. It is the loving radiance of our true nature.

This absolute view of altruism without concept invites us to consider compassion beyond ideas of right and wrong, good and bad. "Concept" (Tib. *rtog pa*) here refers to our thinking mind, which produces all kinds of intellectual constructs, ideas, and judgments that solidify and fixate our view of reality. But Machig is inviting us to awaken altruism that is not constricted by the dualistic rigidity of judgment. Of course, we judge those who cause harm or injustice; this forms the basis for all our legal systems. But the invitation here is to dive beneath any kind of final and absolute judgment, to puncture the solidity of righteous indignation. Within the vast view of Skymind there can be justice without blame.

If altruism without concept means that we don't demonize anyone or anything, then the challenge is: Can we include in our consideration even the darkest corners of humanity? Can we see the suffering that lies within and often serves to catalyze harm-doing? Can we recognize that the badness that we so easily see "out there," in "others," also has seeds within ourselves? That we, too, have ignorance, bias, hatred. That we, too, are capable of violence, discrimination, harm? In this heartful truth-telling, we may recognize that it's not as easy as separating the right group from the wrong, the good guys from the bad. We are them, too, and they are us.

We can be inspired by the great moral exemplars of history who overturned injustice even as they upheld a vision beyond dualities of friend and enemy. Mahatma Gandhi, Nelson Mandela, Martin Luther King Jr.—all affected profound societal revolutions by holding a view that included and transcended both and all sides. Their work is so esteemed because they did not simply shift power from one faction to another but crafted a vision of greater inclusivity. The political and societal changes they affected were thus sustainable, pervasive, and impactful even beyond their lives. In their book *How Can I Help?* Paul Gorman and Ram Dass pose the evocative question: "What kind of victory is it when someone is left defeated?"[6] This inquiry might encapsulate the guiding vision of great changemakers everywhere. Thus we might ask, what kind of compassion is it when someone is left suffering?

The aim of compassion is not to benefit the good and demean the bad. Indeed, sometimes it is the villains who may need particular compassion, for their suffering is so deep-seated that it causes immense harm to others. That's why Padampa said, "Whoever you think you cannot help, help them!. . . . Go to the places that scare you." He means go to the places where you think you cannot open your heart. Go to the one you think you cannot love. That is where the practice truly begins. That is where compassion is most needed and shines most brightly.

This vast, absolute Skymind compassion is not about "getting" to some absolute endpoint. Like Avalokiteśvara, we will wake again and again not just to the suffering of those around us but to the recognition of the limits of our compassion. Compassion is a lifelong practice; we never achieve or complete it. What's called for is the gentle wakefulness of noticing where we close down, what we want to shut out—including parts of ourselves—and then staying present right at that edge. We meet even our resistance to compassion with compassion. Often the difficult parts of ourselves, like the difficult people in our lives, teach us far more about our compassion than the lovely ones.

One of my (Charlotte's) own lessons in meeting the edge of compassion came after returning home from a solitary retreat. My heart was blown wide open by days of extended practice and contemplation, supported by the sublime views of Tara Mandala's vast landscape of hills, valleys, mountains. I felt deeply in love with all of humanity, all of life, my every cell savoring the warmth of profound intimacy with the world. At dinner that night, Pieter shared with me the news of a school shooting that had taken place while I was away. Like all of us, I was intensely shocked and profoundly saddened.

I awoke early the next morning, stirred and restless. How could I hold the radiant equanimity and brilliant bliss of my retreat experiences with the shattering stories of killing and loss? Was my retreat—which had felt like such an attunement to "reality"—actually just a rainbow bubble of wishful fantasy? Was this reality of loss and pain and suffering more *real* after all?

So I returned to my meditation cushion in the early-morning hours, listening and inquiring into my body, heart, mind. No, came the answer; it was not a fantasy. And so too, this reality of suffering is not a fantasy. Wherever I look in this tragedy I see unfathomable pain: in the children, teachers, parents, the shooter, his family, the police, you, me. Like Avalokiteśvara, we are shattered when we look. We break open. We must break open. And what then? Do we crumble? Do we leave ourselves strewn out on the cold floor of life? No. I think we must love *more*, love *because* we see, love *because* we are shattered. We must love *more* fiercely, fueled by knowing that this brilliant, beautiful, and oh-so-tender life is worth claiming and loving with every last fiber of our being. This love is not against anyone, not against anything. But it is fierce, unwavering, unrelenting.

There's a fierceness and a deep courage in the vast compassion of Skymind, this altruism without concept, because it refuses to grasp the handholds of dualistic thinking. It is fierce because it refuses to leave anyone out; fierce because it acknowledges that the "bad" is not out there; fierce because it recognizes that ultimately we must all be liberated together, that it is never only some who are liberated but only ever all of us, inextricably together.

At times we may feel that we will shatter, like Avalokiteśvara; that we will succumb to despair and hopelessness. Or we may feel the powerful desire to cut off that person, those parts of humanity, those parts of ourselves, that seem altogether vile. It is at these times that we are called to dig even deeper into the fiery heart of bodhicitta, to use the rawness of our pain to love even more, love even more fiercely.

Compassion Without Recipe

But what does compassion look like? How do we act compassionately? Shall we be soft? Or shall we be firm, like a mother's "No" as she pulls her child from oncoming traffic? Shall we speak? Shall we be silent? Shall we engage actively or shall we hold space for the growth that can take place within adversity?

It would be great if compassion had a recipe book, if we could follow a formula for how to heal the pain of living once and for all. All cultures share fundamental guidelines for human behavior: Do no harm. Help those in need. Be kind. Be generous. But what truly benefits another person? What best relieves their pain and suffering? Compassion is not a formula. What is helpful in one situation is not in another. What was beneficial to one person is not to another. Machig suggests,

There are unimaginable buddha qualities
in not fixating on one's own concepts.[7]

Let go of what we *think* will help, even what we know has helped in the past. To truly benefit, meet the moment naked and fresh. When our ideas about being compassionate subside, the natural brilliance of bodhicitta can arise. We can be surprised by what shows up. "Unimaginable buddha qualities" means that awakened compassion can look an infinite number of ways. No single action is always appropriate or inappropriate. The great news here is that we can draw on the full spectrum of human behavior as tools of compassion—gentleness, softness, nurturance; but also directness, silence, humor; and even fierceness, wrath.

It would be a mistake to equate the compassionate "soft spot" of bodhicitta with being a doormat to the world. That would be confusing the basis of our engagement—which is unconditional, unlimited compassion and love for all beings—with the skillful expression of that basis. Yes, we are tender in our openheartedness, but that tenderness is awake, clear, and strong beyond measure. Compassion is unflinching and can express itself in any and all modes. One of our favorite Buddhist deities is Troma, the wrathful, blue-black mother who cuts through delusion with the sharp blade of compassion. Like a brilliant mirror, she reflects uncompromising truth, severing confusion with a single stroke of clear seeing.

Parenting is a never-ending practice of "not fixating on one's own concepts." Of course, we want our children to be happy, to make their lives easeful. We may catch ourselves wanting to soothe the pain as quickly as possible—*Let's go have ice cream, watch a movie, play a game*—as though feeling better is the ultimate goal. We've learned that sometimes we just need to let our child be sad, be upset, be heartbroken. Compassion is not about fixing the pain; sometimes it's simply about being present and holding space for the unfolding of emotions that are part of human life. At times we let our children find their own limits, giving them leeway to make their own mistakes and come to their own realizations. At others, direct and even strict guidance is far more compassionate. One thing we've learned is that as soon as we think we've figured something out, it's bound to change.

The term *idiot compassion* refers to an unaware allegiance to formulaic compassion. We think we are doing something that is helpful, but actually we are making things worse. We have good intentions, but we're not attuned to what's truly needed. Giving someone what they want may seem kind in the moment but may be harmful in the longer term. Idiot compassion is lazy because it relies on *ideas* of compassionate action, but it is not aligned with what's actually beneficial in a given situation. Sometimes we may be trying to relieve someone else's pain simply in order to relieve our own discomfort in the face of difficulty.

True altruism is not about any ideas whatsoever, even—or perhaps especially—the idea of being good. There's some ego gratification that we derive from helping others. It makes us feel good to engage in altruistic action. There's nothing wrong with that, but it can reify the ego. We can slip into altruism with ego, clinging to a self that feels elated because *I am helping those people*. Thus Machig suggests,

> *Be without presumption, free of the inflation of helping or harming,*
> *as are foliage and boulders and such.*
> *You should understand suchness.*[8]

Suchness—things as they are. As you are. We don't construct our identity as someone who has helped (or who has harmed, for that matter). We show up as we are—raw, open, radiant—the ground for altruism without concept. The ground of awakened compassion.

Spontaneous Compassion

Altruism without concept is attuned spontaneity. When we rest in awareness, in Skymind, we can actually trust our heart; we trust that we can respond with skill and intelligence, aligned with the situation in which we find ourselves. Rather than reacting with preconceived notions of what compassion should be, we embody the fundamental intelligence of bodhicitta as it moves in and through us. If you rest in awareness and things occur in your environment, you act spontaneously from a place of self-occurring compassion. You do the most compassionate thing—the right action, right in the moment. This may be reaching out your hand to someone or it may be starting an NGO to relieve hunger.

Though the basic practice is to rest with ease, this path is not easy and should not be confused with any form of apathy. The spontaneity of self-arising compassion means we are always awake, like Avalokiteśvara with a thousand eyes, ever-present like the sky itself. On the path of awakened compassion, we're never off duty.

When we let go of ideas of what to do, we can step courageously into authentic presence nakedly honest, aware, engaged—the precious jewel of bodhicitta. Abiding in vast view, in the loving radiance of Skymind, we meet the moment with the clear-seeing precision of intelligent compassion.

Acts of compassion need not always be grand. In fact, sometimes they are supremely ordinary. Several years ago, we were traveling in Turkey with our two-year-old son and happened into an intense October snowstorm along a large highway leading to Ankara. The traffic slowed and eventually came to a standstill. There was nothing but a white, icy gale beating at our little rental car crammed between large container trucks. For a while we did our best to stay positive, singing Mateo's favorite songs for the thousandth time, the heat of the car cranking. But eventually we began to wonder what would happen when the gas ran out, without proper winter clothes, out in the middle of the countryside of a foreign country. It brought to mind stories you read in the paper about stranded travelers who freeze to death in their cars. The mood became quieter, somber as the clock ticked on. Then suddenly there was a knock at the driver's side window. A young Turkish man motioned to Pieter to roll down his window and gleefully stretched out his naked hand to offer us a cracked-open pomegranate. The bright-red, glistening seeds of the fruit punctured the gray veils of the storm. The smile of the young man shot a ray of warmth into our little car. We could barely say thank you before he turned to climb back into his truck. Nothing was different but everything had changed. A glint of magic to remind us that all would be well. Love shows up in unimaginable ways. A knock at the door. At the window. A pomegranate in a snowstorm.

15

The Full Belly and Satisfied Mind

Machig's teachings have taken us from the vast openness of sky-like mind into the intensity and grittiness of daily life as we know it. Resting in the ground of being, holding the view as we've explored, has implications: No one and nothing is left out—radical inclusivity. Everything matters—radical interdependence. And there's no way out—radical responsibility. With heart and mind blown open, we find ourselves in the expansive fields of awakened compassion, Skymind compassion. How do we hold ourselves within this radical call of Skymind compassion? In this chapter, Machig offers us some helpful metaphors and reminders for accessing and stepping into the fullness of our nature and our capacity to experience true satisfaction as the ground for our compassionate engagement.

The Fine Cow with a Full Belly

Deep into our study of Machig's teachings, we found ourselves re-reading some of her source texts, looking for her words on compassion. Hidden in a lengthy section on self-inflation (that sticky habit of clinging to a small self) we found the lines below, which offer the potent and beautiful metaphor of the full belly of compassion:

Like a fine cow nourishing a small calf,
when she helps herself to a full belly
it sustains the small calves and such.

If one's own inflation is decisively cut off,
sentient beings will surely become liberated.
No doubt the welfare of others will be achieved.[1]

Read at face value, the first lines suggest that we are best able to help others when we are well-nourished ourselves. You can't be of much benefit to others if you are worn out, depleted, running on empty. In modern-day compassion trainings, the suggestion is that compassion for others is inextricably connected to compassion for oneself.

But there is more here, right? Continuing onward in Machig's verses we read that this nourishment of ourselves, which will allow us to benefit others, actually means to "cut off" our "own inflation." This sounds a bit different from the cozier and warmer self-compassion verbiage we might expect if we're thinking about personal nourishment. So what does Machig mean? How do we reconcile this seemingly odd juxtaposition?

In the preceding stanza, Machig points out that a yogi—a spiritual practitioner—cannot simply give instructions "delivered by the lips"[2] and imagine they will benefit others. We can't just talk a good talk. Rather, we must *embody* the teachings ourselves, not through words or conceptual understanding but by thoroughly integrating and living them. Like a cow who has helped herself to a full belly, we must ingest and digest the teachings. We must actualize their truth in our very being. We must *become* them.

What does it mean to *become* the teachings? It means to fill ourselves with the actualization of our true nature—liberated, radiant, unbounded, inextricably connected to all. It means to recognize ourselves as no other than the Great Mother, Prajñāpāramitā, the ground of being. Doors of the heart swung open, mind unconstrained and clear, body present and vibrant. To put these verses plainly, the most effective way to benefit others is for us to wake up.

How to do this? How do we fill our belly? How do we embody our innate wholeness? By "decisively cut[ting] off . . . one's own inflation"! Paradoxically, Machig suggests that we become fulfilled ultimately by emptying ourselves. We empty ourselves of fixed notions of a small, separate self, what she calls inflation. As we've discussed previously, inflation refers to all the ways we divide and separate ourselves from others: me and you, us and them. What's mine and not mine; what's in and what's out. What's part of my world, my beliefs, my way and what's not. Inflation applies to social, political, and global levels as well. The dualizing of self and other lies at the heart of every war, every movement inspired by fear and hatred. From this perspective, compassion includes only those who fit within the boundaries of our narrow world, those "deserving" of our care. This is not the full belly of compassion.

Inflation is fundamentally fixation on the self, which can show up in many guises, none of which are conducive for compassionate engagement. On one end of the spectrum is the inflation of arrogance and pride. Knowing better, being better. History is filled with the inflation of those who think they've got the answer for everyone else. As the annals of politics illustrate, the self-centeredness of narcissism doesn't generally go well with working for the welfare of others. But even at the everyday level, we've probably all experienced a moment of feeling like we have a better way of doing something, we know more, we understand more (or even we feel we are more kind, more compassionate, more awakened). If you feel into it, you might notice the distance that moment of superiority creates between you and those around you.

On the other hand, inflation can show up as self-denigration, as paradoxical as that may seem at first glance. We're referring to that gnawing feeling of inadequacy, of not being good enough, smart enough, accomplished enough. Less than, insufficient, lacking. The acid of self-doubt corrodes our ability to show up, take our seat, reach out. I'd rather hide in my closet with my sleeping cat than step into this day, exposing my mediocrity. So I check out, fading into the background. One might not initially equate low self-esteem with inflation, but just like arrogance, it is based on intense self-involvement, which ultimately distances us from others. Benefiting beings from a place of doubt, uncertainty, and fear is like the mother cow trying to feed her calf on an empty stomach. The milk will be meager.

It's worth noting that both extremes of inflation rest on fundamental insecurity. Beneath the pride of arrogance is the need to prove ourselves. Beneath self-denigration is the feeling that we are less than others. The uncompassionate trap of comparison and judgment binds us in basic instability and doubt regarding our primordial worthiness. Underneath inflation—of the positive or negative kind—is fear and uncertainty regarding who and what we are.

When Machig suggests that our ability to truly benefit others arises from decisively cutting off inflation, she is inviting us to sever all the ways that we separate ourselves from others. Chöd means to "cut through" the tightly wrapped mummy of self-absorption, whether that's about how great or how awful we are. Machig is inviting us to take down the wall that separates us from our neighbor, from the stranger, even from the perceived enemy, and thus limits the fullness of our compassionate potential. The sky has no limits; its vast, all-encompassing nature allows it to embrace totality. So too, to step into our Skymind nature with all our capacity for compassion, love, and care means to let down the narrow confines of self-clinging.

In the preceding chapters, we've discussed various ways that we practice this cutting through of inflation: non-avoidance, radical acceptance, going to the places that scare us. When we cut through inflation, we awaken into a dynamic web of relationship with all others. We rediscover ourselves as an integral part of a vast whole, inextricably connected and interwoven with all things. Here there is no separation, no isolation, no "other than," no "greater than" and "lesser than." This is our Skymind nature. It may feel a bit overwhelming—this intimacy with all things—but it is also supremely empowering as we take our seat in the grand matrix of aliveness. This is the ultimate "full belly," living in the embodied recognition of wholeness, the source from which all our engagement arises and the home in which we can continuously rest.

The AH of Fulfillment

Let's return briefly to this beautiful image of the mama cow with her belly full of sweet grass. Imagine yourself in the moment of satisfaction after a tasty and nourishing meal. Perhaps your hands are on your warm belly; you naturally lean back a bit, relax your body, and exhale a long, gentle *ah*. A moment of enjoyment, the subtle bliss of basic contentment. As Machig says,

Like a simpleton with a full belly,
Rest . . .[3]

There's a pause in this moment, a release of effort, and a resting back into the simple feeling of fulfillment. But what does this very mundane experience have to do with our Skymind nature?

Machig's lovely metaphor of the "full belly" is a reminder that the everyday experience of fulfillment, which we can experience in even the simplest moment of enjoyment, can also remind us of ultimate fulfillment. We might say that whereas the everyday *ah* expresses our satisfaction in a particular moment, the "primordial AH" is the exhale into our unconditional completeness, the belly that was always already full.

In the simplest iteration of the *Prajñāpāramitā Sūtra*, a seminal Buddhist text, the reality of all things is described in one sound: AH. Nature-of-mind teachings and practices often use the seed syllable AH. In sounding AH we visualize the veils of obscuration regarding our true identity lifting like early-morning fog. We see clearly, brilliantly. The fullness and completeness of basic space, of our true nature, is revealed. We rest in the ultimate fulfillment of Skymind.

The primordial AH is always available to us, in every moment, at every turn of life. Because wholeness is the nature of our being, it is always already there. It is our basic goodness that is beyond creation and destruction. We do not need to manufacture or fabricate it because it is the very stuff we are made of. The ultimate purpose of all meditation practices, like our Skymind meditation, is to access and familiarize ourselves with the primordial AH so that it becomes the basic state from which we engage all aspects of our lives. When we rest in open, uncontrived awareness, we experience that ultimate fullness of our being, inseparable from the vibrant, radiant wholeness of all things.

When you practice the Skymind meditation, you might sound the syllable AH out loud as you expand awareness into vast spaciousness. Notice how the vibration of sound fills your body and then extends infinitely into the space around you. Riding on the sound frequency, your awareness opens, opens, opens. Then abide in the unending openness.

We may glimpse the primordial AH through the many small *ahs* of everyday life, the relative ways we fill our bellies through basic self-care. Consider a small pleasure, like stepping into a hot bath on a cold winter's day. Or perhaps more profoundly, the glow after an orgasm. For a moment, we relax, release, savor a sense of fundamental wellness. This moment of arrival is a taste of completeness, the full belly—"*ah.*" And so we can meet all that nourishes us at a more relative level, not just as supports of our individual well-being but as expressions and reminders of the warmth and luminosity of the very ground of being itself, the primordial AH.

And here we come to Machig's final lines in which she suggests that recognizing our true nature ultimately benefits others: "No doubt the welfare of others will be achieved." Why? Because when we have recognized our inherent wholeness, we no longer engage with others in terms of what we need from them or what they can do for us. Others no longer fill our sense of lack or prop up our pride. Neither do we engage them as objects to be "fixed" or even "helped." Finally, we meet them just as they are. We see them clearly as though for the first time—manifestations of the ground of being, expressions of Buddha Nature, ultimately whole, complete, brilliant. Whatever compassionate action arises takes place within a view of fundamental wholeness, basic goodness. Our recognition becomes a mirror, reflecting the wakefulness of another being. Seen and met in their true nature,

sentient beings will surely become liberated.
No doubt the welfare of others will be achieved.

The Satisfied Mind

Machig's metaphor of the full belly aligns beautifully with her teachings on the "satisfied mind." Here is a view that counters much of modern society with its billion-dollar marketing enterprises fueled by unmet needs and the promise of fulfillment at an indeterminate future time. We are tempted to believe that true satisfaction lies just behind that next spectacular skin product, the next abundant meal, the next trip to a faraway and exotic place. Even spiritual life can unfold as a quest for some distant moment of enlightenment that we never quite seem to reach.

The "satisfied mind" also speaks directly to the Buddha's earliest teachings on the primary cause of suffering: craving, clinging, and grasping. We suffer in wanting what we don't have. We suffer in the fear of losing what we do have. The fundamental mindset of craving—the unsatisfied mind, or what Chögyam Trungpa called "poverty mentality"[4]—is a sense of lack in the present and the continual projection of a more perfect reality into some other place and time.

In contrast, Machig suggests that satisfaction is not the attainment of something but rather a quality of mind, a way of being.

Like a person who has finished their work,
rest instantly with a satisfied mind.[5]

"Rest instantly": She doesn't say that we will find the satisfied mind after countless hours of committed practice, study, or productivity. No—now! Instantly. As though the satisfied mind were actually available to us at any moment. And that precisely is her teaching.

But what is satisfied mind? To be satisfied is to be sated, full, and complete. Satisfied, we rest at ease, like the simpleton with a full belly we encountered earlier or as one who has finished their work. We've all experienced relative moments of satisfaction. The satisfied mind points to a more absolute sense of satisfaction. The satisfied mind is a mind at peace, relieved of striving for the evasive *something else*. It is total presence because there is nowhere else to go. The satisfied mind is the mind of acceptance, not because perfection has been achieved but because there is a willingness to be with everything in whatever form of imperfection it arises. The half-baked plan, the broken dream, the road not traveled take their seat at the banquet of the satisfied mind.

The satisfied mind is a mind of compassion as it embraces our insufficiencies as much as our greatest strengths. Satisfied mind holds our regrets and shame as much as our achievements and success. The satisfied mind doesn't need to hide anything. Even our faults become workable, those rough threads in the fabric of who we are. The satisfied mind embraces our sore and tender spots, our perceived weakness, our uncertainty. In satisfied mind we become less preoccupied with ourselves and thus develop the capacity to consider and care for others. Focused less on how to make ourselves happy, we expand our view to genuine interest in and compassion for others. It's hard to turn our attention to others when we are consumed with our own deficiencies, sense of lack, and unfulfillment (remember Machig's teachings on inflation).

There is courage in the satisfied mind because we are not sidling out of life, making excuses for our missteps, apologizing for our not-yet-completed nature. We valiantly embrace the full, messy catastrophe of it all. It's much easier to be unsatisfied with our lives, or with the world for that matter. In an odd way, dissatisfaction gives us permission not to take full ownership and responsibility. Dissatisfaction can easily become a way of sneaking out the back door of the life, family, community, and world we actually have co-created. Satisfied mind does not evade life but rather stands nakedly in the center of it. Satisfied mind is infused with gentle fierceness and grounded power because it's willing to show up, absolutely. In satisfied mind, we glimpse the uncompromising acceptance and courageous presence of Skymind.

Machig proposes that we access satisfied mind "instantly." Taking a "short moment," as we discussed earlier, is a way to come into contact with satisfied mind on the spot. In an instant of vast, open, embodied awareness, we sense the presence of satisfied mind. Open awareness meditation practice cultivates the ability to "rest instantly with a satisfied mind" as we attune to the ground of being itself.

The Art of Savoring

Yet even at an everyday, more relative level, we can practice meeting the satisfied mind, as in the art of savoring. To savor is to relish the richness of a perception, the depth of an emotion, the clarity of a thought. To savor is to embrace our experience fully. Sometimes when I (Charlotte) put a favorite piece of chocolate in my mouth, I like to close my eyes and let my entire awareness focus on the warm, melting sweetness permeating my mouth. All my senses join into a unitary perception; even my thoughts settle into the sensual enjoyment of this one taste. Others may experience this with the first sip of coffee in the morning, the whiff of the first spring breeze, the sight of the full moon rising golden red over the horizon. We are captured by that one experience, savoring the absoluteness of *just this*. Our lives are filled with a rain of blessings. To savor is to turn toward the particular offering of this moment. The ordinary becomes extraordinary.[6]

In Tibetan Buddhism, the practice of "one taste" (Tib. *rochig*) invites us to perceive before and beyond our normal labels of like and dislike. We taste (or see or hear or smell) as though it were the primordial experience of taste, before we decide what we prefer. This means to enter the perception so fully that in some way you become it. Awareness becomes the chocolate, the coffee. At its most basic level, perception does not have preference; it simply perceives. To practice one taste in everyday life is to be willing to meet everything, every person, every situation initially in its original state of just being what it is, before our ideas of right and wrong, attraction and repulsion. We like to think of one taste also as a consideration that *This is the* one *taste, the only taste—there is no other*. This is it, totally and absolutely, even if only for a brief moment. We meet that taste without comparison, without the possibility of lack. Just as we meet sensations in this way, so too we can meet other people: seeing them directly before and beyond any conceptions or judgments about them. And thus one taste can become a profound practice of equity.

One taste means that we are invited to savor more than just the immediately pleasant—sweetness, beauty, warmth. Could we savor uncertainty and the wobbly wakefulness it engenders? Could we enter fully into heartache, tenderness, even fear, and allow them to reveal a deeper layer of softness within us? Could we rest in satisfied mind even when we are not particularly satisfied? Could satisfied mind help guide us through life's narrow passages of not knowing and confusion? This kind of practice calls for a level of trust in the inherent intelligence and value that lies even in life's more difficult experiences.

The art of savoring is also catalyzed in the recognition of impermanence. As our boys become teenagers and prepare to embark on their own life journeys, we relish each hug, each moment of conversation, even just the sound of their voices up in their bedrooms. Simply knowing they are present and well lets us rest in satisfied mind. We realize that there really is nothing more that is needed. To savor is to let the beauty of the ordinary open us to gratitude, appreciation.

The moment of death is perhaps the greatest teacher of this radical as-it-is nature of satisfied mind. Nothing more can be done. Incontrovertibly we have "finished our work." Wherever we find ourselves in the final hour, that instant of life is total and absolute. There is no other moment. May we all be blessed with a final exhale into the rest of ultimate completion.

A final reflection on Machig's verse likening the satisfied mind to "a person who has finished their work": That analogy in itself can give us pause as we contemplate whether we ever take a moment to feel the satisfaction of completion. In a culture centered on doing, her teaching is particularly poignant. Sometimes when I (Charlotte) turn the lights off in the kitchen at the end of the night, I briefly tap into a sense of closure, the end of the day's work. More often than not, however, whatever is completed spills instantly into the next unfulfilled task. For much of my life, I've put off doing things I wanted to do until I was "finished" with my work. A few decades later, I've come to realize that if I'm looking for the glorious moment when my to-do list is empty, I will wait forever. There is no end of things to be done. So Machig's verse is radical right from the start. She's inviting us to imagine what it would be like to finish our work—not even forever but just for right now, for this moment, this day. Savor that.

Pieter and I remember meeting senior monks of Thich Nhat Hanh's community as we were planning a visit by the renowned Vietnamese Zen teacher to Naropa University. As we walked around the stadium where the event was to happen, we spoke about various issues related to the upcoming program. Whenever we spoke, the monks would stop, listen, then respond. Then we would continue walking. We soon realized that we would either walk or talk, but not both. It was a humbling lesson in patience and the possibility of doing just one thing well. And the importance of weighing one's words! This question is enough. This response is enough. This step is enough. In the gaps, satisfied mind has a chance to blossom.

Hidden in these teachings is the message that there is no external state that will provide complete satisfaction; that fundamentally satisfaction is not about what you have or have not accomplished but rather about how you hold your mind in relation to the full, messy, unfinished play of life. There is no ultimate point of completion, no final resolution. Satisfaction lies within the brilliant aliveness of each moment, replete with its worries and joys, insights and unanswerable questions.

What are we learning about Skymind through these teachings? That within that open, spacious, and all-embracing nature of mind lies the invitation to fully and courageously step into our wholeness, our completeness, the always already full belly of our being. We can learn to access this wholeness even in the everyday, mundane experiences of fulfillment, just as a short moment of awareness, a glimpse of Skymind are always available to us. This ongoing practice of savoring opens the way to the satisfied mind, which we might call a relative experience of Skymind—the sense that right now, as it is, is actually fundamentally an experience of wholeness, completeness. The sky is never lacking, never incomplete. In this courageous and total presence, our capacity to benefit others can flourish, like a fine cow nourishing her calf, like the sky embracing with one taste whatever specters of beauty or intensity move within it.

~ EXERCISE ~

The Wish-Fulfilling Jewel

This contemplation was inspired by the traditional Chöd practice formalized by Machig. Chöd involves the visualization of a great feast in which all beings are fed exactly what they need to be truly satisfied and ultimately to awaken to their true nature. At a certain point the practice—which is sung along with a bell, drum, and thigh-bone trumpet—abruptly halts in an extended moment of silence. All beings are completely sated, completely fulfilled; the needs of all beings have been completely met. All dualities are resolved in the expanse of uncontrived great perfection.

What might it feel like to have all your needs met absolutely? As we discussed in this chapter, our "inflation," or tightly wound sense of an isolated self, arises out of our insecurity, anxiety, or doubt regarding who and what we are. This insecurity makes us feel like we need things in order to be truly fulfilled—relationships, success, recognition, wealth, and so on. Some needs are material, others are more emotional or psychological. From the absolute point of view, our true nature already abides in a state of fulfillment. This contemplation invites you to recognize and engage with your needs as a means to taste a sense of fulfillment that may already be present within you.

In this exercise, work with the needs that are arising most strongly at this point in your life. Don't worry about distinguishing between what you simply want and what you truly need; go with whatever you yearn for at any level. You can start with a very basic wish—a break from work, a delicious meal, a good conversation with a friend. You can include "bigger" yearnings such as being appreciated, finding a partner, achieving success in a particular area of your life, manifesting a dream you've had for years. You'll have the chance to work with a few different needs or desires, so just start with what is most alive for you right now.

Guidelines

- ✧ Bring your body into a comfortable yet wakeful position. You may want to close your eyes. Feel the ground of your seat and let yourself rest into the support beneath you. As you exhale, let current tensions or worries release, as best you can, so that you come into the present moment. Rest here for a moment with gentle attention on the breath.
- ✧ Now bring to mind a particular need or wish you have, something that you yearn for. It doesn't matter how big or small it is. Let this need come alive for you right now. Feel into it. Maybe there are specific words that come to mind as you evoke it; maybe it's more of an internal feeling that you generate. Bring this need into your awareness as clearly and strongly as you can. Notice what it's like to feel this need.

- Now imagine this need being fulfilled. Imagine this need is met exactly as you would like. You may think of specific ways this is happening. Or you may not know the details but simply allow yourself to imagine that this desire, this wish is being met completely, absolutely. Play this out in your mind's eye with as much specificity as you like. Begin to feel into a sense of fulfillment and satisfaction. Notice how it feels to have this need absolutely and unconditionally met. Let yourself rest here in this sense of fullness. Let your body, mind, and heart rest at ease in this fulfillment.

- Now again notice another need lurking on the edge of your awareness. What else do you desire? What else do you wish for? Again, bring this need to the forefront of your mind. Notice the details of this need. Feel into it. Lean into the need, the yearning.

- Once more, imagine this need being completely and absolutely fulfilled. Run through the storyline or images of this unfolding with as much detail as you like. Then feel into the satisfaction of this need. Feel it in your body. Let yourself rest here for a while in the experience of satisfaction, fullness, completeness.

- If you like, you can repeat this process with other needs that are alive for you.

- At the end of the contemplation, rest for a while longer in the state of total satisfaction. Rest as long as you like. As you close this practice, notice the sensations in your body, the quality of your mind and emotions. Close with the aspiration that any benefits that have arisen through this practice may contribute to the welfare of others.

16

Inherent Dignity

You may remember the story told in the introduction about Machig's encounter with Tara, the female deity of compassion. In no uncertain terms, Tara discloses who Machig really is: an embodied manifestation of Prajñāpāramitā, the Great Mother. As Machig doubtfully shies away from this revelation, Tara becomes uncharacteristically wrathful: "Yogini, do not be so timid!" It's an unequivocal call for Machig to take her seat, to step into the brilliance of her true nature.

Whether or not we've received a visitation from Tara, we can take her admonition to heart. In the deity practices of Vajrayana Buddhism, the teachings on vajra pride remind us to have "diamond-like" (*vajra*) confidence in our unconditional worthiness, primordial self-esteem. This means trusting and living from the brilliant wakefulness of our true nature, our Skymind nature. This innate sense of dignity gives rise to steadfast, compassionate presence.

We may initially think of pride as one of the seven deadly sins, right up there with lust, gluttony, and avarice. In the Buddhist tradition, pride is one of the five poisons, accompanied by a similar entourage of desire, jealousy, anger, and ignorance.

Ordinary pride is self-importance, a fixation on proving one's status or value; there's little or no room for the care of others, no space for humor or a lightness of heart. Ultimately this kind of pride is based on a sense of lack, an anxiety regarding one's own worth. We are generally distrustful of pride because we feel the vacuum of insecurity that lies underneath. Ordinary pride is unstable. Like the fairy tale about the emperor's new clothes, we suspect that beneath all the hype there's just a naked man. On a side note, socially awkward or shy people may sometimes appear as being prideful even though they are only experiencing self-consciousness themselves.

Vajra pride, in contrast, has nothing to prove but is based on trust in one's inherent worth and value. It arises in knowing one's true, indestructible nature—Buddha Nature—and having the confidence to act from this recognition.

When we talk about the nature of mind, we may be able to conceptually imagine the vast, radiant ground of being out of which all phenomena arise. But in imagining that, do we then realize that there is no difference between that ground and our own essence? In this sense, the boundaries that define the ego-self inadvertently also serve to separate us from a direct experience of our true condition, which is that we are manifestations of pure awareness. From that point of view, we see that it is by giving ourselves boundaries as an ego that we diminish ourselves in terms of what is actually our true condition. Like points of reflexive self-awareness floating in an ocean of awareness, we practice to let go of the boundaries of self and open to our actual situation of interconnectedness with all things. We realize that we are made of the same stuff, ultimately. Like focalizing lenses through which the brilliance of primordial awareness expresses itself in vivid intricacy and diversity, we are not separate from the innate radiance of the ground of being itself.

From within the walled garden of ego, ordinary pride is an attempt to boost oneself, to make oneself important in some way, all within the context of feelings of separateness and lack. Through meditation and the cultivation of big view, Skymind, we can begin to let go of those ego boundaries. Chögyam Trungpa suggests that whereas "confused ego pride . . . is trying to become something else," vajra pride "comes from facing the reality of one's nature . . . being willing to be what one is."[1] There can be tremendous alignment and liberation in this: coming to terms with ourselves and the world as it is rather than how we might want it to be.

Pride of the Deity

In traditional Tibetan Buddhist deity practice, vajra pride is taught as the "pride of the deity." As the practitioner, you begin by seeing the deity or teacher in front of you, imbued with the perfection of wisdom, an expression of enlightened intent. You supplicate them to share those blessings with you. You then become the deity, and tapping into the "pride of the deity," you embody their wisdom and enlightened altruistic intent. As the deity, through the use of mantra, you radiate compassionate wisdom out into the world to benefit all beings. And finally, you dissolve the entire visualization, including yourself, and rest in nondual awareness.

We can consider deity practice, at one level, to be a kind of role-modeling, a skillful way to gradually realize that ultimately there is no difference between ourselves and the teacher or deity. Rather than continuously seeing the deity or teacher as removed from and superior to ourselves, we actually recognize the equal nature of the Buddha Nature within ourselves and the enlightened being. The fourteenth-century great Buddhist master Tsong Khapa quotes this passage from the *Vajrapañjaratantra*: "Through union with the dignity of an enlightened being, enlightenment will not be far. . . . Therefore the technique is to assume the form of success, which is the teacher's form itself."[2] The practitioner assumes the form of the deity as a skillful means to have a direct experience of enlightened dignity, bypassing habitual insecurities and feelings of not-enoughness. The ultimate point is to recognize that the wisdom we so clearly see or visualize outside ourselves is actually a reflection of the innate wisdom from which we ourselves are never separate.

Thus, Machig reminds us:

Even the spiritual powers of . . . deities
arise to the mind from the meditating mind.
Therefore, it is oneself, not another.[3]

Looking into the eyes of the deity is like looking into a clear mirror. Our own mind is laid bare in its inherent brilliant wakefulness. Machig points us to the reality that ultimate wisdom lies not outside ourselves, not in "another" but in "oneself"; not the constricted, inflated self but the self that knows itself as not other than the very ground of being.

Tara's reprimand of Machig's uncertainty is a reminder that our timidity does no one any good. Self-doubt disguised in humility undermines not only ourselves but our capacity to offer our gifts to others, to truly benefit in the unique ways that we can. We've all experienced low self-esteem and the suffering of hesitation it engenders. Continuously monitoring whether or not we are getting approval (from the outer or inner critic), our thoughts and actions are awkward, misaligned, ineffective, and contrived. We're driving with the brakes on, caught in a self-perpetuating trap of insecurity.

Instead, Machig suggests,

Demons and devils and such are subdued by splendor.[4]

The demons of doubt and insecurity are overcome by the natural radiance and splendor of taking our seat in wakefulness. Splendor (Tib. *zil*)—also translated as "magnificence," "resplendence," "strength"—is used in many Buddhist prayers to describe the power of a deity or teacher whose brilliant presence itself has the force of transmission, protection, illumination. In deity practice, visualizing ourselves as the deity, we radiate the light of awareness, compassion, and healing throughout the vast universe. The wakeful, loving radiance within the Skymind meditation is a visual metaphor for the inescapable ways we affect all beings and all beings affect us. With dignity, we extend our presence, warmth, care, and compassion. At the end of all deity practices, the entire visualization dissolves, including ourselves, and we rest in nondual, primordial awareness. It's a reminder that splendor is ultimately not based on anything we can grasp or hold.

The encumbered patterns and obstacles that seem so very real and overwhelming from the point of view of the constricted self are liberated in the radiance of unconditional worthiness. Like shadows dispelled by light, our fears, hesitations, and tentativeness are outshone by the splendor of primordial self-esteem. It's not that all our difficulties go away but the view with which we navigate the twists and turns of being human radically shifts. We can meet our challenges not as continuous threats to our identity but as opportunities to become curious, to learn, and to draw on the diamond-like strength of our heart to face the moment with uncompromising presence.

In another portion of the text Machig offers the image of the garuda, a magical bird, soaring high up in the skies whose view is so vast that it "subdues with splendor the flocks of birds"[5] below. When we relax the tension of trying to prove ourselves—which reflects a distrust of splendor—we actually create the open space for natural vajra pride to arise.

In the embodied splendor of vajra pride, we can move through our lives with basic confidence, simple clarity, and grounded fearlessness. Being of benefit, however that looks in our specific chapter of life, is not a chore but an inspired, joyful call, an expression of our awakened heart. Indeed, in remembering our inherent worthiness, we also attune to the innate brilliance of *all* beings, a visualization that is also included in deity practice. Regardless of the overlay of obscurations and afflictions, at the heart—of ourselves and thus of everyone else as well—is enlightened dignity.

We might rephrase Machig's verse as "remember your birthright of brilliance," a note to self when the demons of self-doubt and small-mindedness nip at our heels. And so too, we can practice remembering the birthright of brilliance that lives in others. We don't want to suggest that this is always easy. But it is possible. Perhaps living from the diamond-like nature of compassionate wakefulness, life does not need to be quite so heavy. Perhaps it is quite fantastic after all.

Strongholds of Confidence

Having taken Tara's words to heart, Machig goes on to teach:

> *Keep to secluded strongholds of confidence without inflation.*[6]

The notion of developing confidence[7] flows through many Buddhist teachings and is a central purpose of meditation. At his death, the Buddha gave his final instruction: "Be a light unto yourself." The point is not to simply believe in some truth or wisdom outside ourselves but rather to come to know and experience it directly within. Thus we are confident. Garab Dorje, the great seventh-century Dzogchen master, in his "Three Points That Strike the Vital Essence," asserts that we must first be introduced to a direct experience of the nature of mind, then decide definitely on the truth of it, and finally develop absolute "confidence."[8] This confidence allows the view to inform everything we do and say. It becomes the foundation for our lives.

Machig invites us to claim these inner strongholds of confidence, much like the vajra pride we have been discussing. The Tibetan word for stronghold[9] also denotes a royal throne or exalted position. Cognizant of our true nature, basic goodness, we take our seat without hesitation. This "fearless confidence,"[10] as Machig calls it elsewhere, is unwavering because it is not built on outer recognition and not broken by failures or unaccomplished dreams. It is a stronghold because it is deep within us, an inner sanctum that we can always draw on precisely because it is not dependent on or impacted by what we have or have not achieved.

This too is why the stronghold of confidence is "without inflation." Based on neither proving nor disproving anything, promoting nor denying anything, this confidence need not bolster itself with arrogance or power. We don't get inflated about seeing the tree outside our window. We simply see it and know it is there. So too, there is no arrogance in resting in our true nature. We don't need to prove or defend it.

We can appreciate expressions of natural confidence in everyday life. If you have to have surgery, would you want a surgeon who is insecure about what they are doing? If you fly, do you want a pilot who is timid about their abilities? No. You value confidence and the sense of ease it engenders. You can also think of a surgeon who's walking around with arrogance—that's conventional pride, which generally doesn't elicit a feeling of ease. Noticing the difference between arrogance and dignified confidence is a good way of distinguishing between small-self pride and vajra pride.

Or think of listening to a skilled musician, being deeply moved by the sounds that open us into transcendent awareness, almost a spiritual experience one might say. It's not because we're so impressed by how expertly the musician is playing their instrument. It's rather that through their uncompromised presence, their confidence without inflation, a doorway opens into a state beyond self and other. One way we might rephrase Machig's verse is "Take your seat. Be confident, without a trace of arrogance."

We can taste this kind of confidence without inflation in our direct experiences as well. I (Charlotte) am thinking of skiing, one of my favorite activities, and the graced moments of seamless alignment. My body becomes my skis, extending into the snow, into the curvature of the mountain—an uninterrupted continuum of movement. There's a sense of confidence, not because "I" am skiing well but because I've actually let go of "me" skiing on "the mountain." I'm not trying so hard anymore. It's only when I think, *Now* that *was a good turn*, that I lose it. Self-referential thinking has crept in and broken the continuity of flow.

We each have our particular activity that carries us into such an experience of effortless alignment with our body, others, the physical world around us. It's known also as "flow state." The unfabricated confidence of that state, and the ease and joyfulness that come with that, can be a reminder of the seed of vajra pride.

Stronghold also suggests a retreat-like quality, translated as "secluded strongholds." How beautiful. Seclusion elicits the opposite of the flagrant exhibitionism of confidence built on outer recognition and circumstances. Vajra pride emanates from our innermost, deepest is-ness, the very heart of our being. It is what lies beneath all the layers of our persona—who we think we are or should be—and is revealed in our bare nakedness. The deities of Tibetan Buddhism, particularly those representing the groundless ground of being, are depicted as naked to reflect that radiant awareness is not a fabrication or supplement but rather the very basis of being.

We are reminded of a phrase in the New Testament after the angels have heralded Jesus's birth: "But Mary kept all these things, and pondered them in her heart."[11] There is a wise tenderness in holding something close to our heart, sensing that something will be cheapened in the telling of it. So too, we hold the warm glow of vajra pride deep within us, a fearless confidence that lets us meet others with a courageously open heart, with radical honesty and trust, that lets us love fiercely.

This inner sanctum of our Skymind nature is our deepest treasure. It's also our innermost vulnerability and sensitivity from which we feel everything. The adamantine jewel of our heart, it is the most precious, simultaneously unbreakable and absolutely tender.

Indeed, it is often in true seclusion, away from the everyday calls of life, that we can tap into the secluded strongholds of vajra pride. Because we've laid down the robes of identity, entered naked into the liminal space of being no one, we can also access a confidence that is life's innate confidence itself. Just like the tiny purple flower springing from a crack in a rock or the beetle in magnificent green armor making its way through the dry grass. For no reason whatsoever, we know we *are*. We have a seat on this earth. We offer our presence without any doubt whatsoever, absolutely. As Machig says,

> *Inspire your own mood by yourself.*[12]

That seed of radiance within us means we do not have to wait for happiness or joy to arrive through the perfect configuration of circumstances. For that we will indeed wait a long time. No, the primordial happiness of beingness itself arises without any circumstances whatsoever because it is who we are, it is what is. It cannot be taken away. But we *can* turn toward that basic goodness as the core of inspiration itself. And thus the experience of vajra pride, the unconditioned and radiant confidence of Skymind, elicits profound joy not because we've gotten what we wanted or finally reached our goal but because we've connected with the source of being itself. We live in the inextricable connection to all things, the ground that holds us all. And that inspires joy supreme.

Tapping Into Vajra Pride

There are many ways to access vajra pride, most notably the deity practices of Vajrayana Buddhism. However, there are other ways that may be more accessible. Here are a few ideas:

- When we are able to *rest in the nature of mind*, as in our Skymind meditation, vajra pride comes naturally, a self-arising experience of doubtlessness. This is why meditation, including those practices offered in this book, are so valuable, both in their own right and to inspire our life in the world.

- ✧ As you contemplate "secluded strongholds without inflation," imagine letting go of all the forms of identity that define you: your work, your role in your family, your position in your community, your talents and gifts. And then notice: What's left? Who and what are you? At first it may seem like you are nothing. Perhaps after some time, something else arises, some basic being-ness. Rest in that. If you're dealing with a particular challenge in life, imagine meeting it from this place, from the basic ground of who you are.
- ✧ Our *physical posture* in Skymind meditation connects us directly with the embodiment of our inherent dignity. The key points of meditation posture settle us directly on earth, where we take our seat, in the literal and figurative sense. When we let our body rest on the earth (floor, cushion, chair), we can feel the unconditional support of the ground. From this stability, the spine rises tall, like a stack of gold coins, to use the traditional imagery, or like a trunk of a huge tree reaching to the sky. We can feel uplifted simply in bringing awareness to the elongation of our spine, extending upward even through the crown of our head as though we were suspended from the heavens. With shoulders relaxed, the chest expands with the courage of openheartedness. For those not able to sit upright, one might tap into ground, sky, and openness even while lying down. We always find ourselves between heaven and earth, so to speak, in the dignity of our aliveness and presence. You might try this right now and see whether it sparks a sense of inherent dignity.

~ EXERCISE ~

Introducing the Avatar

The following exercise is inspired by Vajrayana deity practice, which we've referred to several times in this chapter. In this exercise, we construct an archetypal self-image, an avatar, that is imbued with all the qualities we aspire to: the perfection of wisdom and altruistic intent. If you imagine your wisdom self, imbued with radiance and compassion, what would it look like?

This exercise can be done on its own or added on to the Wish-Fulfilling Jewel exercise at the end of chapter 15.

- ✧ Take a few breaths to ground yourself in the present moment, releasing any and all tensions as best you can.
- ✧ Rest at ease for a little time, attuning to the warmth and aliveness of your body.
- ✧ Now tap into a sense of radiant luminosity within your body, perhaps experienced internally as body heat, vibrancy, or simply energy. See your body infused with luminous awareness, wisdom, altruistic intent, compassion.
- ✧ Imagine there's a radiance emanating from your body, the light of your awareness. You are filled with light and effortlessly radiant.
- ✧ Perhaps you feel there's a gesture or posture that naturally arises within this wisdom body, or maybe you just remain seated as you are.
- ✧ Perhaps as you rest in this simple radiance of your wisdom body, you notice there are adornments or a token or object that are associated with this wisdom body.
- ✧ At this point you may move your awareness outside of your body and look back at yourself. See the radiant wisdom body with its color, gestures, tokens, or anything else that you notice. Then bring your awareness back into your body.
- ✧ Abide in this manifestation of your wisdom self, your body infused with radiance, every cell effortlessly awake and activated. Feel the compassion inherent in this state and embody it fully.

- ✧ Remember what this looks and feels like in your body, so you can find your way back to it in the future.
- ✧ Now relax and let your awareness expand out effortlessly with this radiance, letting your awareness mix with the luminous ground of all things.
- ✧ From this place, send out compassion—whatever that means or feels like right now. Your altruistic intent pulses out into the world, not pushing or efforting but naturally radiating, benefiting beings, bringing relief, help, healing. Just rest like this for a good while.
- ✧ When you are ready, gently bring your awareness back to your body. Notice one final time this wisdom body: what it looks like, how it feels. Then dissolve this body and the entire visualization from the bottom up.
- ✧ Rest in the vast emptiness that remains. Just rest.

Integrating the Avatar with Skymind Meditation

If you feel a strong connection to this wisdom-body avatar, you can bring it into your Skymind meditation. Place your wisdom body in the sphere above your head, where you first rest your attention. Then the sphere, together with this image of your wisdom body, descends into your crown into your heart center, radiating its luminosity throughout your body and eventually infinitely outward. The wisdom body dissolves together with the sphere as you enter into the practice of pure, open awareness. See the full Skymind meditation as outlined in chapter 8.

17

Encountering Death

In Buddhism, regarding death, it is said there is one certainty and three uncertainties. The certainty is that we will die; it is the inevitable conclusion to birth. The uncertainties are when, where, and how. And, of course, this impending demise often creates a lot of anxiety. However, since it is entirely unavoidable, and every one of us will eventually experience it in this lifetime, we may as well come to terms with it sooner rather than later. There are many benefits to examining our relationship to our own death, not from a place of morbid fascination but because contemplating our death can be tremendously liberating. How does Skymind support a fresh and inspired perspective on death? In many spiritual traditions, death is seen as a profound opportunity for practice, a profound teacher.

I (Pieter) grew up in South Africa, and upon graduating from high school I was "called up" for mandatory military service. I was assigned to the Air Force and ended up becoming an intelligence officer. At that time, South Africa, along with the CIA, was supporting Jonas Savimbi's UNITA rebel movement against the Russian and Cuban-backed socialist government of Angola, and I found myself embedded with the legendary and fearsome "Buffalo" battalion[1] deep inside enemy territory. The South African Defense Forces generally prevailed in that war, but one night after a flanking maneuver that failed due to densely forested terrain, and having taken some casualties, we had to bed down for the night in a place that was close to the enemy and exposed to their artillery and aerial bombardment.

We were told to dig "foxholes" for our own safety, but what I ended up digging looked much more like a shallow grave. Hopefully you haven't had to, and never will, but if you have ever tried to dig a hole big enough to fit a body you will know that it is very hard work. So one ends up digging as efficiently as possible, hence the coffin-shaped shallow hole I ended up with.

We were expressly told not to take shelter in our armored vehicles as they were more vulnerable to heavy bombs compared to sheltering below ground level. But as I lay there in my coffin-shaped hole in the Angolan forest, I had the overwhelming feeling that I was lying in my own grave. I couldn't shake this feeling, and sleep was impossible. I was only nineteen and hadn't spent much time contemplating death, although war has a way of quickly changing that. Either way, I got up and went inside the vehicle against orders, spending a long and uncomfortable night in my hard but familiar seat. The disconcerting fear of lying in my own grave weighed more heavily on me than the actual risk of being more exposed.

Right now death is the absolute truth.[2]

These words from Machig sound pretty drastic. But from our relative, dualistic point of view in this life, so convincingly bound by the veils of existential ignorance, it feels very true. This seemingly absolute truth of death is also what makes it such a sobering and potentially powerful ally to us. Given our propensity for self-clinging, it is no surprise that death is such a vexing topic for the ego. We tend to cling to our physical body as the most substantive proof of our individual, separate existence. So the death of the physical body and the loss of everything we know naturally tend to inspire a lot of uncertainty and fear.

This unresolved fear may take different forms. Most often it takes the form of extreme avoidance of anything relating to death. But it could also result in an unhealthy fascination with morbidity or even an unhealthy defiance toward death. But how can we come into alignment with death so that it does not make us contract into fear or escape into avoidance but rather become a source of strength and insight? We may start by gently contemplating our own death. It is, after all, on our path already. There's quite literally no avoiding it. This way we enter into a healthy relationship with our own death, as a practice and as a reality in our daily lives. And, although generally harder, that may also help us come to terms with loved ones passing away.

Contemplating death provides the invitation to reflect on how you would like to die. What state of mind do you want to be in when you die? Freaked out, fearful, and avoidant? Or relaxed, accepting, and at ease? What will you take refuge in and how will you rest your mind when the time comes? For example, if you have strong faith and an established relationship with the divine, then that's what you would take refuge in when you die. Depending on your background and traditions, this may be a strong, cultivated relationship with God, a deity, or a loving spiritual teacher. The point is to start cultivating and strengthening that relationship and the ease of access to it right now while you are alive.

In Machig's tradition, we access and stabilize that refuge through our practice of meditation. And that's the practice of resting in the ultimate self-arising nature of mind and its infinitely compassionate resonance, resting in what remains uninterrupted and unbroken through and after death. Chögyam Trungpa says,

> The ultimate instruction on death is simply to try to rest your mind in the nature of ultimate bodhicitta . . . pass your breath in that way until you are actually dead.[3]

Ultimate bodhicitta is the radiant, compassionate nature of mind, Skymind.

One of the reasons we practice Skymind meditation is that it familiarizes us with resting in open awareness, the nature of mind. When you practice, recognize that space of absolute bodhicitta, the natural state. You can rest here within your meditation practice, at any given moment, and at the time of death.

Death as a Process

When contemplating our death there are two helpful approaches. First, assume you have a choice about how you want to die. Second, think of death as a process rather than a singular "moment." Regarding choice, contemplate what your preferences are and set your intention accordingly. Apart from influencing reality, this provides agency and a way of more directly relating with your death in a healthy and empowered way. Regarding death as a process, if you relax in acceptance of each sequential moment of the process, you can be present and at ease in each of those moments. Of course, there are accidental deaths that happen rather suddenly, but even then we don't want to be overcome by shock and surprise. Thus we practice to relax and surrender while we are alive, to be at ease and present in *every* moment. It's a profound prescription for both living and dying.

Thus, where we want to rest our mind at death also informs where we rest our mind in everyday life. Could we be at peace with death without also being at peace with everyday life? And how do we find peace in everyday life? The answer is the same: to rest in the ground of being as profound and ultimate refuge. That's where we came from, and that's essentially what we will find our way back to. We can do that in our lifetime. We can live our lives in the same way we want to die: with openness, ease, presence, kindness, and curiosity. We go through all kinds of contortions, journeys, and trips in our lives, looking for answers. But really what we're looking for is what we've never actually lost: the blissful ocean of compassionate awareness that we all arise out of, the nondual primordial mother we are all born from. And so, in short, our practice becomes about more and more identifying with that vast nature, more and more relaxing into it, falling back into it. When we meditate, we practice accessing and stabilizing this absolute refuge. We condition ourselves to be able to let go completely, without anxiety and concern. This is what we surrender into at the time of death.

Machig, when impermanence is upon you, where will intention take you?
There is no intention within the unborn
There is nowhere to go within the unceasing.
Still, once naturally liberated without reference—
. . . just vivid, quiet, radiant . . . [4]

You may recall the wave metaphor from chapter 1, where we likened this life to a wave on the ocean. Even though we may be completely identified with our waveness, no one will deny that we are also ocean. As a wave, we're completely absorbed in our immediate surface environment, moving along the currents of the ocean with the other waves playing around us. Then, one day, we peer over the crests of the waves ahead of us, and there in the far distance we see a sheer cliff face. As we approach, we see wave after wave slamming into the rocks, shattering into countless droplets. We realize with certainty that as a wave, our complete destruction is imminent and unavoidable. This gives rise to great fear, and we try everything we can to avoid that cliff. However, recognizing that we are also ocean, the scale of our view suddenly changes and becomes much vaster. From the perspective of the ocean, the crashing waves are a playful spectacle of beauty and brilliance. All apprehension evaporates like foamy spray cast up into the shimmering sky. Thus Machig encourages us: Let us surge as ocean waves upon the impending cliffs of impermanence, "naturally liberated . . . just vivid, quiet, radiant."

Death in Buddhism

There are many references and resources related to dying in Buddhism. In a beautiful teaching in the *Sutra on Wisdom at the Hour of Death*, the Buddha says,

> [W]hen the time comes to die, [one] should cultivate wisdom at the hour of death. Wisdom at the hour of death is as follows: . . .
> Since all phenomena are naturally pure,
> One should cultivate the clear understanding that there are no entities.
> Since all phenomena are connected with the enlightened mind,
> One should cultivate the clear understanding of great compassion.
> Since all phenomena are naturally luminous,
> One should cultivate the clear understanding of nonapprehension.
> Since all entities are impermanent,
> One should cultivate the clear understanding of nonattachment.
> Since the mind is the cause for the arising of wisdom,
> Do not look for the Buddha elsewhere.[5]

Here again the Buddha presents a pretty radical view of ultimate reality and a clear invitation to experience enlightened mind directly at the time of death, without fear or apprehension. Conditioned by our spatial perception in this dualistic world, we may think of the death process in different ways: as a profound transformation, or as a narrow passage into a different world or reality that will be experienced by the same "I," the same self that is experiencing this life. But in doing so we may inadvertently be projecting a familiar dimensionality onto the post-death state. Popular afterlife narratives further support this: heaven or hell as a "place" where suffering or delight is experienced in three dimensions; the ferryman taking us to the realm of the dead; the eternal fighting and feasting in Valhalla. But what if this 3D reality we so solidly find ourselves in collapses in on itself, the way a dream collapses upon waking in the early morning? In the Buddha's words, "Since all phenomena are naturally pure . . . there are no entities." Is there spatial awareness in a dream? And what happens with that space when the dream dissolves upon awakening? Where is the world located where that dream took place? Out of what did the dream arise? The entire dream took place in the space of mind. It arose out of mind, and it completely dissolved back into mind. Is it reasonable to think this reality is ultimately any different?

The *Tibetan Book of the Dead*[6] contains very detailed explanations of the dying process and what the dying person experiences in the different stages of death, including instructions for the dying person and for those attending to them. It is well worth reading. It also talks about the various bardos, or intermediate states, that we transition through in life and death. But perhaps the key point is the opportunity for complete liberation during the process. In the culmination of the death process, there's a moment where all the constituent elements have dissolved and there's a direct experience of the clear light of dharmata, the uncontrived and unconditioned nature of reality. The idea is to be already familiarized with it, and to be present and at ease enough to recognize it and abide in that realization. The suggestion here is that Skymind is a continuum of awareness stretching beyond this life. To recognize Skymind now is to know it always. Thus we practice this mode of abiding during this life so that we may be able to recognize and rest in it at death. If we don't recognize, it is said that our mindstream continues and the cycle of rebirth in an embodied form starts again.

In the Vajrayana there's also the advanced practice of *phowa*, transference of consciousness, where we have the opportunity to eject our consciousness from the fontanel at our crown at the moment of death and propel it into a Buddha realm or pure land—or into absolute reality. Here again, we are presented with a view of death as a profound and powerful opportunity for awakening.

The caveat here is to be careful not to turn our death into an accomplishment or to approach it with a road-map mindset and the accompanying apprehension of taking a wrong turn somewhere. Too many instructions and we may end up with too much doing for dying. Rest. Relax. Let go of all accomplishments. If our nature is truly self-arising, we can let go completely of all our grasping, all our holding, all our striving. Let go and be buoyed by what is already there—our primordial self-existent nature. That's the invitation: Completely surrender into simple presence. Present awareness does not diminish when we let go. Unobscured and unfettered by attachment and striving, its inherent radiance and compassion shines brighter. And to this we surrender with openness and curiosity.

Being free of striving . . .
You will dwell on the ground of the unborn. . . .
the ground of no birth and death.[7]

Machig's words here could also be seen as a reference to her severance tradition and the associated Chöd practice. During the highly ritualized practice, we visualize offering our body to our detractors to satisfy them but also to help condition ourselves not to cling to our body as a solid "self" and to open into a direct awareness of the "unborn" and the "ground of no birth and death."

The Death of Loved Ones

The death of loved ones can be far more challenging to contemplate or experience than our own. If we had to consider what we fear most, the loss of a loved one would probably be at the top of the list for many of us, especially if you have children. Because we experience ourselves as being so realistically "here"—and only here—the passing of a loved one naturally results in intense feelings of loss and grief. Not only do we miss their presence deeply, but the closer to us they were, the more intertwined they were with our sense of self, our very identity. So it is very much as if we've lost a part of ourselves. Apart from the grief and loss, we may feel that we have to find ourselves anew, reconstruct a new identity in their absence. There is no shortcut way of dealing with this, except perhaps to open to the grief and pain, to seek support, and to grieve in community with other loved ones. It may also be helpful to think of others, known or unknown, that are currently in the same situation, that have experienced a similar loss, and grieve in compassion with them. However, our practice, the extent to which we've come to terms with our own death, and in particular our view of the ultimate nature of reality, can also help us to accept and integrate the loss of a loved one.

When we want to provide support for the dying or the bereaved, our own relationship with death may often color our behavior and capacity to be helpful. Rather than being fully present, we end up projecting our unprocessed thoughts and fears about death onto the situation, tripping over feelings of awkwardness and hesitancy. The more resolved and integrated our own issues around death are, the more we can show up for others with undistracted presence and unforced compassion.

Birth, Death, and Transformation

In the abiding nature of mind itself, birth and death, clean and dirty, enemy and friend, and so forth are not at all established.[8]

Let's zoom out for a moment from the relative point of view, from the immediacy of this lifetime. If we assume for a moment that reincarnation happens and that we have in fact lived previous lives, it could change our perspective on death. Let's say you have lived a hundred lifetimes on this planet. In that case, you will have experienced death many times already. And you've gone through many births. It may even be likely that birth is a more difficult process to go through than death. Our body, in this reality, may be the evolutionary pinnacle of three-dimensional biotech, but we could assume it is still jarring to come from a more expanded non-embodied state to a sudden squeeze into physicality—with its biological limitations and the impacts of gravity.

Still, we are ecstatic at the birth of a baby, yet we fear death. This only makes sense from the limited perspective of being alive in this reality with its accompanying veil of not knowing. We are experiencing the delight of gain and the pain of loss. But from the point of view of the person who is experiencing their own birth or death, it may be very different, even reversed. Even if you don't think you've had other lifetimes: Well, you've certainly experienced birth, and if you are reading this, you've obviously made it through okay. So it may be quite reasonable to assume you're going to be okay when you die.

In chapter 3 and in this chapter, we talk about the importance of surrender and how it does not mean to give up or let others take advantage of you but rather to relax in ever-expanding arenas of all-inclusive awareness. Especially when it comes to our death process, this idea might make a lot of sense. But what does it actually look like, this process of expanding beyond our boundaries, boundaries that are often delineated by fear?

Many years ago, I (Pieter) was at a large spiritual gathering in Bohemia, Czech Republic, where I participated in a ceremonial sweat lodge. We spent the entire day building the lodge and preparing, resulting in an exceptionally powerful experience that lasted throughout the night. Inside the lodge, the heat was far more intense than anything I had ever experienced before, causing extreme discomfort to all the participants. After a long period of utmost challenge, I finally stopped resisting the fear that I was dying and surrendered completely to whatever was happening, including the possibility of physical death. At that point I lost outer consciousness and entered into a deep inner journey, reexperiencing my birth process in great detail. This process of extreme discomfort and resistance, and the eventual surrender repeated several times that night, each time leading to further breakthroughs with the profound accompanying experiences of freedom, transcendence, and deep natural ease.

All of us go through transformations and passages in life, whether brought on by internal or external circumstances or seemingly coming out of the blue. As you move through these passages in your own life, you may have noticed this same pattern of extreme discomfort, resistance, and contraction, followed by finally letting go and surrendering to what you have been avoiding and the resulting rebirth or liberation. Bringing conscious awareness and intentionality to these life passages will not only make them more meaningful, but it is also a good way to prepare for death.

Precious Human Birth and Impermanence

In the preliminary practices of the Vajrayana path there is a contemplation called the Four Thoughts That Turn the Mind to the Dharma. The first of those is the preciousness of human life. The famous parable to illustrate this is of a blind turtle that lives at the bottom of a vast ocean and surfaces only once every one hundred years. On the surface of the ocean floats a single yoke, a wooden frame used to harness oxen. The chance of obtaining a precious human rebirth is compared to the likelihood of this blind turtle surfacing with its head through the floating yoke. The intent of the story is to encourage us to see this life as a great gift and to inspire us to practice and develop.

The second of the Four Thoughts is about impermanence and death. Reflecting on the transient nature of life, we are reminded that all things, including life itself, are temporary. Because death can happen at any time, that inevitability should inspire us to pursue the spiritual path. It also encourages us to appreciate the gift of this life specifically because it is not lasting and permanent. (The third thought is karma; the fourth the reality of suffering.)

Conversely, these stories may induce us to want to cling to our body and to life even more desperately. But we cling to life for all the wrong reasons. Apart from the primordial urge for self-preservation, we also cling to life because this reality is all we know. The natural consequence is to become completely identified and attached to this life and to experience existential fear of the unknown beyond the end of life as we know it. It's quite a bind: Death is inevitable, and yet we have no clue as to what to expect from it. There are many examples of behavior fueled by this core insecurity in our world: from wars to profound environmental catastrophism to niche pursuits of the wealthy like cryonics, perhaps the ultimate gambit for some kind of entrenched dualistic immortality. It entails preserving one's body at extremely low temperatures after death with the hope of future revival. In truth, there are much greater liberties to be attained in this life than having the same frozen corpse be reanimated in some high-tech future for another go-around. This seems desperate, unnecessary, and based on an important misunderstanding. The spiritual technology at work all around us is already much more interesting and advanced than that. We are already uploaded. Relax and enjoy.

One morning in Angola, during the same war as in the earlier story, we were having an open-air meeting of all the officers in the fighting group I was assigned to. It was being led by a major sitting in a camp chair, and there were a few armored vehicles parked nearby. Suddenly an enemy mortar exploded close to us, and rightly expecting more to come, we all dove underneath the nearest armored vehicle for some protection—everyone except the major, who continued to sit in his camp chair through several more explosions, unperturbed and mildly amused at our scramble. Although quite renowned at the time for his exploits as a modern-day warrior, I don't think the major was a particularly spiritual man. But he had thoroughly come to terms with the inherent risks of his profession and carried that air of inspired, present-in-the-moment fearlessness in his demeanor.

Overall, the invitation here is to engage with the reality of our death in such a way that we don't have an unreasonable fear of it. When we relax into Skymind view, life remains infinitely valuable. But not desperately valuable. Not "at all costs." It is profoundly beautiful and therefore expansively valuable. But there's no need for contracted, small-minded, fearful clinging. We practice for a sense of spacious, surrendered enjoyment.

The Carnival of Life

The veil of existential ignorance that we described in chapter 4 gives rise to an interesting paradox. On the one hand, we desperately cling to life. On the other, we feel a yearning for escape from it, a yearning for transcendence, liberation, salvation. This is the fertile ground of spiritual practice and religion—really, the birthplace of religion. Because this experiential reality is the totality of what we know, we cling to it—and for the very same reason, we may also feel stuck in it at times. This feeling of being stuck may come out of periods of hardship, suffering, emotional or physical pain, witnessing injustice and the suffering of others, or sometimes just feelings of tedium and meaninglessness.

In this regard it may be interesting to explore the following popular thought experiment: In some transcendent, formless, off-planet reality, a vaster conscious aspect of ourselves made a choice to show up in this reality in an embodied form. Now that we're here, with no memory of that, all we want to do is escape. It's a little like a child crying and nagging to go to the carnival that came to town. And finally when they go, get freaked out by all the noise and people, and get tired. After just a short while, they're now desperately crying to go home. Sometimes, without realizing it, our spiritual practice is like this. We want to escape the suffering of everyday profane, mundane life. Yes, we carry histories and trauma. And yes, we experience suffering. But from an already-liberated point of view, from the spacious perspective of unsurpassable freedom, being here right now is just simply incredible. Embodied and replete with sense perceptions and a rich emotional landscape, we are perfectly equipped to experience the ceaseless unfolding of the play of duality. This spacious yet present view is the birthplace of deep and simple joy.

We started this chapter with the one certainty that we will most certainly die, and the three uncertainties of when, where, and how. The primary directive for preparing for our death, from the Buddha, Machig, and other teachings of the tradition, is to practice resting in the primordial nature of our minds, to rest in the ground of being, in Skymind. And as all the pages of this book have already suggested, that is also the primary focus of meditation and everyday life. The ultimate preparation for death is to relax in the recognition that we are already always prepared. We don't have to fret about getting ready or being ready when the time comes. We are ready now, and thus we can relax. We can trust the groundless ground of being, even as all that we know at a relative level dissolves. Our practice, then—in waking, sleeping, living, and dying—is to open and surrender into the luminous, spacious lap of the Great Mother. Then indeed, whenever, wherever, and however our death meets us, we will be ready.

~ EXERCISE ~

The Wave and the Ocean

In this practice, we'll explore what it may feel like to release all that we consider "me" and return to the experience of unification with the ground of being. We'll work with the image described earlier in this chapter—the wave crashing onto the shore, returning to its oceanness.

- ✧ Begin by coming into a comfortable position, either sitting or lying down. Close your eyes.
- ✧ Imagine that you are a wave on the vast, open ocean. This wave encompasses your entire life, all that you value, all your experiences, your entire identity. Around you are other waves—your family, friends, acquaintances—with whom you are relating in this life. You are all moving in the same direction, enjoying life together.
- ✧ Now, all of a sudden, you become aware of the sound of waves crashing on a distant beach. Looking over the tops of the waves in front of you, you see wave after wave disappearing as they wash up on the beach, then running back into the ocean. You look around, seeing all that you love—your life, your family, your friends—moment by moment getting closer and closer to the beach, and realize you will no longer be a wave. Take your time to feel what this feels like. Are there any feelings of contraction, sadness, resistance, or anything else?
- ✧ In the meantime, you've come very close to the beach, ready to break and roll out onto the sand.

- Now you're crashing, catapulting up and over onto the sand. Feel yourself go out onto the beach like a final arrival, without any resistance, releasing, completely letting go and surrendering your waveness.
- Slowly you flow back as water, reabsorbed back into the ocean. Now feel the vastness of the ocean, the vastness that you are. Feel the connection to all you love, your friends, your family, but now from the point of view of the ocean.
- Rest in this open, all-embracing vastness of ocean. Just rest.
- When your contemplation feels complete, reconnect with the warmth and weight of your body, bring gentle movement into your limbs, and open your eyes.
- Offer the wish that any insight generated in this practice may be of benefit to others.

Part Three
FRUITION

18

Liberated from Accomplishment

[T]he person who is liberated from accomplishing
is said to have the unmistaken fruition.[1]

One of my (Charlotte's) favorite classes in graduate school was a seminar devoted to the work of the great British American poet T. S. Eliot. I remember walking to class in the early morning, reading a thick volume of Eliot's collected poems. Hidden in his brilliant *Four Quartets* are a few lines that have rightfully become well loved and well known:

We shall not cease from our exploration
And the end of all our exploring
Will be to arrive where we started
And know the place for the first time.[2]

Fruition is arrival. It is the final destination of the path. But where, after all the twists and turns of our journey, do we find ourselves? Paradoxically, right where we started.

Fruition is the recognition of the ground that we never left in the first place. It is the realization that there was never any lack to be filled. There was nothing we had to complete, nothing to achieve. Some call this the cosmic joke: We work so hard to learn, to practice, to make ourselves better, and finally when we peel away the final layer of the onion, we realize there really was nothing to *get*, or at least not in the way we thought we would be getting or achieving something.

About eight hundred years before T. S. Eliot, Machig taught, "[T]he person who is liberated from accomplishing is said to have the unmistaken fruition." The ultimate fruition, the unmistaken fruition, is the realization that there was nothing to attain in the first place. There really was nothing to accomplish.

Our drive to accomplish means we want to make something happen. We want to attain something, prove something. No, says Machig. Unmistaken fruition is beyond any accomplishing whatsoever because the ultimate attainment is Buddha Nature—fundamental wakeful wholeness—and that is not something we create. It is already always there, from the beginningless beginning.

Even the path, from this point of view, is part of the ground. We can have the experience of feeling separate from the ground and searching to find our way back, but that doesn't mean that we ever left the ground. We *cannot* actually leave the ground. In fruition, there's simply a deep recognition that everything that arises—all phenomena, all experiences—are expressions of the ground of being, including the path itself and our inclination to walk it. Everything we perceive, even when we are afflicted, even the very affliction itself, is a reflection of the ground of being.

It may sound like Machig is encouraging us to just submit to an indolent and avoidant life without a second thought. But the subtle key here is that we have to clearly and directly realize that there is really nothing to accomplish. This is the paradox, the punch line to the cosmic joke. It's like Dorothy and her companions' great quest in *The Wizard of Oz*, where the elusive wizard turns out to be just an ordinary man, and they discover that they already possessed the qualities they thought they lacked. But would they have come to this realization had they not undertaken the journey and peeked behind the curtain in the first place?

The crux, then—the difference between the beginning and the end of the path—is recognition. To realize or not to realize our inseparability from the ground of being, that truly *is* the question. The teachings suggest there is one ground, two paths—recognizing or not recognizing—and two ensuing results. Either we are plagued with this utterly convincing sense of being separate and thus caught in the resultant cycle of trying to make ourselves and the world whole, right, and complete. Or we live within the embodied knowledge of that wholeness, our true nature. In the absence of recognition, we strive and we fixate, and that dualistic fixation robs us of our freedom.

The path of Skymind we've been traversing in the preceding chapters is a path of coming into recognition. Supreme inclusivity: realizing that within the view, the space of totality, everything is held and nothing is left out. Thus we are catapulted into radical acceptance: avoiding nothing, rejecting nothing, but rather leaning in, even into darkness, with a tender and fierce open heart. Embracing supreme responsibility, we take our seat with dignity and compassionate presence. In this process we begin to realize that the ground of being is everywhere. Wherever we turn, that is the ground of being. No matter what arises, it is not other than the ground. Every wave is also the ocean. Fear—of the unknown, the other, failure, loss, even death—opens into curiosity. Our apprehension of losing touch with the ground, of missing it or falling from it, dissolves into the tender wakefulness of bodhicitta and the joyful ease that comes with it. When we are liberated from accomplishment, we stop trying to make something else happen. When we stop trying to make something else happen, we arrive more fully in the already-wholeness of this heart-broken-open being that we think of as *me*, in this overwhelmingly chaotic and magical world just as it is.

Nature can be a wonderful teacher regarding fruition and accomplishment. Plants are continuously moving through a cycle of arising and falling away. Buds open to leaves, to flowers, to fruit; flowers wilt, fruit drops. As we write, the last golden leaves are falling from the ash trees outside our window. What does the tree accomplish? Certainly there is a brief, glorious moment of harvest—the red apple, the perfectly ripened peach. But that too decays. Is there some final endpoint we are busy getting to besides the joy of this moment?

Another great eleventh-century teacher, the Indian scholar Atisha, whose fifty-nine *lojong* (mind training) slogans inspired our use of Machig's verses, offered this wisdom:

Abandon any hope of fruition.[3]

It's not that fruition doesn't happen. Fruition is happening all the time. Right now is a moment of fruition. What we abandon is the *grasping* for accomplishment, for arrival; the *hope* of fruition. To be liberated from accomplishing is not the end of accomplishing; it is the liberation from the self-imposed weight of our doing. Lifted from what should be, our doing becomes just what it is, simultaneously aspirational and fruitional in every moment of its arising. In the big view, the bud is no less complete than the open flower.

Of course, we make peace even with our grasping to accomplishment, that powerful propensity to want to get somewhere. In abandoning all hope of fruition, we add a bit of humor to the situation. We don't take ourselves quite so seriously. We see both the beauty and the folly of our desire to accomplish, which frees it up so that we can put a spring in our step even as we go about our business.

What might it mean to accomplish freely? Already in this moment a breath is accomplished; at the very least, a heartbeat. Perhaps a thought arises, a memory passes through awareness, then falls away, accomplished, completed. Even this writing—this effort of letting a phrase take shape, move into the fingers, the keyboard, and onto the screen—done. But there is no burden in the doing of these accomplishments; their arising, completion, and falling away happen almost simultaneously.

The promise of spiritual accomplishment can be particularly seductive. Yet the very effort of propelling ourselves into a "more enlightened state" can become the obstacle to resting in the awakened state that already is. Lest we grasp to any solid, fixed, and permanent results of our spiritual endeavors, Machig warns,

> *Without the realization that results are unreal,*
> *whatever effort is made toward achieving it*
> *will not become the attainment of freedom.*[4]

It's tempting to look for the results of our spiritual practice—visions, insights, peace of mind—as though these would prove not only our progress on the path but finally establish the ground of our enlightened nature. Yet Machig reminds us, freedom is not an accomplishment built on the results of our spiritual labor. We are already free.

Anything that might suggest that we earn our freedom is misguided. Liberation is not attained because we've finally made something of ourselves. It is the great paradox of spirituality that in giving us nothing to hold on to, it ultimately gives us everything.

You may remember Machig's classification of superior, middling, and inferior practitioners. The superior practitioner rests simply in things as they are

> *. . . within nonconceptual equipoise without fear or anxiety*
> *no matter what [demons] arise.*[5]

She's referring to our inherent capacity to connect instantaneously with the nature of mind, the ground of being. Because our very awareness, our consciousness, and everything seemingly "outside" of ourselves is an expression of the ground, we may assume that we have complete access at all times. We've mentioned previously the practice of "taking a short moment"—dropping all preoccupation and contrivance, even intentionality, and just letting go into our basic nature, Skymind. We're not creating some enlightened state or finally finding a pocket of awakening. We're not grasping or accomplishing anything. In the extreme sense, we're not even realizing anything. We just let go into what is already there, awareness itself.

When you're practicing Skymind meditation, notice if there is any subtle sense of "getting somewhere." Are you trying to accomplish something? Are you trying to be a "good meditator"? What would it mean to release any grasping for the perfect meditation? What might it mean to simply let be, to rest in your natural state?

Being liberated from spiritual accomplishment radically changes our relationship to formal practice because the goal-oriented impetus is removed. What begins to emerge is an experience of the path of practice as a spacious, joyous dance; an expression of the ground in all its clarity and complexity, just like life itself. Thus our practice integrates with everyday life. (See our chapter on non-meditation below.)

On a final note, we can liberate accomplishment by giving whatever we've accomplished away. Much like the dedication of merit at the end of Buddhist meditation practices, we send out whatever goodness, wisdom, or beauty we have generated to the benefit of all beings.

It's a wonderful way to get up with our pockets empty, unburdened by any sense of having "gotten" something, or having to hold on to anything. We are liberated from even that. Whatever you accomplish—give it away, metaphorically or literally. Parenting is a great practice for investing all you have and then giving it away. I offer so that you can be free, so that you can dance your way into the grand adventure of your life. I don't need to keep anything. As every parent knows, we have already received enough. Our greatest accomplishment is liberated, even from the very beginning. The sweet, unencumbered joy of unmistaken fruition.

19

The View of No View

There's a delicious unraveling that begins to take place in fruition. The scaffolds and structures that guide the path fall away into the radiance of simple presence. Resting in the natural state, Skymind, is a way of being that is completely without contrivance or manipulation, free of constructs altogether. Even the cherished guidelines by which we measure our spiritual development as more or less awakened, aware, or compassionate fall by the wayside.

In the "Path" section above, we explored all three aspects of path: view, meditation, and action (or conduct). View is the understanding of the groundless ground that we come to realize through meditation and that unfolds in our daily conduct as supreme acceptance and compassionate presence. As the path opens into fruition and comes full circle to where we began—where, in fact, we have always been—the inherent emptiness at the heart of these teachings becomes clear. In the next few chapters we will explore this unraveling as it relates to view, meditation, and action. Any clinging, even to this prized framework of the teachings, evaporates into the spaciousness to which they point.

The supreme Severance is no view. . . .
The meditative stability of not meditating—
that is the supreme meditation. . . .
. . . the supreme conduct of no conduct.[1]

Rather than a literal set of instructions from Machig on fruition, we can view these verses as written from the perspective of having already realized no-self. As such, they are brightly colored signifiers of lucidity, like messenger birds flying through the vast sky of basic space, leaving no visible trace. If we read it like a directive—*Right now, relinquish all view, all meditation, all conduct*—we get stuck in paradox, the trusty sidekick of dualism. "I've stopped meditating because I want to realize non-meditation" would be a good example of this. At this point, the question of how to attain fruition liberates into the vast view of no fixation. When there is no clinging, dualistic notions of enlightened and unenlightened resolve effortlessly of their own accord. Thus Padampa Sangye says,

The root of samsara and nirvana is in your own mind;
People of Tingri, the mind is free of any true reality.[2]

Here we may be snared into adopting this subtle view of no view as some kind of conceptual spiritual high ground, telling ourselves that we are somehow liberated from mundane duality. *I don't have any views on anything whatsoever* or *I don't need to meditate* or *I don't do anything because I've realized non-action* would be missing Machig's point. No view doesn't mean you simply don't have an opinion; non-meditation doesn't mean you simply don't meditate; and no conduct doesn't mean you just do whatever you want. Actual fruition is self-clarifying and cuts through any egoic pretense, however subtle it may be. Simply put, if there's a *me* that's not meditating, then it's not the liberation of non-meditation. If there's a *me* that is enlightened, then it is not enlightenment.

The View of No View

Our view comprises the lens through which we perceive life. It is the ground for all that we believe, the basis upon which we construct our existence, our sense of self and other; it informs our decisions and motivates our actions. At a relative level, our views are how we make meaning of our world, what we consider most true or real. As such, our views offer us security. To feel we know *something*, *anything*—concretely and absolutely—is relieving because the phenomenal world becomes more solid and reliable. We know what to expect when we wake up in the morning. And thus we also know who *we* are in a more solid way. We feel like we exist concretely, reliably.

While our views give us a helpful compass for directing our decisions and actions, they can also become fossilized, solidifying around labels of "good" and "bad," "right" and "wrong," "for me" and "against me." Regardless of our experience, we stick to our beliefs. Our perception, conditioned by our views, becomes narrow and selective: We see what we want to see. In our search for dependability and meaning, all of us have this fundamentalist propensity within us, however broad-minded we like to think we are. We establish a false ground of certainty and derive much solace from clinging to our familiar and valued beliefs.

Our demons are good clues for where we have solidified our views. The common demon of always staying busy arises out of a view that it's only through doing that I am worthy. The external demon or enemy shows us where we draw a solid line between acceptable and unacceptable, right and wrong—often, of course, rationalized with seemingly reasonable justification. When Machig suggests we tenderly surround ourselves with our demons,[3] she is inviting us into greater awareness of the views we hold, particularly the ones we cling to.

And here, in this radical teaching, Machig suggests we release *all* view. The supreme severance—that is, the ultimate thing to let go of—is our *attachment* to any particular view, however spiritual, grand, or correct we may imagine it to be. It's an invitation to abandon the solid ground that our beliefs seem to grant us. In Machig's severance tradition, the primary practice is to cut through our clinging to a solid, reified self. Our view—and the values, beliefs, and narratives that it consists of—is a cornerstone of our construct of self. Thus Machig suggests that "the supreme Severance is no view," also rendered as "the best view is no view."[4]

Any one view, of course, is limited, necessarily partial, incomplete. The more we cling to any one perspective, the more we lose access to others. We find ourselves caught in a game of proving and disproving, locked in a static posture that gives rise to defensiveness, self-righteousness, or zealotry. Unfortunately, human history is filled with conflicts and wars stemming from this kind of fundamentalism, however subtle or gross.

But the ultimate truth, the absolute view, is beyond any particular view, otherwise it too would be limited and partial. The absolute view includes an awareness of the possibility of all views and simultaneously transcends all views. The ultimate view is unconstrained, unlimited. Thus a dharmic saying suggests "Truth has no handles." Truth, the ultimate view, gives us nothing to grasp, nothing to stand on. Supreme severance is about letting go of all of our clinging in the realization that there is nothing we need to hold on to. It is our holding, in fact, that binds us. Thus Machig says sever your views! And perhaps in the space that remains we can rest in a view that is beyond concept, beyond perspectives; that is in fact "no view" at all.

This teaching lies at the heart of the famous Prajñāpāramitā mantra, dating back two thousand years to the Mahayana teachings that developed in the first millennium: GATE GATE PARAGATE PARASAMGATE BODHI SVAHA. Translated from Sanskrit, it means "Gone, gone, gone beyond, gone completely beyond, to awakening, so be it." Or one could say, "Let go, let go. Let go even more. Let go completely, to awakening." Traditionally the mantra is seen as cutting through the various ways we try to solidify our ideas of reality: reality is *this*; reality is *not this*; reality is *both this and that*; reality is *neither this nor that*. You can replace "this" and "that" with "good" and "evil," "solid" and "empty," "for me" and "against me," or any other binaries. The mantra cuts through any ideologies of eternalism (everything exists solidly, permanently), nihilism (nothing exists), and any variation in between. It is the supreme mantra that cuts through any kind of a view. And then what are we left with? *Bodhi*, "awakening." So be it.

What happens when I imagine living without views? Letting go of every belief, every label, every identity, every handle on reality, I let myself sit with the shakiness of not-knowing, allowing myself to rest into the felt experience of that emptiness. What reveals itself is something profoundly tender and simultaneously expansive. This is bodhicitta, the awakened heart—naked, open, and vast beyond measure. It's as though my eyes have been lifted from counting grains of sand. I raise my gaze to the vast clear sky, spreading evenly in all directions.

There is nothing to cling to. And it is all here: clear, brilliant, free. Not because I have lost anything but because I am open to everything.

From the point of view of our habitual embeddedness in dualistic perception, relinquishing absolutely all views will always sound confusing, idealistic, and impossible. But again, Machig is speaking to us from the other side of the dualistic divide. Within that, no view, no meditation, and no action is not only viable but self-evident. It is the truest and deepest refuge. Why? Because we are resting in totality. When you follow any one dearly held view to its root, you might first find idealism, but eventually you almost always find fear. The notion of relinquishing absolutely all our views may also inspire fear. Fear, however, is a product of the unknown, which is only possible in a dualistic environment. But Machig's land of no view is the nondual, all-good ground of being, the absolute nature of our mind. What Machig keeps reminding us is that this land is not far, far away. No, it is actually our home. Really, no view means to rest in totality rather than clinging to one view as opposed to another. This is why and how the view of no view cuts through fear so decisively.

> *Being without reference is itself unsurpassable genuine complete enlightenment.*[5]

When view is released, we open our arms into vast, unconditional embrace. We become the eyes of the universe. Like Avalokiteśvara, the bodhisattva of compassion, with their one thousand arms and eyes, we see more, engage more. We step into another's shoes. And another's. The seed of great compassion sprouts. From here, all views are accessible, all perspectives can be explored, all possibilities for action and non-action arise.

This may sound highly aspirational. Perhaps we can glimpse the possibility of a life unconfined by the yoke of our views. But does this mean that we never again espouse any view? Do we not vote for one candidate over another? Do we not pursue justice when we see the harms of injustice? The question is how we can hold the absolute view while living in the relative reality of everyday life. Here we offer the insightful words of the great Vietnamese Zen master Thich Nhat Hanh:

> The awakened man lives in the world of things like everyone else. When he sees a rose he knows that it is a rose, like everyone else. But the difference is that he is neither conditioned nor imprisoned by concepts. Concepts now become marvelous "skillful means" in his possession. The awakened man looks, listens, and distinguishes things, all the while being perfectly aware of the presence . . . that is the perfect and nondiscriminative nature of everything.[6]

Similarly, within the great severance of no view, we are no longer "conditioned or imprisoned" by our allegiance or defense of any particular view. Views now become skillful means of compassionate engagement, intelligently pliable rather than resolutely solid. We ask ourselves, *Which view is needed in any given situation to promote the most compassionate action?* Then, because we're not staking our identity on it, we let it go, like a useful but temporary tool. When we encounter "other" views, we may move from contempt and aggression to curiosity and compassionate inquiry. What is the thread of intelligence that lies at the heart of even this view? What can be learned here? Our fundamental point of departure is always the recognition of inseparability, indivisibility, and the shared ground of being that unconditionally holds us all. Thus, when we release our tight grasp to any *one* way, *all ways* reveal themselves as potential access points to truth.

These teachings are exquisitely profound, pointing beyond any concept, thought, structure, system into the ineffable, unceasing spacious radiant awareness of suchness itself, the natural state of Skymind. At the same time, they are about utter and radical simplicity. To let go of what we think and believe, to let go of the story about what's right and what's wrong, the judgments of what should be and what shouldn't, lands us squarely in the here and now, face to face with this moment. This is it. Right now. To awaken is to experience life *as it is*. I notice the sunlight on my page, the chirp of the midday crickets, the distant whir of a plane. Being completely with any one thing opens us to the totality of all things. Nothing is beside the point. We arrive just so. Incredible simplicity, ordinariness—supreme severance.

From the everyday point of view, we may never fully grasp this teaching; that itself would go against its prime message. But it can serve as an ongoing reminder. What can I release? What happens when I let go of this view? Do I feel the ground falling from beneath my feet? Can I relax into that unknown space and still return to my path in the world, my work, my responsibilities? Perhaps with a mind more flexible, a heart more open.

We cannot end these reflections without pointing to the irony inherent in this teaching. Supreme severance must include even letting go of any attachment to the ultimate dharmic view of no view. At some point on our path, we may have a sense that we "got it." There's an aha moment, and however subtly, we grasp, we hold, we want to retain that knowing, that meditative experience, that flash of insight. But even that seeming perfection of wisdom we must release and sever. Machig is pointing to a truth, a dharma beyond words, beyond preservation and solidification. This verse, if it is to mean anything, is written with self-erasing ink. We may put it in our pocket, but when we pull it out, all we see is a blank, open page.

Thus Machig warns,

Do not cling to anything at all.
Do not reference even the nonreferential.[7]

Ultimately Machig is inviting us not to create a foothold in the vast open space of no view. Don't let the glimpse of freedom become another shackle, another handle to grasp on to. Then it is no longer freedom. If the infinitude of nondual spaciousness is our true home, our very nature, we need not cling to it. It will be there no matter what. Clinging is distrust. Words are only pointers. We can rest back, over and over again, into the lap of the Great Mother.

20

The Meditation of Non-Meditation

The meditative stability of not meditating—
that is the supreme meditation.[1]

The meditation of non-meditation, a teaching often associated with the "highest"-level teachings of Dzogchen and Mahamudra, refers to the state of abiding continuously in the nature of mind, an ongoing wakefulness in which the notion of "practice" becomes moot. The great Dzogchen master Tulku Urgyen Rinpoche writes,

> When there is no more distraction throughout day and night,
> you are very close to the dharmakaya throne of non-meditation.[2]

At that point, meditating would be like a fish taking a break in order to go for a swim; it's been in the ocean all along. This non-meditation may seem out of reach, but there are helpful teachings tucked in Machig's verse that may benefit all of us.

The meditation of non-meditation arises in the recognition that there is ultimately no path to travel. As long as meditation is understood as a practice of gaining *something* or getting *somewhere*, it misses the ultimate point. So the supreme meditation, the absolute practice, is a state of non-meditation that strives for nothing, abiding simply and stably in spontaneous primordial awareness:

Everything is self-occurring mind,
so a meditator does not meditate.[3]

If we realize this—that everything we perceive is self-occurring mind that is inseparable from us, from "our" mind—then what is there to meditate on? With the realization of the integral nature of everything, there's the understanding that meditating or not meditating does not actually bring us closer or remove us further from our true condition.

Buddhahood is not conditional,
so how could one achieve it by conditioned effort?[4]

But what about the earlier chapters in this book and the detailed meditation instructions there? Simply put, in the absence of having realized the nature of mind, meditation remains one of the best things one could do with one's time in the meantime. Furthermore, meditation is not the only way to realize our true nature in this life, but it is arguably one of the best.

From a relative point of view, meditation is a method designed to focus our attention, develop insight and compassion, and stabilize awareness. More fundamentally, meditation is meant to familiarize us with our true nature, to come to know directly the ground of our being. But as a method, it is considered a means, not the endpoint. Like a good healer who makes themselves obsolete when the patient is cured, so too meditation—if its methods are skillful—points beyond itself. At some point we stop practicing and just let go into the brilliance of awakened mind itself.

Speaking from our personal experience, we know there is strength and purpose to the delineations and guidelines of any given practice. Our formal practice steers us to contemplations of this precious and impermanent life and invites us to an embodied remembrance of our web of interconnectedness, awakening the heartful, aching wish for the relief of suffering anywhere and everywhere. Unrelentingly, each practice holds up a mirror to our own minds, judgments, obsessions, doubts; our pride, hopes, and fears. Like polishing a dirty mirror, formal meditation gently—and sometimes not so gently!—wipes clean awareness. A radiance arises, the luminosity of cognizance. It's as though the world comes alive—the treed hillsides in their blanket of green, the piercing blue of the afternoon sky, even the haunting wail and whip of the unending wind. A palpable dissolution of the ordinary boundaries of self opens into vast spaciousness. There are moments when totality in all its magnificence arises—not as a thought, not as a feeling, just as is. Whatever effort we've been making vanishes. "I" am no longer "practicing" anything. The formality of "meditation" falls away into pure beingness.

Supreme meditation is beyond all attempts at cultivating a state of mind or heart. It is resting—simply, stably, doubtlessly, and without fixating on anything—in suchness itself. Meditation can help give a glimpse of what already is, of the reality of things as they are, but it is not creating anything that wasn't already there from the beginningless beginning. At a relative level, meditation is key to training the mind. Yet at a more absolute level, that which we are looking for is not to be found by effortful searching.

There are times when even our ideas about the ultimate goal of meditation become an obstacle. Thus Machig suggests,

> *Do not make the unborn a point of reference. . . .*
> *Do not meditate on nonthought.*[5]

The "unborn" refers to the nature of mind, the ground of being. It is unborn because it has never not been. It does not come into and out of existence the way all other things that arise from it do. Thus the ground of being is unborn and unceasing. It is tempting to hold this ultimate realization as a point of reference, as the highest aim of meditation. But Machig is saying, no, let go of any and all reification, even of that most absolute of goals. Having our true nature be a point of reference would be like a bird flying through the sky looking for space. It's not to be found in the way we normally find things. You might remember the verse of Machig's we discussed earlier that says just this: "[L]ook in the way of not looking. Your mind will not be seen by looking."[6]

The second line, "Do not meditate on nonthought," seems to undercut the very best meditation instructions we may have received. To free ourselves from the tight leash of thinking, even if only for a brief moment, is indeed a relief. At an everyday level, it is critical to know the possibility of nonthought, to realize that we do not have to be run by the seemingly perpetual motion of our thinking mind. Ultimately, in glimpsing and resting in the nature of mind, thought vanishes naturally. Not through effort but because there is absolutely nothing to hook on to, no duality to solidify. Tulku Urgyen Rinpoche notes,

> In the moment of unconfined empty cognizance there is no thought present.[7]

Even though the ultimate recognition of the nature of mind is free of thought, Machig warns us not to "meditate on nonthought," not to chase the state of not-thinking. We do not want to make nonthought yet another goal, a reified point of reference. In fact, within pure awareness, thoughts themselves are not really an issue. As Machig writes,

> *When one realizes mental nonengagement,*
> *mental activity need not be stopped;*
> *like a mirage, it vanishes in its own ground.*[8]

This is referred to as the "self-liberation" of thoughts, spontaneously releasing into the radiant space of awareness itself.

We might begin to sense some relief here as the tight grip on getting it right, on performing the correct meditation, begins to open. But what then should the object of our practice be?

> *In fact, there is no object to meditate on;*
> *that individual who is liberated from meditating*
> *is said to have unmistaken meditation.*[9]

No object. Nothing to meditate on. That's Machig's ultimate instruction for meditation!

To have an object of meditation means we are in a state of duality. It is implicit in our attempt to have a particular experience or reach a particular state that we are not already there. Ironically, our searching could thus be the exact thing that stands between us and the recognition of our true nature. There is no object to meditate on because the ground of being is not a *thing* to be found, a realization to be had, an insight to discover apart from who and what we already, incontrovertibly are. The liberation from meditating *on* anything is the liberation from searching altogether. And thus the unmistaken meditation, like non-meditation, is: Be as you are.

"Liberated from meditating, . . . unmistaken meditation" brings us face to face with the supremely ordinary. We're reminded of the wonderful stories of the mahasiddhas, the "great adepts," Tantric masters who lived outwardly simple lives as sesame seed grinders, arrow makers, fish flayers, shoemakers, tailors.[10] Their work was their meditation; they threaded the luminosity of reality through the eye of their sewing needle, shaved away dualistic delusions while planing the shaft of an arrow. Tantipa, the mahasiddha known as the Senile Weaver, sings

> I . . . weave the entirety of phenomena
> I weave the nonduality of expanse and awareness.[11]

One of our favorite stories is about Manibhadra, who had been introduced to the teachings secretly as a young girl and spent her days as a homemaker and mother. One day, as she was returning from the well, her pitcher of water fell to the ground and shattered. In that moment of rupture, she awakened to the recognition that there is no difference between inner space and outer space, whole and broken; she realized the vast totality of all. She stood there until late into the evening, when her concerned family found her still gazing speechless at the shards at her feet. We might say that it's not so much that she "got" something as that the normal confines and projections of her subjective reality burst, literally and figuratively. In that breaking open, she arrived fully, completely, with nowhere else to go. Aside from the tremendous impact of a seemingly small event, Manibhadra's story suggests that everyday occurrences can just as well be moments of recognition. How many times have you broken a glass?

Part of the beauty of the stories of the mahasiddhas is the seamlessness between their spiritual practice and ordinary activities. The demarcation between meditation and non-meditation is so porous that their whole lives can be considered the supreme meditation of non-meditation.

For those of us who have not yet attained the level of the mahasiddhas, we might experience this seamlessness in the simple ways that our meditation seeps into post-meditation, the times that follow any kind of formal practice, basically the rest of life. I (Charlotte) find this to be particularly true in my lengthier solitary retreats, when I have the great fortune to spend a couple of weeks up at Dragon's Nest, a remote cabin at Tara Mandala built into the rocks of a steep ridge. From the meditation platform, just the size of a large meditation cushion, I look out miles upon miles to the San Juan Mountains in the east, the La Plata Mountains in the west. I do a lot of meditating here—all kinds, from complex Vajrayana visualization practices; to highly ritualistic Chöd with its thigh-bone trumpet, drum, bell, and ancient melodies; to simply resting in open awareness. Sometimes I find myself just gazing out into the enormous space around me, marveling at the jet-black crows who effortlessly ride the buffeting winds like a riff of a dance tune. Sometimes I think about people I know, things I'd like to do, what my next meal will be. And sometimes I don't think at all.

Although solitary retreat is usually structured around four formal practice sessions per day, there's a hidden and secret purpose to this intensified alone time. Subtly, sometimes imperceptibly, the lines between formal meditation and whatever else I do begin to blur. There's a certain expansiveness of mind, lightness of body that I sense even as I wash my few dishes, comb my hair, go out to refill the water jug. Awareness becomes more pervasive, easefully moving from meditation to non-meditation. My contemplations of the boundlessness of the human heart are no different from my connections with the tiny ants I help out of the water bowl or the intimacy I feel with the chipmunk who visits every morning. So what is my meditation? Where does it begin? Where does it end?

So what, then, is the distinction between the seemingly mundane activities of the mahasiddhas and the everyday activities that fill our modern lives: driving to work, loading the dishwasher, downloading an app? On some level we might wonder whether we should have scrapped all our meditative efforts and simply watched a good game of soccer with a cold drink and a bag of chips. And yes, at one level, seen from the outside, these various activities are not so fundamentally different. But we'll remember Machig's initial verse, which highlights "the meditative *stability* of not meditating." This stability allows true rest to occur regardless of the activity, throughout the day's happenings. This stability allows the mahasiddha Tilopa to chop off the head of a fish as though he were slicing through confusion into the vast expanse of primordial awareness. The issue with ordinary non-meditation is that we're not aware, not awake, not cognizant. We're simply not meditating, but there is no meditative stability within that nonpractice. Formal meditation trains us in this stability so that we have the capacity to truly rest—ultimately, irrespective of whether we are meditating or not. And then, indeed, you might be resting in your true nature in a meditation posture or on a porch swing watching the neighborhood going about its daily business.

Finally, what can you do with these verses? Given that most of us, at least for now, are not mahasiddhas, how might they be useful in our lives? For one, they can remind us not to get stuck in our practice, not to make golden chains of our spiritual aspirations. To be "liberated from meditating" can invite us not to take ourselves so seriously but instead to hold our practice lightly. So often as we speak to fellow practitioners, they share a feeling of the weight of needing to accomplish something in their practice. At times, we suggest they stop meditating altogether, clear their day of any "spiritual" duties, expectations, and goals. Just let be. See what arises. When we liberate ourselves from having to meditate, meditation—when we find ourselves there—can truly be liberating.

Machig's verses also underline that we are never going to "get" it. We will not find the nature of mind, box it up nicely, and put it in our pockets. Luckily. This also undercuts any kind of spiritual arrogance that might arise in the development of meditative expertise, what Machig calls the demon of elation. If liberation is attained by cutting through ego-clinging, there is no self to become enlightened anyway. The "I" is wholly relative—a creature of duality. If enlightenment is anything, it is liberating from the "I." In all my meditative exploits, "I" am not busy getting somewhere. Indeed, it is actually all about the shattering of "I," like a pitcher of water falling to the ground.

21

The Action of Non-Action

In fact there is no object of activity;
that one who is liberated from acting
is said to have unmistaken activity.[1]

Activity—the creating, maintaining, destroying of things—is ceaseless. We move and we are moved, always, without fail. The wind moves the leaves of the ash tree outside my window, which moves threads of thought in my mind, which flows onto the page, into your eyes, which moves or stills your mind . . . Who or what has acted on whom? What is the object of activity?

We cannot cease from engaging. Stillness engages, motion engages. Silence engages, speech engages. Know that everything and anything you do moves something, someone. Because you are inescapably inseparable. You cannot escape activity.

All that moves moves within the expanse of inseparable continuity. There is no break, no gap. The activity does not start with me, nor does it end with me. There is no "one" acting. This is what it means to be liberated from acting.

It is foolish to think the wave can act apart from the ocean. It is foolish to think that I can "act" on anything independently of anything else. It is also foolish to think that I can choose not to "act" at all.

Machig says: liberate yourself from the notion that you are doing anything independently of anyone or anything else. Also liberate yourself from the notion that you could actually do nothing.

"Unmistaken activity" means: know yourself as ocean. Know that your activity as a wave is no other than the activity of the ocean. You can free yourself from the yoke of "I am doing something." Thus all doing is recognized as the great currents of the ocean itself.

To some extent, the conceptual mind may struggle to make sense of these teachings. Like water, they run through the sieve of our mental constructs. Yet they are not altogether foreign to other streams of thinking. Systems theory offers a similar view of interconnectedness that counters the supposition that action is ever an isolated occurrence. First articulated in the 1940s, Systems theory[2] suggests that one can best understand any component of a system by examining it in relation to all the other components within the system, and each system in relation to other systems. To truly understand the cell, for example, we must look at the body; to understand the body, we must understand the environment in which the body moves. Indeed, nothing functions or exists in isolation from the context in which it functions but always inextricably in relation to all others it is influenced by and influences. The person raises the hand, which lifts the hammer, which falls upon the nail, which pierces the wood. Together, reaching infinitely backward and forward, these movements link together as a continuum. There is no component that has acted independently from the others. In Machig's words, "There is no object of activity." Thus, we can understand non-action as the dynamic expression of nonduality.

You will recall Machig's verses quoted a couple of chapters ago on "no view" and the supreme meditation of "not meditating." She follows these by pointing to:

> *The supreme conduct of no conduct.*[3]

Conduct, like right action, means to choreograph our behavior in accordance with moral laws, ethical guidelines, and societal regulations. We follow. We do as we should. It is how we survive, as a culture, as a city, as a town, as a family. We drive stakes in the ground so that goodness and respect can prevail.

But supreme conduct arises from the unscripted knowing of our hearts, from the innate wakefulness that is our truest nature. The ultimate moral conduct arises without any rules whatsoever, free of any law or obligation, liberated from any reward or recognition. We do "good" when we are aligned in awakened relationship to all things. No prescribed "conduct" as such is necessary. Compassionate right action arises spontaneously.

Supreme conduct does not arise from doing what you should, nor from doing simply what you want. It does not mean anything goes. No. Supreme conduct is far more precise and subtly attuned with arising conditions than following either a whim or the letter of the law. Conduct is supreme as a dynamic expression of absolute wakefulness. There is no recipe to follow, not even your own. Whatever formulas have served you in the past are released in favor of the vibrant aliveness of total presence. It is acting from the unscripted, absolutely awake space of Skymind.

Thus, when Machig queries:

> *How should one engage in the activity methods of the conduct?*

—that is, how should I act in order to be a good human being?—the response is:

> *In fact there is no conduct to reference.*[4]

At ease, we are so attuned to the awakened heart-mind within us that our actions arise without effort as uncontrived, limitless compassion. We act not from our ideas or concepts but from the whisper of our Buddha Nature, the inner knowing of wholeness. From here we can, actually, trust ourselves, absolutely.

Joanna Macy, the brilliant Eco-Dharma teacher and author, writes about the development of the "eco-self," a broader notion of self that extends beyond our own skin into the natural world of which we are an integral part. Just as we don't need moral codes to remind us not to cut off our own leg, so too, she suggests, when our sense of self expands to include the trees and oceans and other sentient beings, we do not need ethical laws to remind us to act with compassion and care toward our environment: "Moral exhortation [becomes] irrelevant," Macy writes in *World as Lover, World as Self*.[5] Codes of conduct fall away when action arises from an embodied understanding of inseparability, the lived experience of inextricable interdependence.

At a relative level, we can appreciate the teaching on the action of non-action as a brilliant counterweight to our culture's idolization of doing for doing's sake. Busyness in and of itself relays status, importance, value. In contrast, traditional teachings warn of "lazy busyness," the continuous activity that lacks underlying intelligence regarding its purpose and motivation. We are busy in doing and lazy in wakefulness. The injunction to "just *do* something" is similarly mindless. There's a tempting relief that comes from staying busy. Like the roadrunner of the cartoons who runs off the cliff but keeps running midair, we feel that as long as we stay busy, we don't have to fear falling. We are *someone*; we are the one who is doing. To contemplate the action of non-action is to glimpse the possibility of activity arising not for its own sake but as an enlightened expression of basic aliveness.

What does the action of non-action mean for us in everyday life? Perhaps we can effort less. Perhaps our engagement can arise from a gentler inspiration than the aggression of getting stuff done or the numbness of obligation. Perhaps we can trust that in relating more directly with that which we love, with joy itself, compassionate conduct will arise of its own accord.

Supreme activity is action without effort.[6]

We've been inspired by the teachings of Barbara Dilley, the founder of Contemplative Dance Practice and founding faculty member of Naropa University, who teaches movement as meditation.[7] In this practice, movement does not follow a choreographed script to get somewhere or do something but rather unfolds as an outer expression of an inner dynamic. We surprise ourselves by our movement because there is no preconception and no expectation to make something particular happen. What is on stage and off stage becomes less important, less interesting of a distinction. The "pedestrian dancer" emerges. We recognize that all movement can be dance, the creative expression of embodied mindfulness. There's that beautiful moment of not knowing what will occur, surrendering into an experience of *being moved by* rather than trying to move one's body according to some preformulated choreography. It's not so easy at all. Just like the supreme action of non-action is not easy: neither flopping on the couch and doing nothing, nor mindlessly following a script step by step. It's a tightrope walk of supreme wakefulness and supreme relaxation.

When I release the bonds of "me" "doing" "something," the dance of life unfolds in a seamless interplay of movement. I am moved by and I am moving. The dance is certainly happening, there is no doubt. But it is not just me dancing. You are dancing, too; we are all dancing, actually. Like our ancestors have done for ages, we are dancing the world into existence, into the wholeness that it is.

22

Joy, Beauty, and Play

A wonderful sense of freedom arises in the liberation from beliefs, guidelines, and formulas for how to be and what to do. Without negating or rejecting any aspect of our existence, we come to see and love the phenomenal world with its luscious, painful, tender, and thorny occurrences as the very display of the ground of being. The possibility of joy, beauty, and play in everyday life arises. To recognize our true nature, to know and live from the ground of being is the ultimate source of joy. Thus, Machig inspires us to

> *Spread the news of dharma that arouses joy.*
> *Sing little songs about experience.*
> *Melancholy arises while you are thinking about what to do.*
> *Wherever you are is equable.*[1]

"Equable" here means of equal value or having a sense of equalness; wherever you are is not better or worse than any other place. Wherever you are is the right place; we might even say, the only place to be. It's our ruminations about being elsewhere that lead to melancholy, to doubt, anxiety, depression. The gap between where we are and where we imagine we should be creates the ground for dissatisfaction. Claiming where we are as worthy, as valuable, allows us to stand on our own two feet rather than leaning into an imagined alternate reality. Standing on our ground, we have the capacity to look around, to enter fully and intimately into the rich experience that is only ever happening now.

But Machig is suggesting even more. Claim joy in this moment, she says. Right as you are, right where you are. There's something quite revolutionary in this invitation to be with things as they are—one of the translations of the word *dharma*—and to find joy in this.

Joy, of course, has many layers. Traditional Mahayana Buddhist teachings describe the four immeasurables of loving-kindness, compassion, sympathetic joy, and equanimity as qualities of the awakened heart that we cultivate in our aspiration to benefit others. Immeasurable joy is often referred to as "sympathetic" as it arises in seeing and partaking in the happiness and fulfillment of others, thus pointing to its transpersonal nature. It is also described as "the joy beyond all sorrows," not because we have overcome all sorrows but because we have resourced a deeper wellspring—the joy of being itself, the joy of life itself. Not because anything has gone particularly our way but simply because there is worth, value, and brilliance in being aware, being awake, being alive. This joy is immeasurable because it cannot be quantified by the number of reasons we may or may not have for being joyful. It is also immeasurable because it is unending and infinite in its capacity. Once recognized, this joy can be shared with all, just like the air we breathe. This joy is never limited by circumstances. It is a human birthright that can never be rescinded or denied. This joy lies at the very heart of life itself.

The Tibetan teachings similarly point to a more absolute notion of joy (Skt. *mahāsukha*; Tib. *dewachen*) described as great bliss. This bliss is considered the very essence of what and who we are. At our core, we are made of bliss, both at the level of the subtle body and as the very nature of pure awareness. At the physical level, this is traditionally understood in terms of subtle energies that compose and move through the body. An intricate map of our subtle body outlines an array of channels, currents, and essences. Various meditative practices bring consciousness to this network, allowing clarity, radiance, and awareness to suffuse the body. The body itself awakens to its natural state of bliss.[2]

Fundamentally, our awakened nature *is* great bliss. Again, this is not just the bliss that arises as a result of particularly pleasurable experiences but the primordial bliss of abiding in our true nature, the luminous and vast radiance of beingness itself. We may come to know this bliss, this ultimate joy, through meditation in glimpsing the nature of mind, but it is never created or manufactured. Rather, in glimpsing the nature of mind, we see the great bliss that has always already been there. We see the fuel and source of life that activates all our doing, knowing, being. We see ourselves as we are; reality as it truly is. To know our true nature is to know great bliss. To know great bliss is to know our true nature.

Sometimes joy is quite simple, even ordinary, met unexpectedly in the gaps between whatever we're busy doing. The sudden ray of sunlight across the page, the smile of a stranger, the warm belly of the cat lying on my lap—these moments can elicit an inner joyfulness even in their fleeting simplicity. Indeed, Machig invites us to "sing *little* songs about experience," not the great aria of our most sublime insights. It's more like singing in the shower, whistling in the car, humming while taking out the trash. Claiming the joy of the ordinary moment. This too is a practice, one that we can cultivate at any moment of time.

I (Charlotte) remember my Austrian grandmother, whom we lovingly called Matsch, as an exemplar of simple, ordinary joy. As a child, I considered her the happiest person I knew. She was probably the poorest as well, living in a tiny two-room apartment with no bathroom, a shared toilet two flights down, in a small industrial town in Styria. Her life was not easy, spanning two world wars, raising three children with minimal means. Yet I remember her taking joy in the simplest of things: dancing to her only record, a Harry Belafonte single; savoring the homemade sausage from the local butcher; cooking the apricot-filled potato dumplings I loved so much. My favorite photo is of her standing beside a tall, pink rosebush, her face lit up in total delight at the sight of the exquisite blossoms, which seem to be opening in response to her admiring gaze. It is the joyful look of unequivocal appreciation of simple beauty. Her lesson to me was that it doesn't take much to find joy. In fact, if we look around, we can discover joy and beauty in the smallest of life's infinite offerings.

Our relative experiences of joy can reveal to us the possibility of ultimate joy. Usually we establish a link between our experience of joy and its cause. *If* I get X, *then* I am happy. *If* I get love, recognition, acknowledgment . . . *then* I will feel joyful, content, fulfilled. But, of course, this is circumstantially dependent joy, always reliant on X. It is far from immeasurable. Conditional joy is just that; it arises when the tides are in our favor and falls when they are not. Spiritual traditions tend to reject relative experiences for this reason; because they are conditional, they are unreliable. Conditional joy is not a lasting refuge. It pulls us into a cycle of hope and fear, wishing that we meet the right conditions, fearing we will not.

The problem here is not really the relative nature of joy. It's rather our *clinging* to the particular conditions that elicit our joy, as though our joy were dependent upon those specific circumstances. In fact, it's about clinging, period. If we allow ourselves to relax into the felt experience of joy, however it was brought about, we can tap into a more unencumbered, liberated, and unconditional form of joy. We can afford to loosen the tight grip on the object of our joy—the compliment, the success, the newly bought item, the rose. In fact, we must because, like all things, the objects of our joy are themselves changeable and impermanent. Instead, holding it lightly, we recognize and appreciate the object not only as a gift of joy but as a reminder of the inherent capacity for joy that lies within us as a human birthright, an essential expression of our being. Then when we pass the rose again and see that it has wilted, we can smile at the unconditional joy, the "joy without sorrow" that still courses through our veins.

When we come to trust joy as innate to our being, the smallest ordinary joy becomes a reminder. Or as Walt Whitman so beautifully wrote, "I find letters from God, dropped in the street, and every one is signed by God's name."[3] The ray of sunlight isn't a random moment of awareness but an invitation to recognize—with supreme joy!—the very ground of being that's been there from the beginningless beginning.

There's an invitation here to become intimate with all things, to allow the edges as well as the soft curves of the world to touch us in the intensity of tenderness. Perhaps we can lean in to listen to the distant hum of the plane, the gurgling whisper of the mountain stream. Soak in the warmth of rock. Wonder at the green sprout that pushes itself through the sidewalk crack. To be intimate is to trust. To be intimate is to let my skin reveal itself to yours, to let us exchange across evanescent boundaries. Perhaps we can, after all, abide in the ever-unfolding joy of making love with our beautiful, brilliant, ephemeral world.

Beauty

Joy and beauty are close cousins. Just as mundane joy can open the way to unconditional joy, so too the appreciation of beauty can expand to sacred view. In the Vajrayana tradition, the practitioner trains in pure perception (*dak nang*) through which all phenomena are recognized as ultimately pure, beyond the temporary illusions of good or bad, pretty or ugly. In a post-meditation prayer written by the great seventeenth-century teacher Terdag Lingpa, the practitioner aspires to regard all beings as buddhas; all sounds as sacred (*mantra*); and all thoughts as awakened mind (*rigpa*).[4] A vision of sacred world recognizes that *all* things, no matter how we might perceive them, are actually emanations of the ground of being.

Sacred view is the fruition of the path, arising naturally as we relax into the groundless ground that supports and holds us unconditionally. Machig describes the world as

> *the adornment of dharmakaya.*[5]

"Dharmakaya" refers to the ultimate nature of reality; the empty, radiant source of all. And here Machig suggests that the world and all appearances arise as the adornment of the dharmakaya. We generally think of adornment as an add-on, as that which takes place after the essential matters have been taken care of. First you put on your pants, shirt, and socks; then, if you have time, you might adorn yourself. But here the suggestion is that absolute reality, the ground of being, is expressed in and through all things ultimately. Manifest reality is the effortless adornment of ultimate reality. Like a mountain meadow coming alive with a thousand wildflowers, the colorful, chaotic multiplicity of everyday life is the radiant face of the absolute. The ocean wave glistening in the evening sun, the tender green leaf bursting from its bud, and even the discarded cigarette butt on the city sidewalk—they all are expressions of the ultimate source that is infinite, radiant, inherently pure. The ground of being reveals itself *as* beauty, naturally and of its own accord. Beauty is not imposed from the outside. It's not adventitious, a supplement, or incidental. Sacred view is when we recognize reality as an adornment of the ground of being.

Machig further elucidates:

Self-arising without attachment is not inflation.
It is said to be the adornment of dharmakaya.[6]

"Self-arising" refers to natural unfolding without contrivance. There is no attachment, nothing to hold on to. We can't own the beauty of the world. We can't possess the adornment of the dharmakaya. Nor do we need to work harder to look for beauty. By relaxing more, we come to rest in the beauty that is and that is also us. In perceiving and appreciating it, we simultaneously let it go, just as the wave recedes into the ocean.

Like the beauty produced by a lovely face,
self-occurrence adorns itself—
there is no cause for arrogance.[7]

This beauty has no self-importance, no self-consciousness, no inflation. It self-arises naturally and effortlessly, without a goal or motive. Just as the beauty of a lovely face is not fabricated and cannot be considered a personal achievement, so too the beauty of reality is not manufactured or objectified. Adornment happens. Beauty happens.

Since this is fruitional beauty, we may ask what this all means for us in daily life? It's a powerful invitation to see beauty wherever we can, finally even in that which we might initially consider mundane or even ugly. To find beauty entails allowing an intimacy to arise with whatever we encounter, until the line between self and other opens into vibrant, living relationship. It means to let the thing itself speak to us, reveal itself so that its inherent beauty self-arises as clearly as its shape, color, and size, like the rose exposing itself to the loving eyes of my grandmother. Then no matter where we look, beauty simply is.

Machig probably would have appreciated haiku, a form of poetry developed in Japan beginning in the seventeenth century, as the supreme "little song about experience." We might say that the great haiku poets were continuously resting in the nature of mind, in supreme intimacy with their surroundings, free from subject-object duality. Thus the most ordinary perception could be appreciated as an exquisite and unique expression of ultimate reality. Haiku puts into words what is seen, heard, or sensed directly in the moment. Its three lines are uncomplicated and direct, intimating the profundity of undistracted presence.

Evening prayer bell –
ripe persimmon
thumps to the ground[8]

The haiku poet appreciates the smallest occurrence as an exquisite reflection of the whole. In entering fully into the simplicity of things as they are, in laying bare the absolutely ordinary, haiku exposes the deepest truths of life. In celebrating the ordinary, the extraordinary is revealed.

In the summer rain
the path
has disappeared[9]

The ordinary, like the infinite, offers a refuge from the endless ruminations of meaning-making and deliberation, the entanglements of judgment, the suffering of choice. The magic of simplicity is that it need not take itself so seriously. To write a haiku, like "singing a little song about experience," awakens aliveness, intimacy, the fullness—and fleetingness—of the moment.

~ EXERCISE ~

An Exercise in Simple Beauty

Get up and go for a little walk—around your room, to the window, outside if you can. Or simply turn your head, open your ears, your sense perceptions. Notice what you notice: the color and shapes of things, the silence or clang of things, the touch and feel of things. Gather your perceptions. Then write them into three short lines. The traditional haiku format is three lines of five syllables, seven syllables, five syllables. Keep it simple. Nothing fancy.

Play

To enter the path without myself, delightful! . . .
To cut the rope of saving face, delightful!
To tear down the wall of conformity, delightful!
To be free of all fixation, delightful![10]

Here, in the fruition of the path, we have the bandwidth to appreciate the sheer magnificence of this particular situation we find ourselves in, what we call our life, and the exquisite intimacy, complexity, and intensity of being alive in this moment.

We are invited into the possibility of play, not as an idle activity relegated to the young but as a vibrantly creative, delightfully spontaneous, and joyful response to the life force that pulses inside of us. As we've noted previously, resting in the ground of being does not mean there is no activity. "Just rest" is nowhere near an invitation to dispassionately disengage from life. Activity occurs always, unimpededly, irrepressibly, just as the wind moves and the waves rush. Life is movement. Even in death, the apparent stillness of a corpse composts into the next iteration of emergent life. But within fruition our activity arises from a different place: the embodied knowing of wholeness. Action is not a response to lack but rather an expression of primordial fullness.

The Hindu tradition considers the movement of life *līlā*, "divine play." The Tibetan Buddhist tradition speaks of *rolpa*, "display" or "play," to describe how wisdom spontaneously manifests as appearances. In either case, the heavily contracted, stolid seriousness of reality is freed into exquisite playfulness, a supreme lightness of being. This is not simple frivolity, an escape from reality, but rather the essential nature of it. It comes from an even deeper immersion into the immense potentiality that lies in every ounce of life. Indeed, in play anything and everything becomes possible; nothing is confined to a singular, solid identity. Everything is alive. This is the magic of play and why it is indeed divine.

When we truly realize that the origin of absolutely everything is the nondual, all-good nature of mind, we cut the root of fear. Existential fear is a product of dualistic fixation. There's a way whereby people get more serious the more "sacred" they think things are. But realization brings an absence of fear that leaves lighthearted joy in its stead.

When our children were young, our living room was transformed into a landscape of caves, tunnels, and castles. Sheets and blankets became silken canopies, fortress walls, tall turrets. The white enamel pot became a throne. The ladle a sword. The clothespin an iron gate. Everything could become anything. In play we open our minds to include whatever we encounter. Nothing is too meager, secondary, or beside the point. We drink water like wine and sing like an angel. When children play, they engage absolutely, immerse themselves without doubt. When we awaken to our true nature, to Skymind, we live in the brilliant fullness of all things. The spontaneity of play is without hesitation or second-guessing.

Machig frames her teachings on play like this:

[Y]ogins with . . . realization
need not block carefree conduct.[11]

The yogin (Tib. *naljor*) is literally one who is in union with the natural state, joined with fundamental reality. They recognize things as they are: self, other, and all phenomena as integral, continuous, and infinitely colorful manifestations of the ground of being. Carefree conduct is spontaneous action that arises as an expression of this recognition. Freed of self-interest, it becomes the most appropriate, skillful, and compassionate response to any given moment. Rather than knee-jerk reactivity, this spontaneity is the play of wisdom itself.

When you rest within great effortlessness
in the nature of phenomena, once free of inflation,
blessing occurs without exertion.[12]

Blessings are the basic goodness of life itself that radiates endlessly through all things, all beings. Not sometimes, not conditionally, but always. Blessings are not deserved or undeserved. They are like the warm rays of the sun that shine continuously. They well up from inside. They are, after all, our true nature.

As we come to the end of our Skymind journey, we arrive, as we might expect, where we began: abiding in the brilliant wholeness of primordial awareness, the radiant nature of all. Machig's words of wisdom point beyond themselves, like rainbow arrows that are already dissolving into the supreme wakefulness of your own mind.

Conclusion

You may remember the story from Machig's early life in which her teacher, Sönam Lama, inquires into her genuine understanding of the *Prajñāpāramitā Sūtra* that she was so skilled at reciting, recounted in chapter 11. It was in ensuing deeper personal contemplation of the text that she awoke to a fresh understanding, leading her to make changes in her life and enter a path of radical, honest practice. Similarly, Machig gives us this encouragement to make her words of wisdom come alive and take root in our direct experience:

To be wise in words is not to be wise;
to be wise in meaning is to be wise . . .
Meaning is the realm of unborn emptiness . . .
Rest in the meaning, noble child.[1]

Having glimpsed Skymind, how do we apply these insights to the everyday fabric of our lives? How can we be wise in meaning so that our being in the world is infused with genuine understanding?

If we take Machig's teaching to heart, it means that the very brilliance and wakefulness of our true nature calls on us to meet ourselves and others with ongoing fresh curiosity, openness, and unending compassion. In our own experience, meditation has been the most helpful practice to remind ourselves of this truth and to stabilize our embodied awareness of this deeper nature.

What the ongoing path of meditation looks like will differ from person to person. For many, a regular daily practice creates an unquestionable support, like weaving a thread of luminous wakefulness through the fabric of the everyday. In this case, you can begin your day with twenty to sixty minutes of Skymind meditation, or find a time of day that best suits your temperament and schedule. This discipline, although difficult to establish for some, can have incredible delight and joy in it as it connects us regularly with the most profound source of inspiration.

Longer periods of solitary retreat can often provide the opportunity to remember and reconnect at a much deeper level with the innate wakefulness that is our very nature. Our experience of long periods of Skymind meditation in solitary retreat has been profound. Traditionally, a retreat day includes four formal meditation sessions during the course of the day. It is ideal to find a place for retreat where you will have no contact with other people for the duration of your retreat and, if at all possible, one that offers spacious views, so that the expansive environment around you can support expansive awareness within you. If you've never engaged in a solitary retreat before, you might start with three to five days, then extend your retreats. It is best to receive some guidance from a meditation instructor or teacher to support your retreat.

Once you have established your Skymind meditation practice, short moments of open awareness, many times a day, can serve as sparks of recognition even as we move through our busy lives. What might it be like to abide in Skymind continuously?

We hope you've encountered verses from Machig in the pages of this book that will continue to echo in your heart and mind. Take them with you into your meditation and onto the road, so they can serve as ongoing reminders and pointers, rainbow arrows that shoot into the brilliant sky-like nature of your awareness.

The point is to find your own way. What your way looks like may change over time. Follow your joy, follow your inspiration. Or as Lama Tsultrim would say, "Let your wisdom lead you to wisdom." You might consider your relationship to meditation like a love affair: At times you are deeply attuned, magnetized, inspired; you can't wait to sit down to practice. At other times, you feel your practice is quite ordinary, maybe even mundane. And again there may be times when you feel quite frustrated with your practice; it annoys you, bores you. But as in all long-term relationships, the point is to keep meeting your practice in all its varied forms. Then its depth, brilliance, and profound gift can reveal itself. The gift of recognizing your true Skymind nature, the nature of all.

Appendix: Machig's Verses

The verses quoted in this book come from the following sources:

Chöd: The Sacred Teachings on Severance. Vol. 14 of ***The Treasury of Precious Instructions: Essential Teachings of the Eight Practice Lineages of Tibet.*** Compiled by Jamgön Kongtrul, translated by Sarah Harding. Snow Lion, 2016.

- ✧ *AB*: "Another Bundle: Answers to Questions on the Esoteric Instructions of the Perfection of Wisdom," by Machik Lapdrön.
- ✧ *EB*: "The Essential Bundle: From the Severance of Evil Object, Esoteric Instructions on the Perfection of Wisdom," by Machik Lapdrön.
- ✧ *EUA*: "The Eight Uncommon Appendices," by Machik Lapdrön.
- ✧ *GBP*: "The Great Bundle of Precepts: The Source Text of Esoteric Instruction on Severance, the Profound Perfection of Wisdom," by Machik Lapdrön.
- ✧ *HTW*: "A Hair's Tip of Wisdom: A Precious Treasure Trove to Enhance the Original Source Text of Severance, the Esoteric Instructions on the Perfection of Wisdom," by Machik Lapdrön and Drung Sarupa Kunga Paljor.
- ✧ *VP*: "Vajra Play: Questions and Answers on the Profound Severance of Evil Object," by Machik Lapdrön.

Machig Labdrön and the Foundations of Chöd. Jérôme Edou. Snow Lion, 1996.

- ✧ *MLI*: "Machig's Last Instructions." Translated from Kunpang Tsoöndrü Sengé, *The Concise Life Story of Machig Labdrön*, fols. 445–457.

Machik's Complete Explanation: Clarifying the Meaning of Chöd. Translated and edited by Sarah Harding. Snow Lion, 2003.

- ✧ *QGM*: "The Questions of Gangpa Muksang"

Women of Wisdom. Tsultrim Allione. Snow Lion, 2000.

- ✧ *WOW*: "The Biography of Machig Lapdron (1055–1145)"

Verses

Listed in the order they appear in the book

Don't you consider the enemy in a dream
as coming from yourself?
GBP23

Once one's mind is recognized for sure,
there's no need to establish buddha from elsewhere.
GBP23

The defining characteristic of mind
Is to be primordially empty like space;
The realization of the nature of mind
Includes all phenomena without exception.
MLI166

Since it abides inherently, release anger and desire.
Since it occurs naturally, don't take it up in mind . . .
Since it is unborn, don't mentally cut it off.
Since it is unceasing, don't construct a support.

Since it is transparent, don't be biased.
Since it is all-pervasive, don't take sides.
Since it is oneself, don't hope for another . . .
Since it is without contrivance, stay natural . . .
Since it is without meeting or parting, don't set a time . . .
Be utterly certain that it is like space.
HTW119–120

Since there is no path to traverse,
rest in the basic ground, noble child.
AB137

Leaving oneself behind and searching,
even after many millions of aeons
of practicing, [one] will not attain it.
GBP18

Don't search, don't practice; rest in your nature.
GBP18

In fact there is nothing to see . . .
AB135

There is no intention within the unborn.
There is nowhere to go within the unceasing.
Still, once naturally liberated without reference—
Just *lhang nge lhan ne lham me* (vivid, quiet, radiant).
AB138

Awakening is actualized by realizing rootlessness.
So then rest relaxed . . .
Rest just so with everything.
GBP20

The measure of freedom from inflation is fearlessness.
VP141

[R]est the body in the way of a corpse.
Rest in the way of being ownerless.
Rest the mind in the way of the sky.
AB131

[Demons] are classified as four:
tangible [demon] and intangible [demon],
the [demon] of exaltation, and the [demon] of inflation.
All are included in the [demon] of inflation.
GBP14

That which is called "[demon]" is not some actual great big black thing that scares and petrifies whomever sees it. A [demon] is anything that obstructs the achievement of freedom. . . . [T]here is no greater [demon] than this fixation to a self. So until this ego-fixation is cut off, all the [demons] wait with open mouths. For that reason, you need to exert yourself at a skillful method to sever the [demon] of ego-fixation.
QGM117

The root [demon] is one's own mind.
The [demon] lays hold through clinging and attachment
in the cognition of whatever objects appear.
GBP14

[J]udging the appearances that arise to our senses,
negating or affirming them, is the tangible [demon].
GBP14

Decisively cutting through inflation liberates fixation to real things.
As in cessation, appearances do not stop.
GBP18

[A]ll thought-provoking mental hopes and fears
are one's own [demons] rising up to oneself.
GBP15

. . . [M]ental attachment in which one delights and exalts . . . causes great arrogance and pride and becomes an obstacle on the path to freedom.
QGM119

Conduct yourself without fixating on yourself.
GBP23

[O]ne errs in the distraction of loving and hating friend and foe.
Attachment and aversion are the [demons] of self-fixation.
HTW109

Other than your own decisive cutting through inflation,
nothing at all will happen externally.
HTW116

Those of superior scope rest within nonconceptual equipoise without fear or anxiety no matter what [demons] arise. Those of middling scope seek the one who has the feelings [of demons arising] and understand that [demons] are their own mind and rest within mind's unborn nature itself. Those of inferior scope give over the body to the dangerous obstructors and rest in non-action within the state of mental nonrecollection.
EB155

Remain like a bunch of straw cut loose.
MLI167

From the realm of phenomena's great expanse of clarity
any thoughts and memories whatsoever may arise.
GBP15

This body of ours is impermanent like a feather on a high mountain pass,
This mind of ours is empty and clear like the depth of space.
Relax in that natural state, free of fabrication.
MLI167

Therefore you should abide without distraction in the meaning of the equipoised mind itself. Remaining undistracted in the meaning of the abiding nature in that way will bring about the power and energy of blessing.
EB156

Here is the method of resting in suchness:
in being unimpeded and fixation free,
you rest naturally without contrivance . . .
[T]here is nothing to do on purpose . . .
Relinquish fixation and rest at ease.
HTW118

While concentrated by concentration, relax by relaxing.
Released by release, let go freely.
Freed by freedom, rest by resting.
That's the resting place of meditation.
EB148

[L]ook in the way of not looking.
Your mind will not be seen by looking.
Not seeing in itself is the nature of phenomena.
If you see [something,] it is not the nature of phenomena.
AB130

All teaching of phenomena is mere symbols.
Do not dwell on books; do real practice.
HTW107

In the same way, mind itself
Has no support, has no object:
Let it rest in its natural expanse without any fabrication.
MLI165

At first, you came alone. In the end, you will go alone. So now also you must train alone.
VP142

If you don't know occurring circumstances as supports,
even with a lofty view, you will lose your way.
AB134

[Not to dwell in the space of the Great Mother,]
although performing characterized virtuous acts,
is to remain a long time in cyclic existence.
AB127

People who engage in negative actions
are like little kids clutching fire . . .
It produces your own sorrow. . . .
. . . [T]o commit negative actions
is exceedingly stupid.
AB125

Carry the load of appearing conditions. . . .
If you don't carry the load of all phenomena,
the remedy of peace and happiness can't liberate you.
GBP27

At the time that adverse conditions occur,
it is crucial to know the vital point of taking it on.
HTW110

No matter what sickness occurs in the manifesting
    circumstances,
know that each one is a training exercise.
AB134

Confess all your hidden faults,
Approach all that you find repulsive!
Whoever you think you cannot help, help them!
Anything you are attached to, let go of it!
Go to the places that scare you, like cemeteries!
Sentient beings are as limitless as the sky,
Be aware!

Find the Buddha inside yourself!
(Words of Padampa Sangye)
WOW181

Buddha enacts the welfare of sentient beings
as in the example of the precious jewel:
through altruism that arises without concept.
There are unimaginable buddha qualities
in not fixating on one's own concepts.
AB136

Be without presumption, free of the inflation of helping or harming,
as are foliage and boulders and such.
You should understand suchness.
HTW110

Like a fine cow nourishing a small calf,
when she helps herself to a full belly
it sustains the small calves and such.
If one's own inflation is decisively cut off,
sentient beings will surely become liberated.
No doubt the welfare of others will be achieved.
GBP21

Like a simpleton with a full belly,
rest in the complete eradication of concepts.
GBP22

Like a person who has finished their work,
rest instantly with a satisfied mind.
GBP22

Even the spiritual powers of yidam deities
arise to the mind from the meditating mind.
Therefore it is oneself, not another.
GBP23

Demons and devils and such are subdued by splendor.
GBP21

Keep to secluded strongholds of confidence without inflation.
HTW104

Inspire your own mood by yourself.
HTW104

Right now, death is the absolute truth.
EUA179

Being free of striving . . .
You will dwell on the ground of the unborn. . . .
the ground of no birth and death.
AB127

In the abiding nature of mind itself, birth and death, clean and dirty, enemy and friend, and so forth are not at all established.
EUA184

[T]he person who is liberated from accomplishing
is said to have the unmistaken fruition.
AB135–136

Without the realization that results are unreal,
whatever effort is made toward achieving it
will not become the attainment of freedom.
GBP26

The supreme Severance is no view. . . .
The meditative stability of not meditating—
that is the supreme meditation. . . .
. . . the supreme conduct of no conduct.
GBP16–17

Do not cling to anything at all.
Do not reference even the nonreferential.
HTW112

Everything is self-occurring mind,
so a meditator does not meditate.
GBP16

Buddhahood is not conditional,
so how could one achieve it by conditioned effort?
GBP26

Do not make the unborn a point of reference. . . .
Do not meditate on nonthought.
AB135

When one realizes mental nonengagement,
mental activity need not be stopped;
like a mirage it vanishes on its own ground.
GPB25

In fact, there is no object to meditate on;
that individual who is liberated from meditating
is said to have unmistaken meditation.
AB135

In fact there is no object of activity;
that one who is liberated from acting
is said to have unmistaken activity.
AB135

How should one engage in the activity methods of the conduct?
In fact there is no conduct to reference.
AB131

Supreme activity is action without effort.
MLI169

Spread the news of dharma that arouses joy.
Sing little songs about experience.
Melancholy arises while you are thinking about what to do.
Wherever you are is equable.
AB132

Self-arising without attachment is not inflation.
It is said to be the adornment of dharmakaya.
GBP20

Like the beauty produced by a lovely face,
self-occurrence adorns itself—
there is no cause for arrogance.
GBP16

To enter the path without myself, delightful! . . .
To cut the rope of saving face, delightful!
To tear down the wall of conformity, delightful!
To be free of all fixation, delightful!
HTW118–119

[Y]ogins with . . . realization
need not block carefree conduct.
GBP25

When you rest within great effortlessness
in the nature of phenomena, once free of inflation,
blessing occurs without exertion.
AB133

To be wise in words is not to be wise;
to be wise in meaning is to be wise . . .
Meaning is the realm of unborn emptiness . . .
Rest in the meaning, noble child.
AB137

Notes

Introduction

1. Dzogchen (literally "great perfection") and Mahamudra ("great seal") are considered the highest teachings in the Nyingma and Kagyu schools of Tibetan Buddhism, respectively, and espouse a nondual view.
2. We are particularly grateful to Sarah Harding's translations found in *Chöd: The Sacred Teachings on Severance*, vol. 14 in *The Treasury of Precious Instructions: Essential Teachings of the Eight Practice Lineages of Tibet*, compiled by Jamgön Kongtrul (Snow Lion, 2016); as well as Jérôme Edou's translations in *Machig Labdrön and the Foundations of Chöd* (Snow Lion, 1996), which have made Machig's source teachings available to a broader audience.
3. A koan is a riddle that Zen Buddhists use during meditation to help them unravel greater truths about the world and about themselves. Zen masters have been testing their students with these questions or phrases for centuries.
4. Dampa Sangye's teachings on *Zhije*, the Pacification of Suffering, are found in Sarah Harding, trans., *Zhije: The Pacification of Suffering*, vol. 13 in *The Treasury of Precious Instructions*, compiled by Jamgön Kongtrul (Snow Lion, 2019).
5. For more extensive biographies of Machig Labdrön, see Jérôme Edou, *Machig Labdrön and the Foundations of Chöd* (Snow Lion, 1996); Tsultrim Allione, *Women of Wisdom* (Snow Lion, 2000); Sarah Harding, trans. and ed., introduction to *Machik's*

Complete Explanation: Clarifying the Meaning of Chöd (Snow Lion, 2003).

6. Machig Labdrön, "The Great Bundle of Precepts," in *Chöd: The Sacred Teachings on Severance*, vol. 14 in *The Treasury of Precious Instructions: Essential Teachings of the Eight Practice Lineages of Tibet,* comp. Jamgön Kongtrul, trans. Sarah Harding (Snow Lion, 2016), 23.
7. Allione, *Women of Wisdom*, 196.
8. At times depicted as a female deity, Prajñāpāramitā is a representation of the ground of being. *Prajñāpāramitā* (Skt.) refers to transcendent wisdom (literally "wisdom across the other shore"); it is not knowledge that involves the duality of a subject (knower) and an object (that which is known). Rather, it is the wisdom that transcends all dualities, the awareness of the ultimate nature of reality. In the early Mahayana, in the first–second centuries, Prajñāpāramitā was envisioned as the Great Mother who gives birth to all the buddhas; she is the primordial wisdom out of which awakening arises.
9. Edou, *Machig Labdrön and the Foundations of Chöd*, 152.
10. Machig Labdrön, "Great Bundle of Precepts," 23.
11. Machig Labdrön, "Machig's Last Instructions," in *Machig Labdrön and the Foundations of Chöd*, by Jérôme Edou (Snow Lion, 1996), 166.
12. *Lojong* (mind training) consists of fifty-nine slogans developed by Chekawa Yeshe Dorje in the twelfth century, based on the teachings of the eleventh-century Bengali teacher Atīśa Dīpaṅkara Śrījñāna.
13. Transmission in the Vajrayana tradition is given from a qualified teacher to a student in order to engage in various meditative practices. It generally includes an explanation (Tib. *tri*), an oral transmission (Tib. *lung*), and an empowerment (Tib. *wang*).

1. The Basic Ground

1. "Basic goodness" is a term used by Chögyam Trungpa in reference to Buddha Nature. See *Shambhala: The Sacred Path of the Warrior* (Shambhala, 1988), 35.

2. Machig Labdrön, "A Hair's Tip of Wisdom," in *Chöd: The Sacred Teachings on Severance*, vol. 14 in *The Treasury of Precious Instructions: Essential Teachings of the Eight Practice Lineages of Tibet*, comp. Jamgön Kongtrul, trans. Sarah Harding (Snow Lion, 2016), 119–20.
3. What we refer to as "ultimate reality"" is *Prajñāpāramitā* in the original translation, literally "transcendent wisdom" (see note 8 in the introduction).
4. Āryadeva the Brahmin, "The Grand Poem on the Perfection of Wisdom," in *Machig Labdrön and the Foundations of Chöd*, trans. Jérôme Edou (Snow Lion, 1996), 17. Āryadeva was a teacher of Dampa Sangye and is thus in a direct lineage with Machig Labdrön.

2. Rest in Your Nature

1. Machig Labdrön, "Another Bundle," in *Chöd: The Sacred Teachings on Severance*, vol. 14 in *The Treasury of Precious Instructions: Essential Teachings of the Eight Practice Lineages of Tibet*, comp. Jamgön Kongtrul, trans. Sarah Harding (Snow Lion, 2016), 137.
2. Machig Labdrön, "Great Bundle of Precepts," 18.
3. Machig Labdrön, "Great Bundle of Precepts," 18.
4. Joko Beck, *Everyday Zen* (HarperCollins, 1989), 24.
5. Chögyam Trungpa, *Cutting Through Spiritual Materialism* (Shambhala, 1987), 13.
6. Machig Labdrön, "Great Bundle of Precepts," 23.

3. Groundless Ground

1. Machig Labdrön, "Hair's Tip of Wisdom," 119–20.
2. Machig Labdrön, "Another Bundle," 135.
3. Question #28 to Machig in "Another Bundle," 138. Sarah Harding's translation includes the original Tibetan, showing the poetic alliteration, followed by the verse in English. We have reversed the order here.
4. Machig Labdrön, "Great Bundle of Precepts," 20.

5. Machig Labdrön, "Vajra Play," in *Chöd: The Sacred Teachings on Severance*, vol. 14 in *The Treasury of Precious Instructions: Essential Teachings of the Eight Practice Lineages of Tibet*, comp. Jamgön Kongtrul, trans. Sarah Harding (Snow Lion, 2016), 141.
6. A phrase commonly used by the Dzogchen teacher and translator Keith Dowman. See, for example, Keith Dowman, trans. and ed., *Old Man Basking in the Sun: Longchenpa's Treasury of Natural Perfection* (Vajra Books, 2006), xx.
7. You may recall this verse from chapter 1, describing the ground of being: "It is without meeting or parting." Machig Labdrön, "Hair's Tip of Wisdom," 120.
8. Machig Labdrön, "Another Bundle," 131.

4. The Problem of Self-Clinging

1. Ken Wilber, *The Eye of Spirit: An Integral Vision for a World Gone Slightly Mad* (Shambhala, 2001), 290.
2. Chögyal Namkhai Norbu, *The Crystal and the Way of Light: Sutra, Tantra, and Dzogchen* (Routledge & Kegan Paul, 1986), 26.
3. See chapter 5. In the Buddhist tradition, *karma* (literally "action") refers to intentional, deliberate actions performed through body, speech, or mind that have future consequences. It points to the chain of cause and effect.
4. Machig's four demons are related to but slightly different from the traditional four maras of early Buddhism, representing key obstacles to awakening.
5. Machig Labdrön, "Great Bundle of Precepts," 14.
6. "The Questions of Gangpa Muksang," in *Machik's Complete Explanation: Clarifying the Meaning of Chöd*, trans. and ed. Sarah Harding (Snow Lion, 2003), 117.
7. "Questions of Gangpa Muksang," 117.
8. Machig Labdrön, "Great Bundle of Precepts," 14.
9. Machig Labdrön, "Great Bundle of Precepts," 14.
10. Machig Labdrön, "Great Bundle of Precepts," 18.
11. The Four Noble Truths is a foundational teaching of Buddhism: the truth of suffering, the cause of suffering, the cessation of suffering, and the path to cessation.

12. Machig Labdrön, "Great Bundle of Precepts," 15.
13. "Questions of Gangpa Muksang," 119.
14. Carlos Castaneda, *A Separate Reality: Further Conversations with Don Juan* (Simon & Schuster, 1971), 4–5.
15. Machig Labdrön, "Great Bundle of Precepts," 23.
16. Dogen, "Actualizing the Fundamental Point (Genjō Kōan)," from Dogen's masterwork *Shōbōgenzō*, trans. Robert Aitken and Kazuaki Tanahashi, in *Moon in a Dewdrop: Writings of Zen Master Dogen*, ed. Kazuaki Tanahashi (North Point Press, 1985), 70.
17. The Tantric view embraces the totality of experience on a path of developing sacred view in which even that which is traditionally considered impure is transformed into wisdom.
18. Machig Labdrön, "Hair's Tip of Wisdom," 109.

5. Cutting Through Self-Clinging

1. See chapter 4.
2. The term *interbeing*, meaning interconnectedness, was coined by Thich Nhat Hanh.
3. Machig Labdrön, "Hair's Tip of Wisdom," 116.
4. Machig Labdrön, "Essential Bundle," in *Chöd: The Sacred Teachings on Severance*, vol. 14 in *The Treasury of Precious Instructions: Essential Teachings of the Eight Practice Lineages of Tibet*, comp. Jamgön Kongtrul, trans. Sarah Harding (Snow Lion, 2016), 155.
5. This is radical inclusivity, discussed in the next chapter.
6. Machig Labdrön, "Essential Bundle," 155.
7. Machig Labdrön, "Great Bundle of Precepts," 23.
8. Machig Labdrön, "Great Bundle of Precepts," 18.
9. See Pieter Oosthuizen, "The Meaning of Phet," www.skymind.us. For further explanations on this powerful sound, see Chögyal Namkhai Norbu, *Chöd* (Shang Shung Edizioni, 1999), 48–49; here he also warns about using this sound without appropriate awareness of its potential impact.
10. Machig Labdrön, "Machig's Last Instructions," 167.
11. See chapter 10 on the relationship of Skymind to morality, honesty, and authenticity.

12. It should be noted that the mystic branches within many traditions focus on union with the divine, which can be understood as an experience of nonduality.
13. Machig Labdrön, "Essential Bundle," 155.
14. See Tsultrim Allione, *Feeding your Demons: Ancient Wisdom for Resolving Inner Conflict* (Little, Brown, 2008).
15. Namkhai Norbu, *The Crystal and the Way of the Light* (New York: Routledge & Kegan Paul, 1986), 163.
16. See chapter 7 for more details.
17. See chapter 7 for more details.
18. Attributed to the ninth-century Ch'an master Qingyuan Weixin.

6. Radical Inclusivity

1. Chögyam Trungpa called this Buddha Nature "basic goodness." See *Shambhala: The Sacred Path of the Warrior* (Shambhala, 1988), 35.
2. Machig Labdrön, "Machig's Last Instructions," 166.
3. Limpid: Clear, transparent, or pellucid, as water, crystal, or air. Free from obscurity; lucid. Completely calm; without distress or worry.
4. Laṅkāvatāra Sūtra 3.65.37.
5. Thich Nhat Hanh, *The Other Shore: A New Translation of the Heart Sutra with Commentaries* (Parallax Press, 2017), 21.
6. King, Martin Luther, Jr. *Letter from Birmingham Jail.* (Penguin Classics, 2018).
7. Machig Labdrön, "Great Bundle of Precepts," 15.
8. See, for example, Trungpa's discussion of the "territory" of the ego in *Cutting Through Spiritual Materialism* (Shambhala Publications, 1973), 142–44.
9. In Mahayana Buddhism, *bodhicitta* (awakened mind) is the mind (*citta*) that is aimed at awakening (*bodhi*) with wisdom and compassion for the benefit of all sentient beings.
10. See also the "Element Meditation: Space," outlined by Lama Tsultrim Allione in *Wisdom Rising: Journey into the Mandala of the Enlightened Feminine* (Simon & Schuster, 2018), 157. Tulku Urgyen Rinpoche describes the traditional Dzogchen sky-gazing practice in *Rainbow Painting*, trans. Erik Pema Kunsang (Rangjung Yeshe, 1995), 59.

7. Attention, Awareness, and Loving Radiance

1. "Machig's Last Instructions," from *The Concise Life Story of Machig Labdrön* by Kunpang Tsöndrü Sengé (thirteenth century), fols. 445–457, in *Machig Labdrön and the Foundations of Chöd*, by Jérôme Edou (Snow Lion, 1996), 167.
2. Our own experience is deeply steeped in the Tibetan Vajrayana tradition, which serves as the primary influence on our perspective.
3. *Ānāpānasati*: Pali, meaning "mindfulness of breathing"; the primary meditation technique taught by the Buddha.
4. The earliest schools of Buddhism tended to emphasize meditation with an object, whereas later schools tend toward meditation without an object of focus.
5. See Chögyam Trungpa's chapter on boredom in *The Myth of Freedom and the Way of Meditation* (Shambhala, 2002), 67–73.
6. Machig Labdrön, "Essential Bundle," 156.
7. Machig Labdrön, "Essential Bundle," 156.
8. Ken McLeod, *Wake Up to Your Life: Discovering the Buddhist Path of Attention* (HarperSanFrancisco, 2002), 28.
9. Machig Labdrön, "Hair's Tip of Wisdom," 118.
10. *Dharma*: Sanskrit; used in Buddhism to refer to the Buddha's teachings that outline the basic nature of reality. It also very simply refers to phenomena, and thus a description of the way things are. In this quote, we can read *Dharma* as "ultimate reality."
11. Karma Chagme, from the practice text "Supplication to the Great Mother Machig Lapdrön," compiled by Lama Tsultrim Allione (Machig Publications, 2020), 4.
12. Tulku Urgyen Rinpoche, *Rainbow Painting*, trans. Erik Pema Kunsang (Rangjung Yeshe, 1995), 126.
13. Machig Labdrön, "Essential Bundle," 148. Tib. *krim gyis bsgrim la lhod kyis glod / shigs kyis bshigs la phyal gyis thong / lhugs kyis klug la cog gis zhog / bsgom pa'i bzhag sa de na yod*. The first line of Machig's most famous instruction is translated in various ways, including as "While concentrated by concentration, relax by relaxing" by Harding. Tulku Urgyen Rinpoche's commentary renders the phrase as "tighten tightly and loosen loosely."

14. Tulku Urgyen Rinpoche, *Rainbow Painting*, 126.
15. Karma Chagme, from the practice text "Supplication to the Great Mother Machig Lapdrön," compiled by Lama Tsultrim Allione (Machig Publications, 2020), 4.
16. Tulku Urgyen, *Rainbow Painting*, 126.
17. Ido Amihai and Maria Kozhevnikov, "Arousal vs. Relaxation: A Comparison of the Neurophysiological and Cognitive Correlates of Vajrayana and Theravada Meditative Practices," *PLoS One* 9, no. 7 (2014): e102990, www.ncbi.nlm.nih.gov/pmc/articles/PMC4106862/.
18. The five aggregates (Skt. *skandhas*) are form, feeling, perception, mental formations, and consciousness. Together they create a sense of self and serve as the basis for clinging and craving.
19. Āryadeva the Brahmin, "The Grand Poem on the Perfection of Wisdom," in *Machig Labdrön and the Foundations of Chöd*, by Jérôme Edou (Snow Lion, 1996), 18.
20. Machig Labdrön, "Another Bundle," 130.
21. *Nyams* are traditionally described as meditative experiences of emptiness, clarity, or bliss, all of which suggest some progress in one's practice but which one should not cling to. They are like smoke, which suggests the presence of fire but is not itself the fire (actual realization).

8. The Skymind Meditation

1. Machig Labdrön, "Hair's Tip of Wisdom," 107.
2. Vairocana, or "Great Sun Buddha," is a major buddha in Mahayana and Vajrayana Buddhism. He represents the absolute wisdom body of the historical Gautama Buddha.
3. *Sushumna*: Sanskrit, lit. "very gracious, kind" (Tib. *uma*). The primary central channel in the subtle body through which energy flows, according to traditional Indian and Tibetan medicine and spiritual theory. It runs from the crown of the head down to the base of the torso, and connects various energy centers.
4. Known as the *kati* channel, it is said to run from the heart to the eyes, acting as a pathway through which awareness can travel. The practice leads to the realization that outer appearances

are none other than manifestations of internal awareness. Christopher Hatchell, *Naked Seeing: The Great Perfection, the Wheel of Time, and Visionary Buddhism in Renaissance Tibet* (Oxford University Press, 2014).

5. The vajra (Tib. *dorje*) is used in Buddhist Tantric practice as a symbol of the diamond-like indestructible nature of primordial awareness. It also represents the masculine aspect of skillful means or compassion that is balanced by the feminine aspect of wisdom or emptiness within the practitioner's experience. The double vajra—two crossed vajras—represents the stability of meditation.

9. A Deeper Look at Open Awareness

1. Keith Dowman, *Maya Yoga: Longchenpa's Finding Comfort and Ease in Enchantment* (Vajra Publications, 2010), 13.
2. Machig Labdrön, "Great Bundle of Precepts," 18.
3. Machig Labdrön, "Essential Bundle," 148.
4. Āryadeva the Brahmin, "Grand Poem on the Perfection of Wisdom," 17.
5. Karma Chagme, from the practice text "Supplication to the Great Mother Machig Lapdrön," comp. Lama Tsultrim Allione (Machig Publications, 2020), 4.
6. Machig Labdrön, "Machig's Last Instructions," 165–70.
7. *Perfection of Wisdom in Twenty-Five Thousand Lines*, Lhas Kangyur (rKTs-K9), f. 391.b. In Machig Labdrön, "Hair's Tip of Wisdom," 111.
8. Tulku Urgyen Rinpoche, *As It Is*, vol. 2, trans. Erik Pema Kunsang (Rangjung Yeshe, 2000), 160.
9. "Training is simply short moments of recognition repeated many times." Tulku Urgyen, *Rainbow Painting* (Rangjung Yeshe, 1995), 84.
10. Keith Dowman, ed., *Maya Yoga: Longchenpa's Finding Comfort and Ease in Enchantment* (Vajra Publications, 2010), 58–59.
11. Dowman, *Maya Yoga*, 56.
12. Dowman, 57.
13. Machig Labdrön, "Vajra Play," 142.

10. The Liberation of Morality

1. See, for example, Tulku Urgyen Rinpoche, *As It Is*, vol. 2, 81.
2. Machig Labdrön, "Another Bundle," 134.
3. Machig Labdrön, "Another Bundle," 127.
4. Prajñāpāramitā, the perfection of wisdom, the ground of being.
5. Machig Labdrön, "Another Bundle," 125.
6. For example, the Hindu Upanishads highlight the potent totality of sound: "om—this syllable is this whole world . . . the past, the present, the future—everything is just the word om. And whatever else that transcends threefold time—that, too, is just the word om" (*Mandukya Upanishad*). Or the New Testament of the Christian tradition: "In the beginning was the Word, and the Word was with God, and the Word was God" (John 1:1).
7. The famous mahasiddhas, or great adepts, were early Tantric masters in the period 750–1150 c.e.

11. The Path of Radical Responsibility

1. Tsultrim Allione, *Women of Wisdom* (Snow Lion, 2000), 182.
2. Sarah Harding, trans. and ed., *Machik's Complete Explanation: Clarifying the Meaning of Chöd* (Snow Lion, 2003), 68.
3. Jérôme Edou, *Machig Labdrön and the Foundations of Chöd* (Snow Lion, 1996), 133.
4. Machig Labdrön, "Great Bundle of Precepts," 27.

12. Non-Avoidance and the Path of Radical Acceptance

1. Tsultrim Allione, *Feeding Your Demons: Ancient Wisdom for Resolving Inner Conflict* (Little, Brown, 2008).
2. Machig Labdrön, "Hair's Tip of Wisdom," 110.
3. Carl Jung, *Psychology and Alchemy* (Princeton University Press, 1980), 99.
4. Machig Labdrön, "Another Bundle," 134.
5. Machig Labdrön, "Another Bundle," 134.

13. Go to the Places That Scare You

1. See Sarah Harding, trans. and ed., *Zhije: The Pacification of Suffering*, vol. 13 in *The Treasury of Precious Instructions*, compiled by Jamgön Kongtrul (Snow Lion, 2019), for translations of source texts.
2. Tsultrim Allione, *Women of Wisdom* (Snow Lion, 2000), 181.
3. Chögyam Trungpa, *Shambhala: The Sacred Path of the Warrior* (Shambhala, 2015), 33.
4. Tsultrim Allione, *Feeding Your Demons: Ancient Wisdom for Resolving Inner Conflict* (Little, Brown, 2008).
5. Chögyam Trungpa, *Training the Mind and Cultivating Loving-Kindness* (Shambhala, 1993), 9.

14. Skymind Compassion

1. Machig Labdrön, "Another Bundle," 136.
2. Absolute bodhicitta refers to our Buddha Nature, the vast, luminous nature of our being; relative bodhicitta refers to the ways this nature expresses itself through love, compassion, care.
3. Chögyam Trungpa, *Training the Mind and Cultivating Loving-Kindness* (Shambhala, 1993), 10.
4. Fritz Vincken, "Truce in the Forest," *Readers Digest*, January 1973, 111–14.
5. For an in-depth discussion of compassion from both practice and scientific perspectives, see Matthieu Ricard, *Altruism: The Power of Compassion to Change Yourself and the World* (Little, Brown, 2013).
6. Ram Dass and Paul Gorman, *How Can I Help? Stories and Reflections on Service* (Knopf, 1985), 175.
7. Machig Labdrön, "Another Bundle," 136.
8. Machig Labdrön, "Hair's Tip of Wisdom," 110.

15. The Full Belly and Satisfied Mind

1. Machig Labdrön, "Great Bundle of Precepts," 21.
2. Machig Labdrön, "Great Bundle of Precepts," 21.
3. Machig Labdrön, "Great Bundle of Precepts," 22.

4. Chögyam Trungpa, "Poverty," *The Myth of Freedom and the Way of Meditation* (Shambhala, 2005), 47–49.
5. Machig Labdrön, "Great Bundle of Precepts," 22.
6. We owe the inspiration for this turn of phrase to Chögyam Trungpa, who uses it frequently. See, for example, Chögyam Trungpa, *Great Eastern Sun: The Wisdom of Shambhala*, ed. Carolyn Rose Gimian (Shambhala, 1999), 153.

16. Inherent Dignity

1. Chögyam Trungpa, "The Dawn of Tantra," in *Collected Works of Chögyam Trungpa*, vol. 4, ed. Carolyn Rose Gimian (Shambhala, 2010), 439.
2. Quoted by Tsong Khapa in the fourth chapter of his *Great Exposition of the Poetic Path* (*Ngags-rim chen-mo*). See Jeffrey Hopkins, H. H. Dalai Lama, Tsong Khapa, *Tantra in Tibet* (Snow Lion, 1987). Our reference is from Joe Loizzo, *Sustainable Happiness: The Mind Science of Well-Being, Altruism, and Inspiration* (Routledge, 2012), 267.
3. Machig Labdrön, "Great Bundle of Precepts," 23.
4. Machig Labdrön, "Great Bundle of Precepts," 21.
5. Machig Labdrön, "Great Bundle of Precepts," 21.
6. Machig Labdrön, "Hair's Tip of Wisdom," 104.
7. Wylie: *gdeng*.
8. Garab Dorje, *Tsik Sum Né Dek* (Wylie: *tshig gsum gnad brdegs*).
9. Wylie: *btsan sa*.
10. Machig Labdrön, "Hair's Tip of Wisdom," 109.
11. Luke 2:19.
12. Machig Labdrön, "Hair's Tip of Wisdom," 104.

17. Encountering Death

1. 32 Battalion, a.k.a. "Buffalo," after their insignia, the head of a cape buffalo.
2. Machig Labdrön, "Eight Uncommon Appendices," in *Chöd: The Sacred Teachings on Severance*, vol. 14 in *The Treasury of Precious Instructions: Essential Teachings of the Eight Practice*

Lineages of Tibet, comp. Jamgön Kongtrul, trans. Sarah Harding (Snow Lion, 2016), 179.

3. Chögyam Trungpa, *Training the Mind and Cultivating Loving-Kindness* (Shambhala, 2003), 78.
4. Question #28 to Machig Labdrön in "Another Bundle," 138.
5. *Atyayajñānasūtra (The Sutra on Wisdom at the Hour of Death)*, https://read.84000.co/translation/UT22084-054-003.html#UT22084-054-003-section-1., 1.4–9.
6. *Bardo Thodol* (Tibetan; Wylie: *bar do thos grol*), meaning "Liberation through hearing during the intermediate state," is a revealed text (*terma*) of the great Nyingma master Jigme Lingpa (1326–1386).
7. Machig Labdrön, "Another Bundle," 127.
8. Machig Labdrön, "Eight Uncommon Appendices," 184.

18. Liberated from Accomplishment

1. Machig Labdrön, "Another Bundle," 135–136.
2. T. S. Eliot, "Four Quartets: Little Gidding," in *The Complete Poems and Plays 1909–1950* (Harcourt, Brace, Jovanovich, 1980), 145.
3. Atisha's teachings were formalized by Chekawa Yeshe Dorje in *The Root Text of the Seven Points of Training the Mind*, trans. Chögyam Trungpa and the Nālandā Translation Committee, in *Training the Mind and Cultivating Loving-Kindness*, by Chögyam Trungpa (Shambhala Publications, 1993), 94.
4. Machig Labdrön, "Great Bundle of Precepts," 26.
5. Machig Labdrön, "Essential Bundle," 155. Original translation: "within nonconceptual equipoise without fear or anxiety no matter what devils arise."

19. The View of No View

1. Machig Labdrön, "Great Bundle of Precepts," 16–17.
2. Padampa Sangye, "The Hundred Verses of Advice," in *The Collected Works of Dilgo Khyentse*, vol. 2 (Shambhala, 2010), 453.
3. "With a loving mind, cherish more than a child the hostile gods and demons of apparent existence, and tenderly surround yourself

with them." In Tsultrim Allione, *Women of Wisdom* (Snow Lion, 2000), 41.

4. In Sarah Harding, trans., *Chöd: The Sacred Teachings on Severance*, 542n16.
5. From the *Perfection of Wisdom in Twenty-Five Thousand Lines*, Lhasa Kangyur (rKTs-K9), f.268a–b. Quoted by Machig Labdrön, "Hair's Tip of Wisdom," 113.
6. Thich Nhat Hanh, "Mountains Are Mountains and Rivers Are Rivers," in *Zen Keys: A Guide to Zen Practice* (Thorsons, 1995), 88.
7. Machig Labdrön, "Hair's Tip of Wisdom," 112.

20. The Meditation of Non-Meditation

1. Machig Labdrön, "Great Bundle of Precepts," 16.
2. Tulku Urgyen Rinpoche, *As It Is*, vol. 2 (Rangjung Yeshe Publications, 2000), 149. The "dharmakaya throne" here refers to ultimate realization, resting without effort in the essence of mind.
3. Machig Labdrön, "Great Bundle of Precepts," 16.
4. Machig Labdrön, "Great Bundle of Precepts," 26.
5. Machig Labdrön, "Another Bundle," 135.
6. Machig Labdrön, "Another Bundle," 130.
7. Urgyen, *As It Is*, vol. 2, 167.
8. Machig Labdrön, "Great Bundle of Precepts," 25.
9. Machig Labdrön, "Another Bundle," 135.
10. The mahasiddhas referred to here were Buddhist Tantric masters who lived between the eighth and twelfth centuries. They include well-known teachers such as Naropa, Tilopa, Saraha, and many others.
11. Karl Brunnhölzl, *Luminous Melodies: Essential Dohās of Indian Mahāmudrā* (Wisdom Publications, 2019), 31.

21. The Action of Non-Action

1. Machig Labdrön, "Another Bundle," 135.
2. See the work of Ludwig von Bertalanffy (1901–1972), the founder of general systems theory.

3. Machig Labdrön, "Great Bundle of Precepts," 17.
4. Machig Labdrön, "Another Bundle," 131.
5. Joanna Macy, *World as Lover, World as Self* (Parallax Press, 1991), 191.
6. Machig Labdrön, "Machig's Last Instructions," 169.
7. See Barbara Dilley, *This Very Moment: Teaching, Thinking, Dancing* (Naropa University Press, 2015).

22. Joy, Beauty, and Play

1. Machig Labdrön, "Another Bundle," 132.
2. For further reading on the Tibetan subtle body teachings and practices, see Nida Chenagtsang, *Nejang: Tibetan Self-Healing Yoga* (Sky Press, 2020), and Tenzin Wangyal Rinpoche, *Healing with Form, Energy and Light* (Snow Lion, 2002).
3. Walt Whitman, *Leaves of Grass* (Penguin, 1986), 83.
4. From the "Final Words of Terdag Lingpa" (1646–1714), prayer.
5. Machig Labdrön, "Great Bundle of Precepts," 20.
6. Machig Labdrön, "Great Bundle of Precepts," 20.
7. Machig Labdrön, "Great Bundle of Precepts," 16.
8. Masaoka Shiki, John Brandi, trans., Noriko Kawasaki Martinez, trans., *A House by Itself: Selected Haiku of Shiki* (White Pine Press, 2017), 64.
9. Buson, Robert Hass, trans., *The Essential Haiku: Versions of Basho, Buson and Issa* (Ecco, 2013; Bloodaxe Books, 2017), 106.
10. Machig Labdrön, "Hair's Tip of Wisdom," 118–119.
11. Machig Labdrön, "Great Bundle of Precepts," 25.
12. Machig Labdrön, "Another Bundle," 133.

Conclusion

1. Machig Labdrön, "Another Bundle," 137.

Index

Credits

We gratefully acknowledge the permissions given to reprint excerpts from the following material:

"Little Gidding" from *The Complete Poems and Plays: 1909–1950* by T. S. Eliot: Copyright 1950, 1943, 1939, 1930 by T. S. Eliot. Copyright 1952, 1936, 1935 by Harcourt Brace & Company. Copyright renewed 1964, 1963, 1958 by T. S. Eliot. Copyright renewed 1980, 1978, 1971, 1967 by Esme Valerie Eliot. Used by permission of HarperCollins Publishers.

"Four Quartets: Little Gidding" by T. S. Eliot in *The Complete Poems and Plays 1909–1950* (Harcourt, Brace, Jovanovich, 1980), used by permission of Faber and Faber Ltd.

The Essential Haiku: Versions of Basho, Buson and Issa by Robert Hass, tr. (Ecco, 2013; Bloodaxe Books, 2013), reproduced with permission of Bloodaxe Books. www.bloodaxebooks.com @bloodaxebooks (twitter/facebook) #bloodaxebooks.

Chöd: The Sacred Teachings on Severance by Sarah Harding, tr. (Snow Lion, 2016), used by permission of Sarah Harding.

Machik's Complete Explanation: Clarifying the Meaning of Chöd by Sarah Harding, tr. (Snow Lion, 2013), used by permission of Sarah Harding.

A House by Itself: Selected Haiku of Shiki by Masaoka Shiki, John Brandi, tr., and Noriko Kawasaki Martinez, tr. (White Pine Press, 2017), used by permission of White Pine Press.

About the Authors

Pieter Oosthuizen's journey arcs from the wild edges of apartheid-era Johannesburg to the heart of contemplative practice. He teaches internationally on meditation, Vajrayana Buddhism, and the nondual nature of reality. As a boy, he roamed the veld with a slingshot; by nineteen, he was an intelligence officer in the Angolan War. Afterward, he slung on a backpack and wandered East to life-shifting encounters in the Himalayan foothills and with the Dalai Lama in India. Back in South Africa, he met Namkhai Norbu Rinpoche—the first of many esteemed Tibetan Buddhist teachers. After earning his law degree, he again crossed oceans to Colorado in the US where he served in leadership roles at Naropa University in Boulder and Tara Mandala Retreat Center. These days he also directs the Feeding Your Demons Institute. Across his roles, he continues to ask the question at the core of *Skymind*: How can we meet this moment with compassionate presence and embodied courage?

Charlotte Z. Rotterdam is a Buddhist teacher, contemplative educator, and writer. Raised in New York City, Charlotte's early fascination with life's big questions led her to study philosophy and religion, first at Swarthmore College, then at Harvard Divinity School where she received a master's degree in theological studies. She is a senior teacher (Dorje Lopön) and lineage holder at Tara Mandala, authorized by Lama Tsultrim Allione. She has been fortunate to study with Lama Tharchin Rinpoche, Namkhai Norbu Rinpoche, Lama Wangdu Rinpoche, Orgyen Khakhyab Lingpa, among others. She teaches internationally on meditation, compassion, and a variety of Vajrayana Buddhist practices. Charlotte is faculty at Naropa University where she also directs the Center for the Advancement of Contemplative Education and codeveloped and teaches the Mindful Compassion Training. She has published essays in *Mandala*, *Lion's Roar*, and *Buddhadharma*. Inspired by the simple joys of everyday life and the subtle beauty of the world, Charlotte delights in sharing the insights of the Buddhist tradition so that they may be accessible and transformative in contemporary life.

Pieter and Charlotte live on the sunny slopes of the Rocky Mountains near Boulder, Colorado, and have two sons. They co-lead the Skymind practice community and teach together.